Labour, state and society in rural India

MANCHESTER
1824

Manchester University Press

Labour, state and society in rural India

A class-relational approach

Jonathan Pattenden

Manchester University Press

Published by Manchester University Press
Altrincham Street, Manchester M1 7JA, UK
www.manchesteruniversitypress.co.uk

British Library Cataloguing-in-Publication Data is available

ISBN 978 0 7190 8914 5 *hardback*
ISBN 978 1 5261 3383 0 *paperback*

First published by Manchester University Press in hardback 2016

This edition first published 2019

Printed by Lightning Source

In memory of my mother *Carolyn.*
And of my sister *Lucy*.

Contents

Figures

Tables

Acknowledgements

As with all books, the author's role is part of a much larger story. It is primarily based upon the experiences of labourers and farmers who gave up their free time to talk to me. Much of what little I understand of India, I owe to them, although the necessity of anonymity means that I cannot thank them here directly.

Beyond them are the fellow academics whose insights into similar questions form the terrain in which this book's modest contribution sits. A few stand out: Henry Bernstein, Jan Breman, John Harriss, Barbara Harriss-White, and Jens Lerche who between them appear to have thought of all the things that I have laboured to think of, and long before I thought of any of them; and my contemporaries Isabelle Guérin and David Picherit whose own work is a constant reminder of what researchers can achieve. Jairus Banaji, Jayati Ghosh, Utsa Patnaik, V.K. Ramachandran and Ravi Srivastava are among the many key contributors to the field in India, whose work has both inspired and facilitated my own.

The following friends and research assistants in India were invaluable in a variety of ways: Savitri, Shivaram, Suresh, Hema, Anitha, Sanjana, Sameer, Shravani, Harsha, Eddie, Sree, Devdas, Vasudha, Veena, Chris, Mahesh, Ulrich, Vithal, Venugopal, Kariappa, Devaputra, Halasangi, Narsamma, Hemant, the JMS, the government officers who deviated from the official script, and the late MD Nanjundaswamy who first nudged me in the direction of Dharwad, and of Karnataka. Thanks also to Muzaffar Assadi and to Mysore University for providing me with a base during parts of the research process.

My friends and colleagues Satoshi Miyamura, Liam Campling, and Ben Selwyn have been an important source of intellectual and personal support, particularly in recent years. All three commented on parts of the draft manuscript. Further support has been provided by Benedict, Guillermo, Sebastian T, Yukiko, Kyaw, Jeff, George, Paolo, Alessandra, and last, but not least, Hao. Thanks also to Kim, Eva, Samir, Alice, Jack and Phil, and to Tony Mason of Manchester University Press for his patience. It should be noted that Chapter 6 draws extensively from an article published in Volume 15 of the Journal of Agrarian Change.

I would like to thank Esme for many things, as well as my family members Patricia, John, Jackie, John, Marcus, Ben, Kate and their partners; and above all my mother, Carolyn, whose last moments with me before her sudden departure accompanied the drafting of a first proposal for this book, and whose contribution to its making cannot be fully conveyed.

Abbreviations

ADR	Association for Democratic Reforms
BJP	Bharatiya Janata Party
BOCWA	Building and Other Construction Workers Act
CBO	community-based organisation
CDPO	Child Development Project Officer
CSO	civil society organisation
DWCD	Department of Women and Child Development
GoI	Government of India
GoK	Government of Karnataka
GP	Gram Panchayat (Village Council, covering one large or a handful of smaller villages)
IAS	Indian Administrative Service
IGA	income-generating activity
ILO	International Labour Organisation
JMS	Jagruthi Mahela Sanghathan
LGI	local government institution
MFI	microfinance institution
MLA	Member of Legislative Assembly
MoF	Ministry of Finance
MP	Member of Parliament
NCEUS	National Commission for Enterprises in the Unorganised Sector
NGO	non-governmental organisation
NREGA	National Rural Employment Guarantee Act
NREGS	National Rural Employment Guarantee Scheme
NSS(O)	National Sample Survey (Organisation)
OBC	Other Backward Caste
PC	Planning Commission
PCP	petty commodity production
PDS	Public Distribution System

RSBY	Rashtriya Swasthya Bima Yojana (National Health Insurance Scheme)
SC	scheduled caste
SEZ	Special Economic Zone
SGRY	Sampoorna Grameena Rozgar Yojana (Complete Village Employment Scheme)
SGSY	Swarnajayanti Gram Swarozgar Yojana (Golden Jubilee Village Self-Employment Scheme)
SGY	Swachh Gram Yojana (Clean Village Scheme)
SHG	self-help group
ST	scheduled tribe
TP	Taluk Panchayat (sub-district council)
UNDP	United Nations Development Programme
UPA	United Progressive Alliance (Congress-led coalition government in power 2004–14)
UWSSA	Unorganised Workers Social Security Act
ZP	Zilla Panchayat (district council)

1

Introduction: poverty and the poor

It has been argued that the analysis of poverty in contemporary development studies has been abstracted both from class and other power relationships, and from processes of accumulation in capitalism (Harriss 2007a:9). Debates on poverty reduction seem to ignore the link 'between the enrichment of some and the impoverishment of others, as if the rich and poor somehow inhabit different social worlds with no economic interdependence at all, and that the rich do not rely upon the labour of the poor' (Ghosh 2011a:854). Instead, poverty is reduced to household characteristics, and technical solutions are offered in a manner that serves the status quo and offers no threat to 'the elites who benefit from the existing structures and relationships' (Harriss 2007a:9). The very term 'poverty', by this reckoning, reduces multi-faceted relations to surface phenomena, and the underlying causes of material deprivation to obscurity.

Neoliberalism's renewed focus on poverty has been operationalised since the 1990s through a range of tools including poverty reduction strategy papers, decentralisation, community-based organisations (CBOs) and microfinance. Critics argue that it has been primarily intended to reform 'social and governmental relations and institutions in order to facilitate capitalist exploitation and accumulation on a world scale, building capitalist hegemony through the promotion of tightly controlled forms of "participation" and "ownership"' (Cammack 2003:1).

Instead of structural adjustment programmes that imposed state spending cuts on many developing countries, poverty reduction strategy papers included governments and civil society organisations (CSOs) in 'participatory' decision-making processes, while maintaining the fundamentals of the neoliberal policy agenda (Ruckert 2006). Decentralised forms of government, meanwhile, induced 'people to experience tightly controlled forms of pro-market activity as empowerment', while exerting pressure on the state to deliver resources efficiently and encouraging 'beneficiaries' to contribute to the costs of such services (Cammack

1

2003:1). The proliferation of local institutions was seen as helping to generate 'political space', while participatory bottom-up approaches, the building of social capital and the development of capabilities would 'drive' poor people's agency (Chambers 1983; Putnam 1993; Sen 1999).

In promoting participation, empowerment and democratisation (World Bank 2001), the 'new poverty agenda' reshaped the state–society interface. In many developing countries, local government's budgets and responsibilities grew substantially alongside a dramatic rise in the number of CBOs (Heller *et al.* 2007; Lange 2008; Nordholt 2004; Pattenden 2011a; Sidel 2004). In India, several million CBOs were formed in the first six years of the millennium alone, while a growing share of government activities was outsourced to an expanding array of local non-governmental organisations (NGOs).

Neoliberal approaches to civil society and social capital have been critiqued for eschewing analysis of the distribution of power and resources for a theory that explains uneven development in terms of varying densities of low-cost 'inherently capable' civic associations (Harriss 2001:2, 45). Rather than a move away from the neoliberal orthodoxy of the 1980s, through which the state was to be scaled back, markets liberalised and the space for the private sector expanded, the growth of 'empowerment' and 'participation' in the 1990s and 2000s ensured the extension of the neoliberal project not only by submerging the 'social and political causes of poverty' beneath its characteristics, but by providing cheap self-help-oriented forms of poverty reduction that foregrounded the individual as an entrepreneurial subject (Harriss 2001:2; Herring and Agarwala 2006:329; Kamat 2004:169). By placing the onus for poverty reduction on the poor themselves, such an approach amounted to a 'strongly normalising and moralising set of proposals that effectively blames the poor for their predicament' (Gledhill 2001:123). In Foucauldian terms, it might be said that neoliberalism had become more biopolitical, while in those of Gramsci it could be seen as having become more hegemonic.

While residual approaches view poverty as being 'a consequence of being "left out" of processes of development' (Bernstein 1992:24), the class-relational approach used in this book locates the causes of poverty among the social relations of production, and specific forms of exploitation and domination, in an attempt to shed light both on how it is produced and reproduced by capitalism (Harriss-White 2005), and on how the economic and political conditions of the poor might be improved. Building on a considerable literature that has deployed a class-relational approach in India and beyond, this takes the analysis beyond phenomena such as incomes and institutional arrangements to the underlying processes of dispossession, accumulation and exploitation.[1] The purpose of doing so is to better understand how, where and when pro-labouring class change can be realised – questions asked in this book in relation to a largely informalised and segmented labour force, which is based in the Indian countryside and works in both rural and urban locations.

A class-relational approach, which will be discussed in detail in Chapter 2, understands people's conditions as the outcome of multiple intersecting social relations. Classes are understood in terms of social relations rather than structural locations, while class in more general terms is understood as a plural identity inflected by other forms of difference such as gender and caste. In other words, although it emphasises the process of exploitation, its engagement with the diverse concrete forms of class relations reflects an open-ended and dialectical approach rather than a linear, teleological one (Banaji 2010; Bernstein 2006). The book's class-relational approach to labour, state and society will be expanded upon in the next chapter. In the remainder of this introductory chapter, the book's argument is outlined, along with the levels and trajectories of poverty in India and the fieldwork state of Karnataka. The fieldwork districts will also be introduced, along with the methods used.

Labour, state and society

Drawing on long-term fieldwork in the South Indian state of Karnataka, this book analyses class relations between and among the dominant and labouring classes in rural India. While recognising that the boundaries between the rural and the urban have become blurred, it focuses primarily on 'rural-based labour' who are (i) those who work and live in villages; (ii) those who live in villages but commute into nearby towns and cities; and (iii) those who migrate out of their villages to cities (or other rural areas) for a number of weeks or years, but who keep a house in their home village and return there periodically. The book shows how the forms of domination and exploitation change over time, and assesses the implications for pro-labouring-class change. It does so through a focus on three interrelated areas of analysis: labour relations (and the labour process), collective action and the mediation of class relations by the state.

Analysis of labour relations shows that rural-based labour in India has a number of clear characteristics. It is underemployed, which reflects the presence of a surplus labour force that weakens its bargaining position. It tends to be informally employed, which means that it is usually unprotected by state regulations and unable to access basic forms of social security. It is also highly fragmented due to factors such as caste, but also due to its increased spatial diffusion across multiple worksites. In the terms of Wright (2000:962), it is a workforce with relatively little 'structural power" (which 'results directly from tight labour markets' and 'from the strategic location of a particular group of workers within a key industrial sector").

While the processes of change discussed in this book tend to reproduce the position of the dominant, they are contested in a variety of ways. Sources of weakness, though, can also be sources of strength. Where caste and class overlap to a significant degree, caste ties can strengthen the basis for mobilisation. Meanwhile, the growth of non-agricultural employment and circular migration can improve labour's economic and socio-political position and increase the possibilities for collective action. This has arguably been the primary basis of pro-labouring class change in the Indian countryside over recent decades.

If the institutional changes wrought by the post-Washington Consensus among the class relations of rural India are one of this book's primary frames, another is the relative 'invisibility' of the labourers whose experiences are central to it. They are located at the margins of global production networks as agricultural labourers scattered across the countryside, as informal workers in formal sector industries, and as construction workers who disappear before prominent international companies move in and begin to accumulate from the office-blocks whose foundations they built. Their 'invisibility' reflects forms of control, domination and exploitation operating at multiple levels, while its unevenness reflects, among other things, the agency of labour. The book analyses labour relations in agriculture, in the construction sector and to some degree in industry as well. It compares villages where labour commutes to nearby cities and others where it migrates to more distant ones. It shows how relations between labourers and employers in their home villages vary depending on how they are incorporated into non-agricultural labour relations. It also shows how they vary according to the predominant patterns of accumulation among their employers.

While in some of the fieldwork villages accumulation remains primarily focused on agriculture, in others it has diversified into agribusiness, formal employment and state-related business. There are echoes here of Epstein's (1973) classic account of agrarian change in southern Karnataka in the decades after independence, which showed how variations in levels of irrigation relate to patterns of accumulation, forms of class relations and the patterns of relationships with the state. This book traces similar variations between irrigated and dryland villages.

The second area of analysis, collective action, starts from the premise that rural-based labour in contemporary India is relatively weakly organised. There have long been socially embedded labouring class movements in eastern parts of the country (Kunnath 2009; Wilson 1999), and there are labouring class organisations in both the formal and informal sectors of the economy (Agarwala 2013). There are also signs of a recent upturn in union activity following a long-running decline since the 1970s (see below). Nevertheless, rural organisations actively seeking pro-labouring-class change tend to be relatively small-scale and focused on accessing state resources rather than directly challenging capital (Agarwala 2013; Lerche 2010). This, though, does not mean that they cannot (or do not) play a significant role in attempts to improve the economic and political conditions of the labouring class, or provide one of a number of avenues to more fundamental change. Given the degree of labour's fragmentation and the often weak bargaining position of casual labourers in the informal economy, small-scale organisation and indirect strategies of struggle are often the most pragmatic option – at least in the short term. At the same time, the book argues that the mass of recently formed CSOs are not organisations of the labouring class, but cross-class CBOs that are inclined to reproduce rather than challenge the status quo, and undermine possibilities for pro-labouring-class collective action.

It is argued that although the state (and the book's third area of analysis concerns how the state mediates class relations) is broadly (and increasingly) pro-capital (see also Kohli 2011),[2] it currently represents the most viable terrain for pro-labouring-class action. This argument is made with the following provisos in mind. First, as well as distributing resources to classes of labour through poverty reduction programmes,[3] the state also undermines labour by failing to implement legislation that would improve its position in workplaces. Second, poverty reduction programmes cannot be understood simply as transfers of resources to the poor, but as part of a broader process of the reproduction of state and society. To be more explicit, poverty reduction programmes also help to reproduce stable conditions for capitalist accumulation by preventing social unrest (which may otherwise arise from the particularly harsh labour regime that prevents much of India's labouring class from reproducing itself materially). Poverty reduction programmes also boost the competitiveness of Indian capital by subsidising the low wages that they pay. In other words, the state's mediation of class relations in rural India is located in broader dynamics of accumulation and exploitation on a world scale.

High levels of fiscal decentralisation to local government institutions (LGIs), along with the proliferation of CSOs, have 'thickened' the state–society interface in recent years. They have also made local government a more significant site of class-based antagonism. Although state poverty programmes are as likely to reproduce the status quo as to challenge it, some programmes (notably the National Rural Employment Guarantee Scheme (NREGS)) can modify socio-economic and socio-political dynamics in favour of labour. They do so, as has been argued in analysis of European welfare states (Esping-Andersen 1990), primarily by removing part of the process of labouring class reproduction from the sphere of direct relations between capital and labour. As a result of this reduced dependence, labourers' room for political manoeuvre increases.

Increased levels of pro-labouring-class organisation may be resisted by capital directly (through lock-outs, for example), or less directly through the state. Examples include the erstwhile United Progressive Alliance (UPA) government's watering-down of legislation to provide forms of social security for informal sector workers in 2008 (which fell well short of calls for a 'social floor' made up of a national minimum wage, minimum working conditions and minimum levels of social security; NCEUS 2007; ILO n.d.);[4] or its decision to allow NREGS wages to fall (relative to prevailing casual rural wages) at the end of its period in office (see Chapter 6); or the new BJP government's ongoing weakening of labour regulations.[5] Any concessions extracted by labour from the state are subject to roll-back, and are moments in a much longer process that may or may not lead to substantive broad-based pro-labouring-class change.

The UPA, which was more dependent on labouring class votes than its rivals,[6] was pressed into passing the National Rural Employment Guarantee Act (NREGA) by a coalition of CSOs and left-of-centre political parties, but it did so while leaving workplaces largely unregulated, and remaining pro-capital in a broader sense (see Chapter 4). Nevertheless, the UPA's 2004 election pledges to 'ensure the welfare and wellbeing of all workers, particularly those in the unorganised sector who constitute ninety-three per cent of our workforce' and to expand 'social security, health insurance and other schemes for such workers' have translated into some material gains for labour (cited in Kannan and Jain 2013a:81).

Several recent longitudinal analyses of agrarian change (one of which stretches back ninety-two years) show that while labour relations have become 'increasingly atomised and diversified' (Rodgers and Rodgers 2011:46), social policy and the growth of non-agricultural employment have been the most significant 'drivers of pro-labour change' (Djurfelt *et al.* 2008:50; Harriss *et al.* 2010; Rodgers and Rodgers 2011). These findings relate to those of this book as it moves across different villages and districts, tracing class relations and forms of impoverishment and the ways in which they are shaped by, the state and broader structural change.

The mediation of class relations by the state tends to favour capital, but also throws up possibilities for pro-labouring-class change. How, when and why it does so is particularly important given that rural-based labour in India remains weakly organised, and continues to endure relative political marginalisation (Harriss 2013), harsh working conditions, low pay and a raft of material deprivations. The book agrees with Selwyn (2014:186) that development studies should be 'labour-centred', and emphasises the significance of labouring class organisation in improving labour's conditions and making more fundamental change possible. It argues that in much of contemporary rural India, this depends for now mostly on organising labour around the extraction of concessions from the state – both regulatory concessions and the expansion of labour's share of public resources (which are ultimately based on labour-power) through the expansion of poverty reduction programmes. The combination of these can, in time, make more broad-based labouring class action possible and reduce the extent of material deprivation (poverty) that is endured along the way. Under the recently elected more right-wing government, such a strategy becomes more focused on preventing the erosion of the minor gains made to date, while expanding labour's organisational base in preparation for a more concerted pro-labour offensive after the current government's inevitable demise.

A class-relational analysis primarily understands the conditions of the poor in terms of the relations through which they are dominated and exploited. It operates both at the broader societal level and through detailed analysis of concrete class situations, and their complex and uneven dynamics and trajectories of change across hamlets, villages and districts, thereby helping to inform how labouring class organisation can be strengthened and its share of public resources increased.

The conditions of labour: poverty in India and Karnataka

Before elaborating on what a class-relational approach is, and then applying it to concrete social settings in rural India, the remainder of this introduction outlines the economic conditions of the poor in India and Karnataka and introduces the fieldwork region.

India's economy is one of the ten largest in the world. It is also one of the 'BRICS', an informal grouping of ascendant national economies (encompassing Brazil, Russia, China and South Africa, along with India) that formed its own development bank in July 2014.[7] India's growth rate has been unusually high since the turn of the century, peaking at over 10 per cent in 2010. From 1994 to 2004 its economy grew at 6.3 per cent per annum, and from 2005 to 2010 it grew at a rate of 8.7 per cent.[8] Although the rate has since declined, it remains relatively high.

While India's growth rates have outpaced those of most developing countries in recent years, its rate of poverty reduction has been slower than most (Drèze and Sen 2013:32), and more sluggish than it had been for much of the 1970s and 1980s (Himanshu 2007:499). From 1993–94 to 2004–05, rural poverty fell by just 8.3 per cent to 41.8 per cent of the population (see Table 1.1).[9] In absolute terms the speed of decline has been remarkably slow: between 1993–94 and 2004–05, the total number

Table 1.1 Rural poverty levels

	1993–94	2004–05	2009–10	2011–12
Tendulkar Method (rural)	50.1	41.8	33.8	25.7
Tendulkar Method (combined rural and urban)	45.3	37.2	29.8	**21.9****
Rangarajan Method (rural)	n/a	n/a	39.6	30.9
Rangarajan Method (combined rural and urban)	n/a	n/a	38.2	29.5
NCEUS (poor *and* vulnerable)	n/a	77	69* (2010)	n/a

Sources: GoI MoF (2014:237), GoI PC (2009:14; 2014b:69), NCEUS (2007:i).

Notes: * Estimated projection by NCEUS member K.P. Kannan (2012); ** Currently used by the Ministry of Statistics and Programme Implementation.

of those living in poverty fell by less than four million to 413.3 million, meaning that one in three of those categorised as poor worldwide lived in India.[10] In the second half of the 2000s, though, the rate of poverty's decline doubled, and then more than doubled again in the following two years before falling away again.

While rural poverty is concentrated among landless labourers and marginal farmers (Corbridge *et al.* 2013:67, 88; Gooptu and Harriss-White 2001),[11] it is also significantly more common among the 'scheduled castes' (SCs, or *dalits*) and 'scheduled tribes' (STs, or *adivasis*).[12] There are also marked intra-household variations. There is evidence, for example, that women and girls consume less within the household (Harriss-White 1990). Patriarchy reproduces gender-based inequalities in a variety of ways. For example, brides generally settle in grooms' households, which may put them in a weak position, and their households tend to pay more for marriages, which contributes to widespread ongoing female foeticide (Drèze and Sen 2013:60–62).

Real wage levels have followed a similar trajectory to poverty. Real wage growth for male agricultural wages accelerated to 7.6 per cent from 1983 to 1990, then slowed to 2.4 per cent in 1993–2000 (Srivastava and Singh 2005:409–412),[13] before almost grinding to a halt in the first half of the 2000s (Drèze and Sen 2013:27, 29; Thomas 2012:42; Usami 2011). With growth accelerating and real wages static, inequality rose between 1993–94 and 2004–05, having fallen in the previous decade (Himanshu 2007:499). It did so both within and across states (Herring and Agarwala

Table 1.2 Rural and urban casual wages and consumer price indices for agricultural labourers, 1993–94 to 2011–12

	Combined (male and female) rural casual wages (male/female wages in brackets)	Combined (male and female) urban casual labour wages	All India CPI-AL, 86/7 = 100 (average of all months)
1993–94	20.5 (23.2/15.3)	28.8	
1999–2000	40.2 (45.5/29.4)	58.0	306
2004–05	48.9 (55.0/34.9)	68.7	340
2009–10	93.1 (101.5/68.9)	121.8	513
2011–12	138.6 (149.3/103.3)	170.1	611

Sources: GoI NSS (2014:121), GoI MoF (2013:Statistical Appendix, 55).

2006:324), thereby further exacerbating existing spatial inequalities, as well as those between social classes. The poorest households' share of growth had been 'sharply diminished' (Corbridge *et al.* 2013:49; see also Drèze and Sen 2013; Walker 2008), and while the living standards of India's middle classes rose sharply, those of unskilled informal sector workers stagnated (Drèze and Sen 2013:29).

There was then a marked upturn in real wages at the end of the 2000s, with rural casual wages almost trebling in the six years to 2011–12 (see Table 1.2). This has been corroborated by case studies from different parts of the country, and linked by some to the implementation since 2006–07 of the NREGS, which provides all households with a right to 100 days of employment on public works (Carswell and De Neve 2014; Rodgers and Rodgers 2011:45). More generally, evidence suggests that occupational diversification has been the most significant source of upward pressure on wages in the post-reform period (Srivastava and Singh 2005:420–421). The growth of non-farm employment and circulation has been unable to absorb the labour surplus, but it has broadened dependence on wage-labour beyond relations with local farmers, and modified the socio-political dynamics in labourers' home villages (Basole and Basu 2011:52; Breman 1999; Djurfeldt *et al.* 2008; Gooptu and Harriss-White 2001; Harriss 2013:358; Harriss *et al.* 2010; Heyer 2012; Lerche 1999; Pattenden 2012; Rodgers and Rodgers 2011).

Given that the poor spend much of their income on food,[14] it is unsurprising that nutrition indicators were flat-lining while real wages stagnated. The key nutrition indicator (mean body mass index) rose very marginally for women from 20.3 to 20.5 between 1998–99 and 2005–06, while the prevalence of anaemia among women increased from 51.8 per cent to 55.3 per cent over the same period (IIPC 2000:246, 252, 2007:308, 311). The percentage of children under the age of three who were underweight had fallen marginally over the same period from 42.7 to 40.4, while the percentage below an accepted height threshold had fallen from 51 to 44.9. On the other hand, the percentage of acutely (rather than chronically) malnourished had risen from 19.7 to 22.9 per cent (IIPC 2007:274).

As well as relatively high poverty levels, India has relatively low levels of expenditure on social services: 7.2 per cent of GDP in 2013–14, up from 6.8 per cent in 2008–09 (GoI MoF 2014:232). In 2013–14, spending on health stood at 1.4 per cent of GDP (up marginally from 1.3 per cent in 2008–09), while education spending stood at 3.3 per cent (up from 2.9 in 2008–09) – both significantly below the levels promised by the first Congress-led UPA government's Common Minimum Programme in the mid-2000s, and considerably less than other developing countries such as Brazil, China and Vietnam (GoI MoF 2014:232).[15]

From the 1980s, the state increased its support for private sector healthcare relative to the public sector, providing the former with tax exemptions and government land in urban centres (Iyer 2005:1). Recent research in Karnataka indicates growing health inequalities across gender, caste and class lines, and underscores the prominence of health expenditures in pushing or holding households below the poverty line (Iyer, 2005:x, 37). The UNDP's 2013 Human Development Indicators, which relate to income, health and education, placed India well down the table in 135th position – slightly ahead of Bangladesh, Nepal and Pakistan, but well adrift of Sri Lanka, Brazil and China.

There are significant disparities between and across states. In the late 2000s, life expectancy ranged from seventy-four years in Kerala to sixty-two in Madhya Pradesh. The infant mortality rate in the latter was almost five times greater than in the former. In the fieldwork state of Karnataka, human development indicators in its most south-westerly district are comparable to neighbouring Kerala, while at the other end of the state they match those of India's poorest states (UNDP 2005).

Poverty in Karnataka

Rural poverty levels in the fieldwork state of Karnataka fell by just 1.6 per cent between 2009–10 and 2011–12, which was the slowest rate of decline of poverty of all major states (see Table 1.3). Over the period 2004–05 to 2011–12, its rate of decline only exceeded those of Uttar Pradesh and Kerala.

Karnataka's rural poverty level is slightly lower than the national average, while its net per capita income in 2012/13 was somewhat higher – Rs. 77,309 as opposed to Rs. 67,839 (GoI MoF 2014:236–237). For three

Table 1.3 Rural poverty and rates of decline of poverty in selected states
and at all-India level (Tendulkar Method)

	2004–05 Rural	2009–10	2011–12 Rural	Decline in rural poverty 2004/05–2011/12	Decline in rural poverty 2009/10–2011/12
Odisha	60.8	39.2	35.7	**25.1**	3.5
Maharashtra	47.9	29.5	24.2	**23.7**	5.3
Tamil Nadu	37.5	21.2	15.8	**21.7**	5.4
Bihar	55.7	55.3	34.1	**21.6**	21.2
Andhra Pradesh	32.3	22.8	11	**21.3**	11.8
Rajasthan	35.8	26.4	16.1	**19.7**	10.4
Madhya Pradesh	53.6	42	35.7	**17.9**	6.3
Gujarat	39.1	26.7	21.5	**17.6**	5.2
West Bengal	38.2	28.8	22.5	**15.7**	6.3
Punjab	22.1	13.6	7.7	**14.4**	5.9
Karnataka	**37.5**	**26.1**	**24.5**	**13**	**1.6**
Uttar Pradesh	42.7	39.4	30.4	**12.3**	9
Kerala	20.2	12	9.1	**11.1**	2.9
India	**41.8**	**33.8**	**25.7**	**16.1**	**8.1**

Sources: GoI PC (2012, 2013).

particular social development indicators (life expectancy, infant mortality and literacy), it is ranked equal sixth of thirteen major states (see Table 1.4).

While a number of its economic and social indicators fall around the national average, Karnataka has performed relatively poorly at implementing NREGS. A recent national-level study of the National Rural Employment Guarantee Scheme, which compares National Sample Survey data (based on door-to-door surveys) and Ministry for Rural Development data (reported upwards from local-level officials), indicates an elevenfold discrepancy between officially recorded workdays and actual workdays (Usami and Rawal 2012:88). This is comfortably the highest discrepancy for any state, and the implication (which is elaborated upon below) is that the share of NREGS funds reaching classes of

Table 1.4 Social development indicators in selected states and at all-India level

	Life expectancy (2006–10, male + female)	Infant mortality (2012)	Literacy (2011)	Composite rank for three indicators (out of 13)
India	66.1	42	73	
Kerala	74.2	12	94	1
Maharashtra	69.9	25	82.3	2
Tamil Nadu	68.9	21	80.1	3
Punjab	69.3	28	75.8	4
West Bengal	69	32	76.3	5
Gujarat	66.8	38	78	6=
Karnataka	67.2	32	75.4	6=
Andhra Pradesh	65.8	41	67	8
Rajasthan	66.5	49	66.1	9
Odisha	63	53	72.9	10
Bihar	65.8	43	61.8	11
Uttar Pradesh	62.7	53	67.7	12=
Madhya Pradesh	62.4	56	69.3	12=

Source: GoI MoF (2014:110, 113) (original data from Sample Registration System, Office of the Registrar General of India, Ministry of Home Affairs).

labour in the form of wages is significantly lower than it is in other states (see Chapter 6).

A recent report on the performance of the Rashtriya Swasthya Bima Yojana (a health insurance scheme that is linked to the Unorganised Workers Social Security Act of 2008) shows that although 45.8 per cent of below poverty line households in Karnataka had been registered by November 2012, only 1.2 per cent had used their cards in hospitals (Aiyar *et al.* 2013:20–21). The rate was highest in the more developed coastal districts of Dakshin Kannada and Udupi (6.2 and 5.1 per cent respectively), and slightly higher in the fieldwork district of Dharwad (2.5 per cent).

With somewhat fewer marginal landholdings and slightly greater numbers of large landholdings, Karnataka's distribution of landholdings is slightly less equitable than the national average (see Table 1.5), which has implications for the distribution of power in rural society (discussed

Table 1.5 Distribution of land (%) by size of landholdings possessed (acres) for selected states (and all India), 2009–10

Ranking according to preponderance of marginal landholdings	State	0	0–1	1–2.5	2.5–5	5–10	>10
1	Tamil Nadu	2.3	78.5	10.7	5.2	2.6	0.7
2	Andhra Pradesh	7.2	62.3	14.7	7.7	6	2.1
3	Uttar Pradesh	5	56.4	22.1	10.3	4.9	1.3
4	Karnataka	8.2	50.5	17.2	12.6	8.2	3.4
5	Rajasthan	3.4	32.5	17	19.1	15.9	12
	All India	8.3	56.5	16.1	9.7	6.5	3

Source: GoI NSS (2012:73).

in Chapters 5 and 6; see also Kohli 1987). It had 706,332 industrial workers (in factories with more than ten workers) in 2011–12, above average for India (just over ten million in total), but less than half of Tamil Nadu, and well behind Andhra Pradesh, Maharashtra and Gujarat (GoI CSO 2014:S7–8).

District-level variations

Karnataka's 'average' indicators obscure wide disparities within the state. The two main fieldwork districts fall in two historically distinct regions of North Karnataka (see Figure 1). Dharwad lies in 'Bombay Karnataka', most of which was directly administered by the British colonialists as part of the Bombay Presidency, while Raichur lies in 'Hyderabad Karnataka', which was ruled by the Nizam of Hyderabad until 1956.[16]. Dharwad has a relatively dynamic economy centred on the twin cities of Hubli and Dharwad, which lie on the main Mumbai–Bengaluru highway and draw in daily commuters from the surrounding villages. Raichur city is smaller, less industrialised and less well connected to export markets. The district is home to a relatively high number of circular migrants, many of whom migrate for several months or years to work on remote building sites.

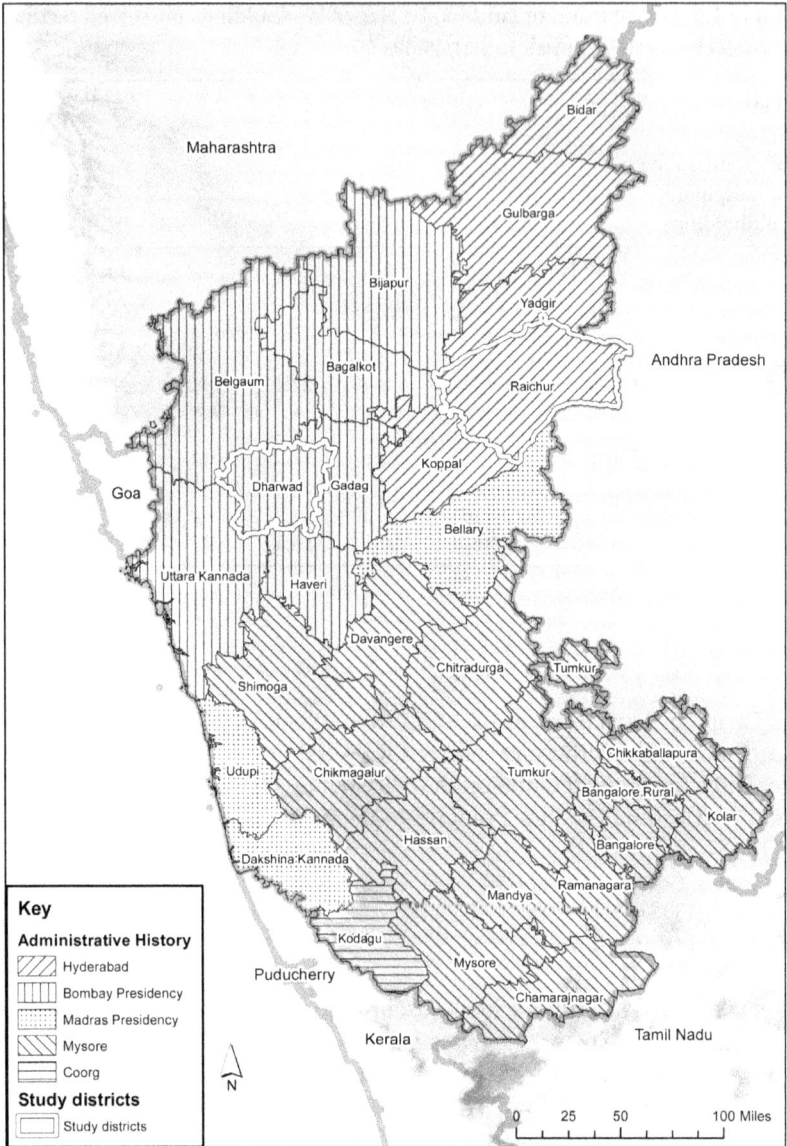

Figure 1 Map of Karnataka showing fieldwork districts and historical administrative divisions. (Courtesy of Oliver Springate-Baginski)

Table 1.6 Human Development Indicators of select states and districts of Karnataka, 2001

State/district	HDI in 2001	Rank out of 15 large states
Kerala	0.746	1
Dakshin Kannada District, South-West Karnataka	0.722	
Tamil Nadu	0.687	3
Karnataka	0.650	7
Dharwad District, North-West Karnataka	0.642	
Madhya Pradesh	0.572	12
Orissa	0.569	13
Raichur District, North-East Karnataka	0.547	
Uttar Pradesh	0.535	14
Bihar	0.495	15

Source: UNDP (2005:15, 29).

Dharwad (one of the two main fieldwork districts) has human development indicators that are close to the state average and higher than those of Raichur (the other main fieldwork district), which has the lowest in the state and the highest poverty headcount (see Table 1.6; UNDP 2005). The human development indicators of the interior south (formerly Mysore, a third distinct historical region) are higher than Dharwad's (one of the two main fieldwork districts), but the highest in the state are to be found in the coastal district of Dakshin Kannada (almost as high as those of Kerala). Its human development indicators are comparable to India's poorest states (lower than Orissa and Madhya Pradesh, but higher than Uttar Pradesh and Bihar) (UNDP 2005:15, 29).

The interplay in Dakshin Kannada of higher levels of social development, greater levels of political equity (in caste and class terms), more labouring class organisation and lower poverty levels is striking (Kohli 1987; see also Damle 1993). Land reform was implemented more effectively there due to its more equitable distribution of power and its major landowning castes' weaker influence over state politics. It had higher levels of landlord absenteeism (as landlords moved to cities) and more organised tenant farmers. Conversely, in the state's interior, major landowners often belonged to the state's two most politically influential castes (Lingayats and Vokkaligas) who had greater leverage over state institutions and weaker opposition. Land reforms were less effectively implemented in these regions (Kohli 1987).

There are also socio-political and socio-economic differences within districts due to land distribution, levels of irrigation, proximity to urban markets and balances of caste power.[17] Class relations and forms of domination and exploitation of labour vary along with levels of class-based organisation and the outcomes of state mediation.

This is where the book's contribution lies. Although it sits in a broader literature that takes a class-relational approach to processes of development, it applies a class-relational approach across hamlets, villages and districts through detailed fieldwork data collected over more than a decade on the three areas of labour relations, state policy and LGIs, and civil society. By doing so, it draws out the uneven dynamics of class relations at different levels and in different social settings, and sheds some light on the impediments to, as well as possibilities for, pro-labouring-class change.

Fieldwork locations and methods

Karnataka is the least researched of India's southern states. Research for this book began in Dharwad district in 2002 in the village of Panchnagaram.[18] It expanded outwards first to the surrounding villages and then to a second cluster of villages around 30 kilometres to the east, and finally to the Raichur villages around 300 kilometres further to the east.

Fieldwork stretched over 12 years (2002–14) and across 39 villages in three Karnataka districts (23 in Dharwad, 15 in Raichur and one in Mandya), a variety of government offices (from *gram panchayats* (GPs or village councils) to state government departments via district and sub-district councils and a range of line departments), a couple of dozen NGOs and two social movements (one small-scale labouring class movement and one state-level movement of dominant class farmers). Methods used ranged from ethnography, census surveys, interviews, interactions with key informants and the collection of official government data (from GP records to large National Sample Survey Organisation datasets). Methods varied across the villages – from ethnography, census surveys and multiple rounds of interviews in 'core' fieldwork villages (and some LGIs), to multiple and single rounds of interviews in 'intermediate' villages, and one-off group and key informant interviews in 'peripheral' villages. Respondents included agricultural labourers, labourers who commuted and migrated to work in construction and industry, farmers of different sizes, NGO workers CBO members, social movement activists and government officials with varying levels of responsibility. Some respondents were interviewed once; others on numerous occasions.

Table 1.7 Fieldwork villages

Key variables	Raichur villages	Dharwad villages
Distance from district headquarters (km)	70–90	6–18
Distance from main road (km)	0–12	3–15
Main bases of labouring class reproduction	Agriculture, construction	Agriculture, construction, industry
Main source of non-agricultural work	Long-distance circular migration to the construction sector	Daily commuting to nearby city
Levels and type of irrigation	Canal-irrigation: 33–95%	Dryland – borewell irrigation: 10–33%
Significant bases of accumulation	Agriculture, agribusiness, city-based formal employment	Agriculture, local state

Source: fieldwork data.

Discussions took place in people's homes and farms, and in village tea shops and government offices.

Fieldwork in Dharwad focused on eight villages in two GPs within commutable distance of nearby cities. Fieldwork in Raichur focused on a larger cluster of villages spanning the sub-districts of Manvi and Sindhanur, and beyond commutable range of any cities. The seven main fieldwork villages spanned five different GPs. The fieldwork-based chapters are not strictly a comparison of different districts. Different groups of villages are analysed in the different chapters. Sometimes the focus is on Dharwad, sometimes on Raichur, and sometimes on both.

Fieldwork villages varied in terms of levels of irrigation, soil types, proximity to urban labour markets, caste distributions, patterns of accumulation and labouring class reproduction, and forms of class relations (see Table 1.7; see also Chapter 4). The Dharwad villages were dryland villages, while those in Raichur had varying levels of canal-irrigation. Scheduled castes were around twice as numerous in the Raichur villages,[19] while the dominant caste in Dharwad had a stronger grip on local politics than was the case in Raichur. Even within districts, there were marked differences between GPs. For example, Panchamsali Lingayats (a farming sub-caste) dominated one of the two Dharwad GPs, while in the other they shared power with Muslims and 'Other Backward Castes'. These differences have a bearing on the forms of class relations and the outcomes of social policy.

Outline of the book

The next chapter outlines what is meant by a class-relational approach to labour, state and society in rural India, and contrasts it to 'semi-relational' analysis. It defines key terms such as Bernstein's 'classes of labour', and distinguishes between class understood as a form of social stratification, and class understood as a social relation. It also defines class as being a multi-faceted rather than a singular identity, and in doing so counters reified approaches to the term. The chapter discusses what is meant by exploitation, and argues that the relations through which it is concretised and labour is impoverished tend to be given insufficient attention in the literature on poverty. It suggests, moreover, that this relative inattention to exploitation is derived in part from Weberian approaches to class, which have been prominent in recent literature on poverty and development.

Drawing on secondary literature, Chapter 3 contextualises the ensuing fieldwork chapters, and begins the process of operationalising a class-relational approach. It does so by outlining some of the key changes in class relations in rural India over recent decades, addressing, in turn, processes of informalisation and segmentation in labour relations (forms of domination and exploitation), state-based mediations of class relations through LGIs and social policy, and neoliberal and class-based forms of organisation.

Chapter 4 is the first of the fieldwork-based chapters, which are all based on analysis of class relations across a variety of rural settings. Chapter 4 focuses on labour relations and how labour is controlled across the agriculture and construction sectors (within the labour process and beyond it). As well as discussing concrete forms of exploitation and increasingly multi-sited patterns of labouring class reproduction, it also assesses the extent to which increased access to non-agricultural employment improves labour's socio-economic and socio-political position. It compares villages where commuting is more common with those where long-distance circular migration is more common. Variations in class relations are also linked to the degree to which accumulation is focused on agriculture, and comparisons are made between wet and dryland villages. As well as agrarian capital, classes of labour in both fieldwork areas have direct interactions with international capital – in the Dharwad villages through factories that they commute to, and in the Raichur villages through the buildings that they construct for international companies in Bengaluru.

Chapter 5 focuses on how the dominant class uses Local Government Institutions (LGIs) to and strengthen its economic and political position. It uses the term 'gatekeeper' to represent how the state–society interface assumes concrete forms among class relations. It is found both here and in Chapter 6 that the influence of gatekeeping on state mediation of class relations is greater where the dominant caste/class is relatively united, and where there are restraints on accumulation in agriculture. Unlike Chapter 4, which analyses class relations primarily in villages where accumulation was primarily based on agriculture, agribusiness or formal employment, Chapter 5 focuses on villages where accumulation is linked more centrally to the state. This has a bearing on the forms of control exercised over labour. More broadly, Chapter 5 also shows how the state comes to be 'constituted' by capital – not least through the fact that the vast majority of individuals in the fieldwork state's elected assembly are capitalists. It also outlines how different regions of the state have clusters of capitalists from different sectors of the economy (such as agriculture, real estate and mining). It does so not because such a finding is particularly surprising but in order to link processes of accumulation, domination and exploitation at village level to the broader workings of the state.

Although LGIs and CSOs are primarily shown to reproduce existing inequalities, they can also play a role in pro-labouring-class change, particularly where labour is well organised and the balance of power more even, and when poverty reduction programmes are universal (available to all). In this regard, Chapter 6 focuses on NREGS. It shows contrasting trajectories of implementation in the different fieldwork villages. In some the scheme initially provided benefits to both the dominant and labouring class. Over time, though, a united dominant class increasingly took control of the scheme and shaped it to suit its interests. In other villages, an initial wholesale subversion of the scheme by dominant-class men who saw it as a threat to their interests, and had sufficient leverage over LGIs to derail it, was subsequently countered by an organisation of labouring class women (with varying degrees of success). Despite its uneven performance, the chapter underlines the potential that NREGS has to strengthen the material and socio-political position of the labouring class.

Chapter 7 argues that the local NGOs, CBOs and self-help groups that have proliferated in recent years represent a neoliberalisation of civil society, which tends to reproduce rather than contest the status quo. In contrast, Chapter 8 analyses a movement of labouring class scheduled caste women. Focusing on associations in three villages, it analyses varying levels of social movement activity and its uneven outcomes. It also assesses different forms of mobilisation, and considers whether small-scale labouring class organisations can be scaled up. A short conclusion follows.

Notes

1 For example, Breman (1974, 1985, 1996, 2007a, 2007b), Guérin (2013), Guérin *et al.* (2009a, 2012), Harriss (1982, 1992, 2001, 2013), Harriss-White (1996, 2003, 2008), Kannan and Breman (2013), Lerche (1999, 2007, 2013), Lieten and Srivastava (1999), Mezzadri 2014, Srivastava (1989, 2011) in relation to India, and Selwyn (2014) more broadly.

2 This varies between state-level governments, with the governments of Kerala and (to a lesser degree) Tamil Nadu being more pro-labour than many other states (Heller 1999; Heyer 2012).
3 The term classes of labour is taken from Bernstein (2006) (see discussion of the term in Chapter 2).
4 http://ilo.org/global/about-the-ilo/decent-work-agenda/lang-en/index.htm (accessed 12 October 2013).
5 Given that these are routinely flouted, this to some degree represents a symbolic gesture intended to please international capital.
6 Voting is certainly more free than it was when labour relations were highly personalised and agricultural workers generally voted according to their patrons' instructions (Robinson 1988).
7 Some of these countries have seen a downturn in their economic position in recent months, but can still be seen as 'ascendant' in the current period.
8 Figures computed from data.worldbank.org/indicator/NY.GDP.MKTP. KD.ZG (accessed 12 September 2014).
9 Long critiqued for underestimating poverty, official estimates of poverty levels rose following the Tendulkar Report of 2009. Its higher minimum per capita consumption expenditure (in part by taking greater account of the costs of healthcare and education) increased rural poverty estimates from 28.7 to 41.8 per cent for 2004/05 (GoI PC 2009:22–23). Estimates for 2011–12 were based on a per capita monthly consumption expenditure of Rs. 816 for rural areas, and 1,000 for urban areas (GoI PC 2009:2), which amounted to $0.51 per day without taking purchasing power parity into account (based on the exchange rate for 31 January 2011). The Rangarajan Committee, which submitted its report in June 2014, has recommended increasing the poverty line by a further 19 per cent for rural India and 41 per cent for urban areas, thereby increasing the numbers classified as poor by 93.2 million (GoI PC 2014:60, 69). A major difference with the Tendulkar methodology lies in the increased weighting of non-food items. Housing rents act as a major contributor to the heightened discrepancy between rural and urban areas (GoI PC 2014:2). Adjusted for purchasing power parity (where $1 = Rs. 15.11), the suggested Rangarajan poverty lines amount to $2.14 for rural areas and $2.44 overall (GoI PC 2014:60). Other estimations of poverty include those of the National Commission for Enterprises in the Unorganised Sector, which included those who were vulnerable to poverty, thereby producing a figure of 69 per cent for 2010 (see Table 1.1), while a recent multidimensional analysis estimated India's poverty levels at over 50 per cent (Alkire *et al.* 2013:3, 24). Although figures based on the Tendulkar methodology are now widely used and are seen as an improvement, official estimates of poverty are still widely regarded as being too low. The real level of poverty probably lies somewhere between the Rangarajan and NCEUS estimates (see Table 1.1).
10 This figure, and the figures in the following paragraph, are all based on official poverty estimates reached by the Tendulkar method.
11 Marginal farmers are primarily wage-labourers given the limited size of their land holdings. They are seen here as part of the labouring class as they are net sellers of labour-power. See Chapter 2 for a detailed discussion.

12 Scheduled castes and scheduled tribes are formal administrative terms with colonial roots. The SCs are also the 'former untouchables' who were (to some degree still are) seen as being at the bottom of, or outside, the Hindu caste hierarchy and who are subject to various forms of discrimination. SCs have generally had fewer assets and been more likely to work as labourers – hence the significant overlap between caste and class (see Lerche 1995, for example). SCs are also known as *dalits* (the oppressed), while STs are also known as *adivasis* (indigenous peoples).

13 The data are based on the Government of India's Rural Labour Enquiry (various years).

14 Over 60 per cent according to one estimate (Himanshu 2008a:31).

15 Additional data drawn from World Health Organisation data on health expenditure (http://apps.who.int/nha/database, accessed 4 August 2014).

16 Althougth the differences between the *zamindari* and *ryotwari* colonial taxation systems (the former exercised through powerful local intermediaries and the latter more directly) are sometimes overplayed (Moore 1966), it is worth pointing out that the taxation system in Hyderabad Karnataka has tended to be closer to the zamindari system while that of Bombay Karnataka has tended to be closer to the ryotwari system (a picture complicated, among other things, by a smattering of small princely states across North-West Karnataka). This is not unrelated to the former's lower levels of development, but there is no space to discuss this here. Mysore (the interior southern half of Karnataka) had somewhat more equal land distribution and a somewhat less oppressive taxation system (see, for example, Government of Karnataka 1989).

17 In some, notably the southern states of Kerala and Tamil Nadu, dominant class/caste power has been significantly dented (see Djurfeldt *et al.* 2008; Harriss 1999, 2003; Harriss *et al.* 2010; Harriss-White 2008; Heller 1999; Heyer 2012; Kohli 1987; Veron *et al.* 2006), and attempts to provide rights and social security for informal sector workers have been significantly more successful (Nair 2004). In parts of West Bengal, meanwhile, state investment in irrigation infrastructure reduced the size of the reserve army of labour. Coupled with party political interventions that were sympathetic to labour, the conditions of migrant labourers circulating through its rice fields had greater bargaining power and were better off, for example, than migrant cane cutters moving through southern Gujarat (see Rogaly *et al.* 2001 for the West Bengal example, and Breman 1990 for the Gujarat example).

18 The names of all places and individuals referred to in this book have been changed to protect anonymity.

19 The Madigas (known as Madars in Dharwad) were the most numerous scheduled caste in the fieldwork area in Raichur. Chalwadis were the second most numerous, followed by Woddars.

2

A class-relational approach

Society does not consist of individuals, but expresses the sum of inter-relations. (Marx 1973:265)

While capitalism presupposes a structural opposition between capital and labour that is rooted in ownership of productive assets and acted out through the performance of surplus labour and its attendant forms of domination, actually existing class relationships are 'almost infinitely more complicated' (Harriss 2006:446). When viewed in concrete historical terms, class is a plural category in terms of its subdivisions (shaped by the 'structural sources of exploitation and inequality inherent in all capitalist production petty and grand, informal and formal') and in terms of the various axes of inequality embedded within it. Class relations may be universal 'determinations' of social practices in capitalism, but they are far from exclusive since they 'intersect and combine with' other 'sources of inequality and oppression', such as gender, caste, race and ethnicity (Bernstein 2007:7, 2010:115).[1] Such a multi-faceted view of class undermines accusations that a focus on class crowds out other forms of antagonism.[2]

This chapter discusses what is meant by a class-relational approach. It proceeds in four steps. Firstly, it defines the terms 'dominant class' and 'classes of labour', and locates them in a typology. Secondly, it discusses exploitation. It then outlines how a class-relational approach differs from 'semi-relational' Weberian approaches. The final section discusses its differences with prominent strands of the recent literature on poverty and development.

Defining 'classes of labour' and the 'dominant class'

'Classes of labour':

comprise 'the growing numbers ... who now depend – directly *and indirectly* – on the sale of their labour power for their own daily reproduction' (Panitch and Leys 2001, ix) ... through insecure and oppressive – and in many places increasingly scarce – wage employment, often *combined with* a range of likewise precarious small-scale farming and insecure 'informal sector' ('survival') activity, subject to its own forms of differentiation and oppression along intersecting lines of class, gender, generation, caste, and ethnicity. In short, most have to pursue their means of livelihood/reproduction across different sites of the social division of labour: urban and rural, agricultural and non-agricultural wage employment and self-employment. (Bernstein 2006:455; see also Lerche 2010)

Bernstein's term 'classes of labour' captures the segmentation of labour across multiple sites of production while underlining their shared position as members of the exploited classes and maintaining focus on the core antagonism between capital and labour (Bernstein 2006, 2007, 2010).[3] By locating labour's fragmentation among class *relations*, it provides the means of explaining the surface phenomena of labour's conditions.

Beyond that, the term is significant for a number of reasons. First, the scarcity of work indicates the presence of a reserve army of labour, which 'disciplines and disempowers those in work, discouraging them politically from struggles over the distribution of wages and profits' (Harriss-White 2005:1243). Second, the term 'classes of labour' underscores the political nature of labour relations, which are 'oppressive', 'insecure' and often located in the informal sector.' This is indicative not only of poor working conditions, but also of the strategies of capitalists, in collusion with the state, to keep labour relations beyond the purview of state regulation (Harriss-White 2010). Third, it points to classes of labour's growing numbers. Each of these are manifested in recent trends in India where labourers are increasingly numerous, but also increasingly fragmented and informalised, and among whom is to be found a growing 'reserve army' of labour (see Chapter 3 for a detailed discussion).

The distinction between classes of labour and the dominant class is based primarily on the net buying and selling of labour-power (see Patnaik 1976), and whether households are surplus or deficit producers (Athreya *et al.* 1987). Both terms are internally differentiated. Classes of labour, understood here as net sellers of labour-power who do not produce a surplus (see Table 2.1), include (i) households that only work as wage-labourers; (ii) those who work more as wage-labourers than on their own land (and/or in other forms of petty production (see below); and (iii) those who primarily work on their own land (and/or in other forms of petty production) but who also work as wage-labourers. The term 'dominant class' refers to net buyers of labour who tend to produce a surplus, and includes (i) those who produce exclusively through hired

Table 2.1 Classes of labour and the dominant class in contemporary rural India

Net buyers of labour-power (**capitalists and petty capitalists**)	Dominant class	Surplus producers	Those whose land is cultivated by hired labour	More likely to diversify accumulation strategies out of agriculture
			Those who primarily use hired labour but also use family labour	May also be involved in petty forms of self-employment outside agriculture
	Petty capitalists and petty commodity producers	Tend to produce a surplus	Those who primarily work their own land but also hire in labour	
'Pure' petty commodity producers (few in number)		No investible surplus	Produce with family labour alone	
Net sellers of labour-power (**classes of labour**)	Classes of labour	Deficit producers	Those who primarily work their own land but also sell their labour-power	May also be involved in petty forms of self-employment outside of agriculture (often as disguised wage-labour).
			Marginal farmers who sell their labour-power more than they work on their own land	Likely to sell labour-power in various sectors and locations
			Landless who only sell their labour-power	

Source: inspired by Bernstein (2006), Lerche (2010), Patnaik (1976).

labour, and (ii) those who produce predominantly with hired labour but also work on the land themselves. Although the term 'dominant class' is a proxy for the capitalist class, it is used in order to emphasise the political aspects of class relations – both in production relations and in their mediation by state institutions. The term is particularly appropriate in India given the interrelations between class and caste and the widespread use of the term 'dominant caste'. The latter is associated with the work of M.N. Srinivas (1963), who understood the dominant caste as those who were numerically dominant, owned more (often most) of the land and tended to dominate village institutions. More recently, Benbabaali (2013) has analysed the more spatially diverse forms through which dominant castes in contemporary India reproduce themselves economically and politically. Although less bound up with land than in previous decades, the power of dominant castes appears to have been dissipated more than it has been diminished (Harriss 2012, 2013). Caste and class cannot be separated in the analysis of Indian society.[4] Caste, as Harriss (2012) puts it, 'entails an ideology that explains and legitimates the material differences of class and power relations'.

An intermediate third category produces mostly with household labour but also hires labour-power. This category tends not to dominate political institutions or control labour in the same way as larger landowners, and hence is not seen here as being part of the dominant class. At its upper levels it includes producers who always hire some labour-power and generate a small surplus that can, over time, be invested in expanded reproduction. At its lower levels there is no systematic buying of labour-power and the size of the surplus, even over time, is not sufficient for re-investment. In other words, it includes petty capitalists and petty commodity producers.

Petty commodity production (PCP) takes place largely through household labour and cannot in itself be seen as capital or labour (Gibbon and Neocosmos 1985). 'Pure' petty commodity producers are understood as the relatively small category of households that produce and reproduce themselves exclusively through family labour. Households that engage in PCP but are net sellers of labour-power whose PCP does not produce a surplus are seen here as part of the classes of labour. Classifying them as such does not obscure those aspects of their material reproduction that are based on PCP, or mask the complex mix of forms of petty self-employment and wage-labour through which they reproduce themselves. On the contrary, as a multi-faceted category classes of labour provides an antidote to such reductionism.

Where PCP is combined with wage-labour it can subsidise the production costs of capital by allowing it to pay wages that do not meet the costs of reproduction – highly significant in particular social settings, but also in the broader context of Indian capitalists' ability to compete in world markets. Many activities that are associated with PCP are better understood as disguised wage-labour, including, for example, petty trading on credit for daily incomes comparable to casual daily wages (Breman 1999; see also Gerry 1978).

While petty commodity producers may be more likely to become 'proletarians' than capitalists (Gerry 1978), petty commodity production's continuing prevalence[5] underlines that it is an integral feature of capitalism that ebbs and flows in significance within households and across societies as forms of reproduction are modified by broader dynamics of capitalist development. Hence distress-related levels of PCP spiked in India in the early 2000s as real wages and employment levels stagnated (Chandrasekhar and Ghosh 2007).

The many forms of wage-labour can be seen as a hierarchy, with formally contracted wage-labour in the formal economy at its apex (those who have a written contract in most cases, some access to social security and a degree of protection through labour regulations); regular informal wage-labourers on the second rung; casual (irregular) informal workers on the third; and bonded labour at the bottom.[6] Formal wage workers have been described as part of an 'aristocracy of labour' and may earn significantly higher wages (for example Parry 2008). Nevertheless, they are categorised here as wage-labourers as they are still net sellers of labour-power and still perform surplus labour. That would only change if they had invested outside of their formal employment in assets that produced a surplus and involved the regular buying of labour-power. Other workers employed on a casual informal basis at the same site may appear to subsidise their wages, but the relationship between workers in one particular place cannot be understood in isolation from the broader relations between capital and labour.

Within households, domestic labour, which 'produces new labour-power for the wage-labour market', is largely carried out by women (and girls) (Gooptu and Harriss-White 2001). Women's contribution to the overall production of surplus-value is often unpaid and concealed from the public sphere. In the sphere of production, women's wages are lower, and they are more likely to occupy lower-grade unskilled positions as well as facing greater obstacles in accessing non-agricultural work (Breman 1990; Da Corta and Venkateshwarlu 1999; Garikipati 2008:629; Gooptu and Harriss-White 2001; Pattenden 2012).

While the fragmentation of labour is derived from the dynamics of capitalist competition and class relations, which drive forces of production and increase the mobility of capital and labour, it is also a consequence of conscious capitalist strategising. Capitalists tend to be better placed to divide labour than vice versa due to their greater political strength (in overall terms, not necessarily in particular places and at particular times). Capitalists shape structurally derived processes of fragmentation in order to weaken labour, cheapen the costs of production and gain advantages over their competitors. They do so in three primary ways: (i) by actively contributing to divisions between labourers (by, for example, mixing together workers from different locations to weaken the links between them), or by increasing the number of wage levels (by gender or task specialisation, for example); (ii) by increasing the extent to which the labour process is controlled through intermediaries who reduce direct interactions between capitalists and labourers, thereby reifying the spaces of class struggle, removing the burdens of direct management; and (iii) by facilitating the informalisation and flexibilisation of the workforce, which allows capitalists to shed labourers during periods when the need for labour-power declines, and reduces its need to provide forms of social security or follow labour regulations. Overall, each strategy lowers the costs of production and weakens labour's political strength within the production process and beyond (see Chapter 4).

Exploitation

Although capitalist labour relations may appear as forms of free exchange in the marketplace, labouring class households are compelled to enter the market to sell their labour-power as they lack sufficient productive assets for their material reproduction following gradual processes of socio-economic differentiation, or more dramatic and sudden processes of appropriation – forcible acts of dispossession such as the enclosures of seventeenth-century England, for example, or the loss of lands to politically connected real estate speculators in contemporary India.

Just as compulsion appears as freedom, so exploitation appears as fair exchange since wages obscure the appropriation of surplus-value (the basis of accumulation and profit) through surplus labour time – the portion of the day when the labourer is no longer working for the costs of her own reproduction but for the capitalist (Marx 1976). This contrasts to Adam Smith's (1970:167) view that 'the produce of labour constitutes the natural recompense or wages of labour'. Wage contracts mediate and mask labour's domination by capital (Banaji (2010:153), while legally formal rights under capitalism 'make it appear that these formal equalities are in fact real equalities' (Selwyn 2011:72).

Labour costs are kept to what is socially necessary for the reproduction of labour (i.e. at a level that neither dents productivity nor threatens the supply of labour through instability, and is shaped by the capital–labour relation within society as a whole), or may be pushed below that level in order to expand market share and increase levels of accumulation (for example Andrees and Belser 2009; Roesch et al. 2009; see also Chapter 3).

The forms of control exercised over labour vary between locations and across time as dynamics of accumulation change, and class relations and strategies are modified. Control is exercised within the labour process but also beyond it through debt relations, or by influencing those charged with regulating labour relations. In other words, exploitation is shaped far beyond the production process, and by relations between as well as within classes. For example, while surplus-value is extracted from labourers by capitalists, the conversion of surplus-value into profits is mediated (among other things) by intra-capitalist competition and patterns of incorporation into markets.

Surplus-value is not only extracted from labour in the production process through the performance of surplus labour, but also by merchant capitalists who appropriate part of the 'total social capital'[7] at various points along commodity circuits; through rents charged for productive assets such as land and machinery; and through usury that can prime both the extraction of surplus-value in the production process and its appropriation through exchange. 'Loans', which act as a form of advance wage that increases access to labour-power, become debts that can be used to press labourers to intensify their work-rate or extend their surplus labour time. 'Interest' rates linked to loans can also mask wage cuts. The combination of buying labour-power, lending money to labourers, trading their produce and providing production inputs increases control over labourers and augments the rate of exploitation (see Bharadwaj 1985).

Finally, capitalist accumulation is derived in part from 'primitive accumulation' or 'accumulation by dispossession'.[8] Marx (1976) used the term 'primitive accumulation' to describe often coercive processes through which land and productive resources are appropriated (often with state complicity). Such resources, with the addition of labour-power provided by those whose assets have been appropriated, provide a basis for capitalist accumulation. Such a process is understood here as not only occurring during the uneven and often protracted transition to capitalism, but as persisting as capitalists seek bases for expanded reproduction. Hence in the contemporary Indian context the appropriation of land for special economic zones (SEZs), dams and infrastructure projects, real estate development and 'all manners of privatizations of natural resources and public wealth' also occurs as an integral aspect of capitalism rather than simply creating the conditions for it (Levien 2011:938). Although often on a grand scale, such processes encompass the more petty acts of accumulation by dispossession that arise from less dramatic processes of socio-economic differentiation that gradually divorce producers from both the means of production and reproduction (De Neve forthcoming; Levien 2011:938). These acts of dispossession increase dependence on the sale of labour-power for material reproduction, swelling the ranks of classes of labour. The Land Acquisition Bill being discussed in India at the time of writing will multiply the number of such acts across the country.

Following Banaji (2010), exploitation is understood in this book at two levels: the forms of exploitation that focus on specific relations between capitalists and labourers in particular places; and the social relations of production, which relate to the broader relations between capital and labour across society. The former exist at any particular moment in time 'in all their complexity', while the latter is a much broader social conceptualisation of relations under capitalism that extends far beyond the labour process (Campling 2014:4). Wage-labour is at once 'abstract, value-producing labour' and the focal point of concrete relationships between capital and labour. The distinction, then, is between the 'concrete or specific ways' in which capitalists control and deploy labour and the 'general forms of domination'.[9] This book foregrounds the former through intensive fieldwork methods while keeping the latter in view.

Labour's spatial extension across different sectors and sites of production means that class relations have to be analysed across a variety of different sites of exploitation, while also reflecting (the tendency towards) intensified interactions with world markets and international sites of production and movements of capital. Class relations are part of a world-historical process – from the broader process of colonialism's widely documented drain on India's economic development (e.g. Davis 2001; Moore 1966; Patnaik 1986; Wolf 1982), or transnational agribusiness corporations' appropriation of surplus-value at some distance from the production process, to the specific histories of particular localities where contemporary accumulation is underpinned by the labour of past as well as present generations.[10]

Forms of exploitation are understood here as encompassing both more direct forms (relations in and around the production process), and the less direct relations that mediate those forms (primarily in this book through class-based organisation and political institutions). Hence direct forms of exploitation include: (i) the relationships between labourers, employers and their intermediaries over the hours and intensity of work, wages and forms of payment, working methods and tasks, working conditions and the nature of the contract (whether it is verbal or written and requires the employer to comply with legislation); and to a considerable extent (ii) relationships among labourers at the worksite (during the production process) or during the immediate process of reproduction (time spent in labour camps or village streets) that influence the degree of unity among labourers, and are influenced by caste, kin, gender, place of origin, language, skill level, task, location of work and affiliation to political parties, unions and other forms of collective organisation; while indirect forms include (iii) forms of collective organisation including small and large social movements, trade unions and political parties that seek to represent the interests of labour, but also civil society organisations that support the status quo rather than challenging it; (iv) observable formal relationships between labourers and the state (whether, for example, they have cards entitling them to the Public Distribution System and NREGS), which affect degrees of dependence upon wage-labour; (v) observable informal relationships between labourers and the state (such as informal access to council representatives); (vi) relations among farmers and other employers (the extent to which they are united or divided along lines of caste, kin, gender, place of origin, language, location, scale of production, level of asset ownership, level of capitalisation, sector, source of labour-power, pattern of market access etc.); and (vii) relationships between capitalists (including caste and industry associations) and the state.

Rather than what Banaji (2010) calls 'forced abstractions', which necessitate generalisations about social reality under capitalism in a manner that is at once both reductionist and teleological, a class-relational approach seeks to engage with the diversity of the concrete and the multiplicity of its determinations. By emphasising complexity, unevenness and lack of linearity, it defies (inherently) ahistorical and teleological views of change. A class-relational approach, by definition, is dialectical rather than linear or teleological.

A class-relational approach analyses forms of exploitation and domination, and their mediation, in order to understand how to improve the material and socio-political position of labour (relative to capital). Unlike situations where labour has considerable structural power (as is the case, for example, with relatively skilled grape producers who are closely connected to global commodity chains through time-sensitive 'export windows'; Selwyn 2009), and is able to use it to augment its organisational strength ('associational power'),[11] the labourers discussed in this book are less visible and have very little structural power (as noted in Chapter 1). As construction workers in Bengaluru, they build the offices of transnational corporations and the living quarters of their middle-class employees, but disappear before the apartments are populated and the offices become part of processes of accumulation. As industrial workers, they mostly perform temporary, unskilled roles that are peripheral to the core labour process and leave their contribution to the generation of surplus-value obscured. As agricultural labourers, they are generally located a long way down commodity chains, performing tasks, such as transplanting rice, that are scarcely discernible beyond the villages where they work in gangs or as individuals. These are informal, fragmented workers labouring on the periphery of global production networks. How can their material and socio-political position improve, and how might their 'associational power' grow?

Weber and 'semi-relational' approaches to poverty

Having outlined what a class-relational approach is, this section addresses what it is not. It sketches some key overlaps and disjunctures between the class-relational approach and the work of Weber, Bourdieu, Sen's *Development as Freedom* and significant parts of the recent policy-oriented literature.

As already outlined, as well as being centrally concerned with exploitation, a class-relational approach views class as a plural category, which is inflected by other forms of difference and antagonism that are partially, but never entirely, discrete from it. The poor are understood not in terms of their characteristics, or as occupying a particular 'structural location', but through their relations with others, which are at once contemporary and historical, particular and reflective of society as a whole.

While the class-relational approach emphasises exploitation and domination and how unequal relations between capitalists and labourers extend beyond the labour process to encompass the entire process of material reproduction (the relationship between capital and labour is constant because while labour is exploited during the process of production, its material conditions and the process of its reproduction are always shaped by the act of exploitation), contrasting stratification-oriented perspectives on class tend to compare and measure the material conditions of labour in isolation from the process of exploitation (Wright 2009).

Such approaches tend not to view class positions as being interrelated. The poor, in other words, are seen in terms of their characteristics and position within a social hierarchy rather than in terms of their relations with the better-off. Categorisation according to key characteristics is useful, but without being linked to the historical and contemporary relations that give rise to them, it tends to obscure both the causes of the poor's conditions and the strategies best placed to redistribute power and resources to them.

Nevertheless, a stratification-oriented approach to class has often dominated development research and policy-oriented discourse in recent decades along with what is termed here as a 'semi-relational' approach to class, which has links to the work of Weber (Wright 2009). Here the better-off defend their position by excluding others ('social closure'). While capitalists own means of production, the middle class exercise a degree of monopoly over the acquisition of education and skills, and the working class are 'defined by their exclusion from both higher educational credentials and capital' (Wright 2009:106). Unlike the first approach, this second approach sees a causal connection between different class positions, but tends to focus on the effects of unequal relations rather than on their causes.

There are similarities between Marx and Weber. Weber recognises the forms of coercion that lie behind the apparent freedom of the market-place, writing that under capitalism, the 'propertyless' are 'compelled to get rid' of 'their labour or the resulting products' in order to 'subsist at all' (Weber 1978:927, see also 110). Weber suggests that 'property' and the 'lack of property' are *the basic categories of all class situations* and the most fundamental source of class division (Weber 1978:927, emphasis added). The propertied have a monopoly on turning wealth into capital, and upon returns to the latter (Weber 1978:927).

Attention is paid primarily to the ways in which unequal distributions of property and productive assets lead to unequal relations in markets, rather than to relations of production and their links to processes of domination. Class position shapes unequal market exchanges: the 'mode of distribution' means that highly valued goods are beyond the reach of the 'non-wealthy', while those who do not have to sell 'monopolise the opportunities for profitable deals' (Weber 1978:927). 'Class situation', Weber wrote (1978:927–928), is 'ultimately market situation'.

The 'class situations' of the propertied and labourers, in turn, are internally differentiated by asset levels and skills (Weber 1978:928, 929). The term 'life chances' figures prominently in these market-mediated trajectories. A class exists, Weber argued, when 'a number of people have in common a specific causal component of their life chances'. That causal component of life chances is 'represented exclusively' by 'economic interests in the possession of goods' and 'opportunities for income'.

Market and life chances, distributions of assets and income are all significant for Weber's approach to class. It speaks to an individual attributes approach in its cataloguing of ownership, while addressing aspects of class relations in its emphasis on how asset distribution shapes interactions in the marketplace. Arguably this amounts to a semi-relational approach to class, which reappears in more recent policy-oriented literature on poverty and development (see below). The focus is on who has what and what they do with it more than on how they got it in the first place. Some mechanisms of surplus-value appropriation are recognised (such as the 'creditor–debtor' relation), but exploitation and discussion of the basis of economic surpluses are largely absent from the analysis as, by extension, are the variations in its forms and their implications for labouring class strategy. In emphasising how control over productive assets shapes life chances more than the ways in which they 'structure patterns of exploitation and domination' (Wright 2005:25; Breen 2005:33–34), Weber is seen here as subscribing to a semi-relational approach that tends to obscure exploitation.

Rather than a neglect of exploitation, Bourdieu's positioning in the same 'semi-relational' category is due more to his opening the door to a fragmentation of relations, and a privileging of the subjective. Recognising the conflictual nature of the capital–labour relation, Bourdieu (1986:83) stated that 'capital is accumulated labour', and referred to social energy being appropriated 'in the form of reified or living labour'. He long accorded primacy to economic capital over cultural, symbolic and social capital, arguing that the former was 'at the root of all other types of capital', although 'never entirely reducible' to it (1986:91).

His use of symbolic capital underlines the significance of status to the reproduction of dominance – manifested, for example, in ostentatious displays of proximity to politicians (Jeffrey 2000). Symbolic capital provides a means of maintaining control over labour without bearing the full costs of its reproduction (Bourdieu 1990:118). In other words, symbolic capital, like cultural and social capital, is part of the process of reproducing dominance and maintaining the extraction of surplus-value.[12] By seeking to persuade rather than enforce, either ideologically or through 'gifts' that 'validate' exploitation, the costs and risks of exploitation are reduced (see also Gramsci 1971).

Bourdieu's disassembling of the term 'capital' has analytical value, and the view that class relations are not reducible to the economic is shared by many Marxists, as it was by Marx (Bernstein 2006; Marx 1976:340–416; Bourdieu 1990). However, *disaggregating the concept of capital* clears the way for those coming afterwards to focus on symbolic and/or social and/or cultural capital *while neglecting* economic capital. In other words, the fragmentation of capital can foster the fragmentation of analysis.

Bourdieu's (1990:55) development of the term *habitus*, a terrain of 'thoughts, perceptions, expressions and actions' bounded only by the 'historically and socially situated conditions of its production' sheds light on the more subjective elements of how people's position and interests relate to their actions and strategies. In the case of Bourdieu, this can be seen as a drawing out of the details of how class relations are reproduced without intending to obscure broader structures (1990). Among some of those inspired by his work, though, it appears to have prompted a privileging of the subjective, which, when combined with the fragmentation of 'capitals', produces analyses that segment the social, neglect the material and take individual subjectivities into the realm of methodological individualism (e.g. Gough *et al.* 2006:20) – a trend that is revisited below in recent literature on poverty and well-being.

Keeping it residual? The 'semi-relational' in the literature on poverty and development

There are two interrelated differences between a class-relational approach and prominent aspects of recent literature on poverty and development, which can be traced in part to differences between Marx, Weber and Bourdieu. These concern the degree of emphasis placed on processes of exploitation, and whether or not different forms of relations are treated as discrete entities. Rather than undermining the obvious analytical significance and intellectual depth of some influential recent contributions to the literature on poverty and development, the purpose of this section is simply to point out their similarities and differences with the class-relational approach.

Sen's (1981) seminal *Poverty and Famines*, and work on public policy and public action (mostly co-authored with Jean Drèze), engaged substantively with the analysis of social relations. In the highly influential *Development as Freedom* (1999), Sen moves closer to residual approaches to poverty by arguing that closer integration into markets will expand people's freedoms – a perspective that conflicts with the class-relational view that markets are arenas of compulsion, competition and antagonism played out among processes of accumulation and exploitation. Sen's capabilities approach is critiqued by Mosse (2010:1158; following Tilly 2007) for 'the pervasive individualism of explanations of poverty that emphasise attributes and capabilities attached to individuals and influencing their life chances'. At times, *Development as Freedom* appears to adopt an explicitly methodological individualist position such as when it states that 'any affirmation of social responsibility that replaces individual responsibility cannot but be ... counterproductive. There is no substitute for individual responsibility.' (Sen 1999:283).

Reference to a shift from bonded labour to 'a system of free labor contract and unrestrained physical movement' strips labour relations back to the dichotomous terms of bondage and 'freedom', negating the coercive element of labour relations, and the ways in which capital (as the next chapter shows) recreates a variety of forms and degrees of unfreedom that have a direct bearing on the political agency and 'participative capabilities' of the labouring classes, and, by extension, its ability to influence public policy (Sen 1999:18–19, 28). In its emphasis on capabilities (in part an echo of Weber's 'life chances'), *Development as Freedom* tends to obscure the often quiet antagonism of everyday relations in capitalist societies (over the extraction of surplus-value), and provides relatively little discussion of exploitation and how it impinges on the capacity to act politically.

The 'freedom to survive' (through access to basic needs such as food, healthcare and clean water), meanwhile, is somewhat detached from politically oriented freedoms based around 'basic civil rights' (Sen 1999:15–17). This can foster approaches to poverty reduction that concern themselves with politics and institutions more than on how they are embedded in the contentious relations of exploitation and production.

In contrast to *Development as Freedom*, Mosse's 'relational approach to durable poverty' has close links to the class-relational approach. It explicitly distinguishes itself from those that stratify primarily according to assets and emphasise capabilities or individual freedom (Mosse 2010:1171). Mosse views poverty as a consequence of the poor's relations with others and of 'historically developed economic and political relations', and critiques poverty research for focusing too much on describing poverty and too little on explaining it (2010:1156–1158). He (2010:1161; Mosse *et al.* 2002, 2005) describes processes of 'accumulation, exploitation, dispossession and differentiation' through which *adivasi* circular migrants are drawn into the Ahmedabad–Mumbai industrial corridor as casual temporary workers who work long hours in harsh conditions with high risks of injuries and wages below the legal minimum, 'tied into relations of dependence and exploitation', and subjected to control by intermediaries.

In placing equal emphasis on poverty as 'an effect of social categorisation and identity', however, Mosse (2010:1156) separates out caste, status and ethnicity from the process of exploitation. Poverty is attributed in part to 'non-class inequalities and systems of exclusion based on social identities of caste, ethnicity and gender' (2010:1162), which may be at odds with a view that although almost no social relations are entirely economic, all social relations are economic to some degree (Bernstein 1992, 2010).[13] As well as capitalist processes, Mosse suggests that exploitation is equally 'embedded in, and reproduced by, social processes which have *their own logic*' and include 'boundary marking and exclusion which give particular importance to the effects of identity and social categorisation (for example, of caste, ethnicity and gender)' (2010:1157, emphasis added). Despite the strong overlaps between Mosse's position and a class-relational approach, there are tensions in bringing together the Marxist concept of class and a Weberian one of social closure, and arguably this, as in the case of Bourdieu, opens the door to a fragmentation of analysis.

Similar tensions between Marxian and Weberian approaches re-emerge in a substantial body of recent publications on poverty (Hickey 2010; Hickey and Bracking 2005; Hickey and Du Toit 2007).[14] Hickey calls for greater emphasis on engagement with the 'political economy of how poverty is produced or reduced ... to address the underlying basis of relational poverty'. 'Class', it is suggested, 'has (re)emerged ... as being of critical importance ... to the politics of poverty reduction on the ground' (Hickey 2010:1152). Despite flagging the significance of political economy (Hickey 2010:1152; Hickey and Bracking 2005; Hickey and Du Toit 2007:5), though, there is a tendency to focus more substantively on institutionalised forms of representation and the politics of citizenship than on relations of production and exploitation.

Hickey and Bracking (2005:851) describe chronic (sustained long-term) poverty as 'an inherently political problem. Its persistence over time reflects its institutionalisation within social and political norms and systems, its legitimation within political discourse and by political elites, and the failure of the poorest groups to gain political representation'. The relative exclusion of exploitation from the analysis of processes through which poverty is (re)produced has the effect, at least in part, of positing poverty as a structural location rather than as a set of social relations linked to the process of production.

The focus on formal political institutions rather than relations of exploitation and class relations at the level of production is in spite of recognition that poverty relates to accumulation as well as avenues of representation (Hickey and Bracking 2005), and that 'citizenship-based strategies rarely alter the underlying basis of poverty' (Hickey 2010:1139). Nevertheless Hickey concludes (2010:1153) that, despite question marks, 'citizenship and broader rights-based approaches to development … seem to bring a political force and rigour to the analytics and strategies of development'. Similarly Chopra and te Lintelo (2011:10) suggest that social contracts constitute a relationship between the state and its citizens that holds the former accountable to the latter, who both bear and claim their rights. Strengthening citizenship, then, is seen as an important part of poverty reduction as it is by Hickey (2010). As well as greater political inclusion for the poor, Hickey advocates the securing of rights and entitlements – a perspective that is echoed in recent work on ('transformative') social protection (Devereux and Sabates-Wheeler 2004), as well as in Sen's work.

This could be seen as a reworking of residual approaches to development with a focus on political institutions, with the assumption appearing to be that greater participation and representation within the existing liberal democratic order will improve the conditions of the poor. Increasing the political influence of classes of labour may improve (and reflect improvements in) its material conditions, but the forms and degrees of classes of labour's political representation, and its access to rights and entitlements, is linked to relations of exploitation and production and requires analysis of them (see, for example, Chapter 6).

Hickey and Bracking (2005) suggest that poverty reduction should be understood within a politics of justice, while Barrientos (2010:7, 15) refers to a 'space of justice' and a prioritarian (almost Rawlsian) approach that prioritises improvements in the well-being of the worst-off (defined as 'those for whom life has not worked out as well as it might have done'). Appeals to 'justice', 'rights' and 'citizenship' have less value if they are not grounded in discussion of the forms of exploitation, as these shape the political space of the poor and the types of relationships it is able to have with the state. In the absence of consideration of forms of exploitation, 'justice', 'rights' and 'citizenship' arguably become liberal norms largely suspended above actual social relations.

Elsewhere the literature emphasises how the position of the household varies across annual and lifetime cycles (Hulme and Shepherd 2003:7–8). Literature that draws out additional characteristics from the poorest households can intensifly analysis of the characteristics of poverty, more than the poor's relations with others. Rather than exploitation, Krishna *et al*.'s (2005; see also Krishna *et al.* 2006) study of thirty-six Indian villages, for example, flags health, marriage/funeral costs, high-interest debt and drought as key reasons for 'descent' (into poverty), while diversification and land improvement are identified as key bases for 'escape' in what is primarily an extension of an 'individual attributes' approach to poverty.

Finally, there is a methodological individualist strand in the literature that builds upon notions of individuals having 'equal opportunities to pursue a life of their choosing' (Engberg-Pedersen and Ravnborg 2010:17). A focus on well-being, for example, emphasises the meeting of human needs, but tends to do so in individualised terms. Hence Camfield's (2012) exploration of 'resilience' takes development debates more clearly into the terrain of methodological individualism, revealing (2012:393) how individuals respond to forms of material deprivation by accessing forms of informal (private) social protection and constructing networks that provide 'pathways to well-being'. Her account is unconcerned with the *causes* of material deprivations, and arguably complements neoliberal hostility to broad-based public provisioning since the forms of resilience she describes might be used to legitimise reduced levels of public welfare spending.

Locke and Lloyd-Sherlock (2011:1132), meanwhile, argue that 'subjective lives' and their 'concrete details', widely rooted in 'constructivist' approaches in which the narrator 'creates reality', are well placed to link experience of poverty, exclusion and vulnerability to 'wider social factors'. However, their detailed subjective accounts are only lightly contextualised. The negative impacts of neoliberal structural adjustment on access to education and employment are referred to, for example, but the social, political and economic processes through which underemployment and exclusion from schooling are produced are left undiscussed. Influenced by multidimensional approaches to poverty, their account has elements of the 'opportunity hoarding' approach associated with Weber, but arguably the way it approaches subjective experience places it closer to the individual attributes approach.

Conclusion

This chapter outlined a class-relational approach as being non-teleological, and as understanding class as plural both in terms of its inflection by other forms of inequality and in terms of its fragmentation into classes of labour. The second half of the chapter pointed to tensions in mixing Marxian and semi-relational Weberian approaches to class, and underlined how a number of accounts flagging the importance of political economy seem to separate the political from the economic, and to pay relatively little attention to forms of exploitation. It also pointed to the usefulness but inadequacy of individual attributes approaches that view class as a structural location rather than as a social relation. Such approaches elucidate the effects of inequality and poverty more than the relational processes that produce them. A class-relational approach stands in contrast to methodological individualism, which largely dislocates the subjective from its social contexts, and fragments analysis of social relations. Class-relational analysis has been sidelined by approaches that separate out axes of domination, and obscure mechanisms of exploitation. This helps more powerful sections of society segment the political and perpetuate the status quo.

Notes

1 In the Indian context, the interplay between class, caste and gender is highly significant (Gooptu and Harriss-White 2001; Lerche 1995). Communal identities are also closely related to class and caste (Berenschot 2011).
2 There are numerous examples of this, even from those who draw upon Marx, such as the new social movement theorists (e.g. Laclau and Mouffe 1985). New social movement theory emerged primarily in a Western European context in the 1970s and 1980s (also to some degree in Latin America; see e.g. Escobar 1995), where everyday struggles over material reproduction were less common.
3 The core antagonism being over the performance of surplus labour and the extraction of surplus-value (exploitation).
4 The significance of caste has changed in uneven ways. Compare, for example, the very different trajectories of change identified by Still (2009) and Picherit (2009; 2012), even though both work in what was until recently Andhra Pradesh (Picherit's fieldwork sites are now part of the new state of Telangana).
5 See, for example, Harriss-White (2012).
6 This typology draws heavily on Lerche (2010), which draws on NCEUS (2007:4–7) and Bernstein (2008).
7 The term is taken from Banaji (2010:278).
8 The two terms are similar, but not identical. See Marx (1976:873–940) and Harvey (2004) for a detailed discussion.
9 This line is adapted from one by Banaji (2010:5).
10 The labour of past generations underpins contemporary accumulation in a variety of ways, be it the digging of canal beds or the laying of roads.
11 The term is taken from Wright (2000).

12 Weber (1978:926) also refers to how 'social honour, or prestige, may even be the basis of economic power'.

13 Mosse *et al.*'s (2002, 2005) analysis of circular migrants in eastern Gujarat supports such a line of reasoning.

14 Their prominence is derived in part from a decade-long research project on Chronic Poverty, which led to the publication of a considerable body of literature by the Chronic Poverty Research Centre, and a number of related publications such as special issues in the *Journal of Development Studies* and *World Development*. It included a number of different perspectives, but the lines of argument referred to here are relatively representative.

3

Labour, state and civil society in rural India

The fieldwork-based chapters of this book explore three co-constitutive aspects of class relations in rural India: those in and around sites of production, and their mediation by both the state and different types of civil society organisations (CSOs). The purpose of this chapter is to set the scene for what follows by drawing out key trends and debates from the broader India literature.

It proceeds in four parts. The first uses government datasets to flesh out a number of points that have already been made in relation to classes of labour – namely that classes of labour are growing in number; that their work is more likely to be informal; that there is a growing reserve army of labour that weakens its structural power;[1] and finally that they are more likely than they used to be to make a living across a variety of locations (in other words, that they have become more spatially fragmented). The second section anchors the statistical trends in a range of recent case studies of labour relations in rural India, which show that the casualisation of labour relations has been partial, uneven and far from linear.

The third section focuses on recent discussion of CSOs in the Indian countryside that involve or are led by classes of labour. It contrasts 'neoliberal' organisations with class-based ones. The fourth and final section assesses debates on the role of the state in mediating class relations. Literature on local government institutions (LGIs) are touched upon before the chapter ends with a discussion of the forms and role of state poverty reduction programmes. It is argued that social policy, despite the fact that the state tends to be pro-capital, is a critical arena of class struggle in contemporary rural India – both as a basis for improving the material conditions of labour, and as a means of ameliorating their socio-political position in order to facilitate more broad-based forms of collective labouring class action.

Table 3.1 Distribution of rural households (%) by size of landholdings possessed (acres), 1999–2000 and 2009–10

Acres	0–1	1–2.5	2.5–5	5–10	>10
All India, 1999–2000	58.2	19.1	11.5	7.3	3.9
All India, 2009–10	64.8	16.1	9.7	6.5	3
Karnataka, 2009–10	58.7	17.2	12.6	8.2	3.4

Sources: GoI NSS (2001:A-257, 2012:73).

Classes of labour in India

A growing majority of India's population belongs to classes of labour. In 2009–10 almost two-thirds of rural households in India (64.8 per cent) were either landless or had less than an acre of land, while 80.9 per cent had less than 2.5 acres – an increase of around one-third from the 1960s (GoI NSSO 2012:73; Table 3.1). The point at which farmers become primarily dependent on the sale of labour-power (and are therefore part of classes of labour) has no neat proxy in terms of the size of landholdings because productivity varies between wet and dryland, black and red soils, and according to cropping patterns. However, fieldwork conducted for this book showed that all of those with less than one acre of land, and all dryland farmers with less than 2.5 acres, were marginal farmers (see Chapter 4). In fact, the cut-off was higher, but even using this underestimate and considering that only just over a third of India's agricultural land is irrigated (35.2 per cent),[2] it can be calculated that the share of rural households that belong to classes of labour is at least 70 per cent.

While many work as agricultural labourers in their home areas, others migrate between different sites of agricultural production (e.g. Breman 1990), and at least forty million circulate out of their home areas to work in cities (as temporary migrants) (Pattenden 2012). Many more commute between their villages and nearby towns and cities to work in a variety of sectors in a blur of multi-sited reproduction strategies. While employment in the manufacturing and agriculture sectors shrank in the second half of the 2000s, employment growth in construction grew at 11.27 per cent every year, with the proportion of male and female rural labourers working in construction doubling and quadrupling respectively over a seven year period (see Figure 2; Srivastava 2012:76).

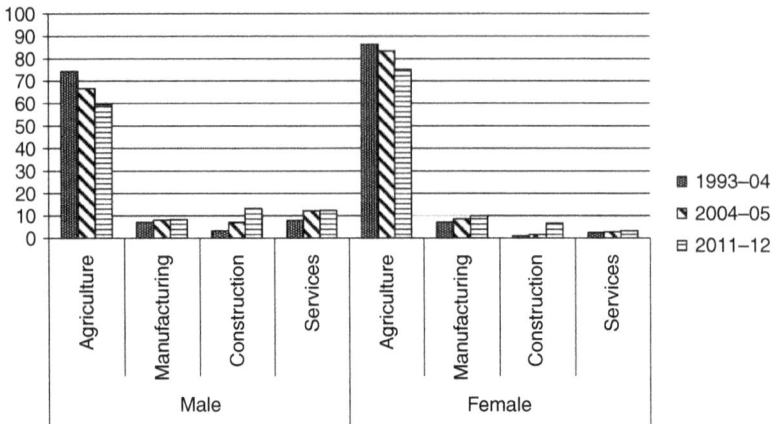

Figure 2 Employment of rural individuals by sector, 1993–94 to 2011–12 (%)

The size of India's reserve army of labour has been expanding. While non-agricultural employment has increased to the point where landless labourers and marginal farmers depend primarily on non-agricultural wage work and petty trade/production (Lerche *et al.* 2013:342), it has not risen fast enough to compensate for the fall in levels of employment in agriculture.[3] The rate of expansion of non-agricultural employment fell in the 1990s and 2000s (compared to the 1970s and 1980s) (Himanshu 2011:48; Thomas 2012:41), and employment growth as a whole fell to 0.21 per cent in the second half of the 2000s. In part this was due to the service sector's growing share of the economy (RBI n.d.:13). By 2012 it accounted for 56.9 per cent of India's GDP (up from 51.3 in 2001), but only 28.1 per cent of employment (RBI n.d.:174)[4] – a marked contrast to the agricultural sector, whose contribution to growth is barely more than one-quarter of its share of employment.

Labour has become increasingly informalised in the two decades since liberalisation. Formal sector jobs fell by 2 per cent in the 1990s, and continued to fall in the 2000s. In 2009–10, 423 million of India's total workforce of 460 million were informally employed (see Table 3.2).[5] Over the previous decade, informal workers grew in number by sixty million as opposed to just four million formal workers. While the vast majority worked in the informal sector[6] (which underlines the extent to which production in India is concentrated in small-scale units, as the informal sector is made up of enterprises employing fewer than ten people and includes all private farming with the exception of plantations and large cooperatives; NCEUS 2007:3), thirty-seven million informal workers worked in the *formal economy*. The formal sector accounts for a large

Table 3.2 Numbers and distribution of informal and formal workers, 1999/2000–2009/10, in millions (and as a percentage of the total population)

Year	Informal workers	Informal workers in the informal sector	Informal workers in the formal sector	Formal workers in millions
1999–2000	362.75 (91.5)	339.71 (93.6)	23.04 (6.4)	33.64 (8.5)
2004–05	422.61 (92.4)	393.47 (93.1)	29.14 (6.9)	34.85 (7.6)
2009–10	423.17 (91.9)	386.02 (91.2)	37.15 (8.8)	37.25 (8.1)

Sources: Breman and Kannan (2013:2); based on NSS figures; see also GoI PC (n.d.) for very similar figures.

proportion of the rise of informal workers since the turn of the century. Informality, whereby workers are employed on an insecure basis, with poor conditions,[7] low rates of pay and a lack of state protection, is being extended into formal parts of the economy – a trend that will be illustrated in the fieldwork chapters.

Informal workers have three key characteristics. First, they work without a written contract and largely without social security (NCEUS 2007:3; Srivastava 2012:77). The numbers of non-agricultural wage workers without any written contract rose from 73.2 to 77.3 per cent in the second half of the 2000s, while the percentage of wage workers with access to social security fell by just over 6 per cent between 1999–2000 and 2009–10 (Srivastava 2012:78–79). Second, they tend to lack forms of representation (unionisation levels in the informal sector are low, and even though there are indications that they are rising, over 90 per cent remain unorganised (Agarwala 2013; see below). Third, they are afforded relatively little protection by labour laws. For example, the Building and Other Construction Workers Act and the Maternity Benefits Act do not apply to enterprises with fewer than ten employees (NCEUS 2007:161–162). Even where labour laws do apply they are routinely flouted through subcontracting and outsourcing arrangements, and due to evasion of worker registration.

Informalisation is being accelerated by the BJP government. Within two months of coming to office in 2014, it had already moved to loosen critical labour laws. The BJP state government of Rajasthan led the way, amending the Contract Labour Act (which imposes limitations on the employment of contract labour) so that it only applies to establishments with more than fifty workers rather than twenty, and amending the Factories Act (which involves, among other things, regulations on health and safety, inspections, hazardous processes, annual leave and working hours) so that it applies to fewer establishments (*Business Standard* 2014; *Indian*

Express 2014a).[8] The following month the national government cleared fifty-four amendments to the Factories Act, and raised the bar for compliance with key labour regulations so that it would only apply to establishments with forty or more workers (*Indian Express* 2014b). Wide-ranging nationwide changes to labour laws are in the offing and are being resisted by unions (*The Hindu* 2014d). To some degree, these changes are symbolic as evasion of labour laws is routine, but they do erode labourers' bases for mobilisation. The BJP seeks to send 'a message' to international capital that they will not be unduly troubled by labour in India, but also to undercut classes of labour's capacity to respond to growing inequality.

Changing class relations in rural India

Recent studies of rural-based labour in India lend weight to the trends shown in the national data.[9] They add analytical depth and indicate why India's labour regime remains particularly harsh, as well as explaining why it varies in form. In addition to its growing segmentation and informalisation, they show that processes of casualisation are far from linear as well as being uneven. In other words, although labour relations are becoming less personalised, new ties are being created.

Some studies focus on areas where class relations remain primarily oriented around agriculture and the village (e.g. Rawal 2006), while others focus on villages where circulation or commuting is commonplace (e.g. Carswell and De Neve 2013). Others still focus on the sites that labourers circulate to (Guérin 2013, Guérin *et al.* 2009a; Mosse *et al.* 2005; Rogaly *et al.* 2001). Some studies move with labour, analysing labour relations both in the villages that they originate from, and the towns, cities and others parts of the countryside that they circulate to (Breman 1996; Guérin *et al.* 2012; Mosse *et al.* 2005; Picherit 2012). Class relations are shown to be inflected by gender and caste relations. For example, Garikipati (2009) underlines the gendered nature of commuting and circulation, with rural male workers significantly more likely to work outside agriculture than women, while Benbabaali (2013) shows how Srinivas's (1963) notion of the 'dominant caste' is stretched spatially as forms and sites of accumulation diversify.

Forms of unfreedom in labour relations

Bonded labour, whereby labourers are tied to a particular employer and unable to renegotiate contractual terms (Srivastava 2009:129–130), has declined markedly in India over the past century, and given way to less personalised forms of labour relations – in part because the agrarian production regime requires fewer workers than before (Breman 2007a; Lerche 2011:113). This has led to greater levels of underemployment partially offset by non-agricultural wage-labour on similar terms, or marginally better ones in the case of urban non-agricultural employment (Lerche 2011).

Traditionally, bonded labour relations often involved a number of family members, including children, and spanned generations (Breman 2007b). The terms of bonded labour were far from uniform: some workers were always at the beck and call of their employers, while others were not. The latter's looser ties may have precluded annual 'gifts' of clothes or more regular ones of food (Breman 2007b:41).[10] Such forms of patronage, or what has been called a 'rude sort of kindness' (Breman 2007b:37; see also Lerche 1995:488), fostered compliance and tended to produce a higher rate of labour productivity.

Although less common, cases of bonded labour persist within contemporary capitalism where employers have the socio-political means to enforce such arrangements, and where they are fostered by production methods and dynamics of competition (see, for example, Roesch *et al.* 2009 and Chapter 4). Bonded labour arrangements push labour costs well below the societal norm of what is 'socially necessary', requiring much longer working days with lower hourly wages, but providing more regular employment. Bonded labourers are more likely to remain on larger irrigated farms where the demand for labour-power is more constant. While in this book's fieldwork villages there were usually only one or two individuals in bonded labour arrangements, ninety-seven bonded labourers were identified in 2013 in one North Karnataka village. Four of the large capitalist farmers implicated were relatives of a BJP minister (*The Hindu* 2013).

As well as casualisation, forms of 'neobondage', which tie labour to a particular employer or labour contractor for a shorter period through advances or loans, have proliferated under capitalism (Breman 1990; Breman and Guérin 2009:3–4; Guérin 2013; Guérin *et al.* 2009a; Lerche 2011:113). 'Advances' increase initial access to and control over labour in the production process, and end-of-season final payments hold the worker in place as well as further reducing his/her bargaining power during the production period (Breman 1990; Breman and Guérin 2009).

Isabelle Guérin and her collaborators' research on forms of 'neobondage' in the brick kiln, rice milling and sugar-cane sectors in Tamil Nadu links different forms of control over labour to different dynamics of accumulation (Guérin 2013; Guérin *et al.* 2009a; Roesch *et al.* 2009). In a rice mill cluster close to Chennai, labour was bonded to cut costs and ensure a continuous supply of labour in a context where proximity to urban labour markets made labour scarcer and levels of competition had increased the power of traders. Production was more labour-intensive and less mechanised, working days lasted up to sixteen hours and the largely scheduled tribe migrant workforce faced physical restrictions on its movement. By contrast, millers further south sold direct to local markets, labour was employed on a casual basis and working conditions were less harsh.

In brick kilns irregular tasks were completed by non-indebted casual labourers while continuous tasks were conducted by debt-bonded labourers whose wages were four times lower (on an hourly basis), and whose working practices were intensified by piece-rated payments (Guérin *et al.* 2009a; see Chapter 4 for a discussion of piece-rate labour). Recruitment was managed by intermediaries who provided a pressure-valve for grievances, while employers increased their control over labour by forging links with dominant men in their villages, as well as collectively fostering links to relevant parts of civil society and the state, which helped employers to persuade officials to overlook labour laws (Guérin *et al.* 2009a; see also Breman 1990, 2007b; Mezzadri 2014).

In other words, capitalists have deployed a variety of strategies to maintain control over labour in contexts of structural change and varying dynamics of competition. Elsewhere it is shown that where labour's bargaining position has remained weak, capital has deployed a range of strategies to increase the rate of exploitation (through the extraction of absolute surplus-value), while in those places where labour's bargaining has increased, capital has tended to accelerate mechanisation and the shift to less labour-intensive forms of production (thereby increasing the extraction of relative surplus-value) (Das 2011; Heller 1995, 1999).

Piece-rated work (where payment is made according to the coverage of an agreed area, or an agreed quantity of produce) has become more commonplace as labour relations have become less personalised (Sarap cited in Ramachandran 1990:122). Such arrangements may be preferred by workers as they earn more in a day, but work is intensified by 'internalising discipline' (Kapadia 1995). Similar intensifications of the labour process occurred in 1830s England: 'paid by piece-rate or gang-rate on the docks or at the navvying, they are tempted to overwork themselves, and to ruin their health and constitution in a few years' (Thompson 1991 [1963]:474). Attempts to increase the speed of work encourage gang leaders to reject slower workers. Those who are hampered by health issues are excluded, along with older women and more inexperienced girls, apart from in cases where a close relative is an influential member of the gang (Kapadia 1995).

As noted earlier, labour's growing access to non-agricultural employment, be it through commuting or circulation, can also increase incomes and strengthen labourers' socio-political position in their home villages (Pattenden 2012). While some circular migrants are debt-bonded and subject to high levels of control (e.g. Breman 1990), others have been found to circulate independently and free from debt in contexts where political parties and state governments that are relatively sympathetic to labour have been able to establish less harsh labour regimes (Rogaly *et al.* 2001).

Labour regimes are often worse in more remote areas that are distant from urban labour markets. For example, in Rawal's (2006) fieldwork area in rural Haryana, mechanisation has reduced demand for labour in a context where access to non-agricultural employment is very limited, land-ownership concentrated, and social hierarchies relatively steep. Control over labour is maintained in part through sharecropping arrangements that are a disguised form of wage-labour (Rawal 2006). Often interlinked with 'loans', sharecropping offloads risk, frees up landowners' time and lowers costs by increasing the rate of exploitation of labouring (sharecroppers') households by encouraging the lengthening of the working day and the intensification of the labour process (Rawal 2006:568, 576). Landowners elsewhere have commented that sharecroppers cultivate with a greater amount of 'interest and diligence' than day labourers (Banaji 2010:113).[11] A hierarchy in the precise terms of sharecropping segments labour, and disciplines it by offering the possibility of improved terms.

Brass (1990), meanwhile, has studied an area of Haryana where non-agricultural employment is more readily available, and greater emphasis is placed on indebtedness as a means of controlling labour (for similar examples from Java, see Hart 1986; White and Wiradi 1989:325). In Lerche's (1999:188–191) fieldwork villages in Uttar Pradesh, where non-agricultural employment had become the primary source of income of most labouring households (see also Srivastava 1989), farmers deployed a greater diversity of strategies to maintain access to labour-power and resist upward pressure on wages – a mix of debt, fragmenting labour by bringing in workers from outside, and attaching conditions to the 'leasing' out of land such as the performance of unpaid labour and the obligation to make household members available to the landowner on a priority basis for wages that were below the going rate (see also Srivastava 1989:500–504; and for similar examples in Indonesia see White and Wiradi 1989:325).

In other words, rather than a simple means of appropriating surplus-value through rents, here 'leasing out' had become a significant means of controlling a more mobile and casualised workforce. Other responses include shifting to less labour-intensive crops; investing in labour-saving machinery (e.g. Das 2011; Viajaybaskar 2010); feminising the labour force to lower wage costs (Da Corta and Venkateshwarlu 1999; Das 2011; Garikipati 2008); and exerting influence over state institutions and CSOs in order to push for subsidies, divide labour and resist/subvert pro-labouring class regulations.

Forms of neobondage remain an integral part of capitalist development, while casualisation is partial, non-linear, contradictory and contested. The ongoing extraction of surplus-value and the inherent antagonism of class relations remain obscured by the appearance of free exchange, but attention to the details of the exploitation process can increase understanding both of how concessions can be extracted from capital, and the possibilities for more radical change.

Civil society and organisations of the labouring class

Although structural change has loosened more personalised village-based forms of control over labour, processes of fragmentation and informalisation impede the organisation of classes of labour and produce an 'amorphous, shifting and diverse relationship to the system of production' (RoyChowdhury 2003:5283; see also Harriss-White 2014). Wage-labour is scarce, takes precarious forms and (for most labouring class rural households) is spread over multiple locations. Hamstrung by multiple forms of segmentation, political action by or on behalf of the labouring class tends to be small-scale and more oriented towards access to basic services and social policy (Agarwala 2013:16; Bhowmik 2008; Chandhoke 2012; Harriss 2007b; Judge 2011; Lerche 2010; RoyChowdury 2003, 2005).

This section assesses discussion in the literature about whether such forms of organisation can improve the economic and political position of classes of labour. It also outlines arguments that the potential for labouring class action in rural India is weakened by the rise of neoliberal CSOs. If the state is now a prominent site of class conflict, then the question arises as to who extracts greater benefits from it and how, and why this varies across different sectors and different villages, districts and states.

The decline in more direct forms of workplace-based action is illustrated by the drop in the number of strike incidents between 1980 and 2008 after industrial disputes peaked in the 1970s (see Table 3.3; see also Agarwala 2013:42). Even informal workers have shifted their demands away from the workplace to 'welfare issues at home' over the decades since independence, as shown by Agarwala (2013:31–36) in relation to *bidi* (cigarette) and construction workers.

Union membership was as low as 8 per cent in the mid-2000s (Shyam Sundar 2008), but increased between 2008 and 2013 (Menon 2013). Membership growth relates mostly to central party-affiliated unions that have largely organised formal sector workers. Among these, though, are unions including those affiliated to the All India Central Council of Trade Unions and Confederation of Indian Trade Unions (linked to the Communist Party of India (Marxist-Leninist) and Communist Party of

Table 3.3 Number of strike incidents (of 10+ workers, and excluding 'sympathetic strikes')

	1980	1990	2000	2008
Manufacturing	1,636	1,091	437	250
Mining	639	438	66	22
Transport, storage, communication	124	30	7	23
Agriculture	72	32	23	25
Other	385	234	123	103
Total	2,856	1,825	656	423

Source: International Labour Organisation, Table 9a. Online: http:// laborsta.ilo.org.

India (Marxist) respectively) that organise among informal workers to a greater degree than some central unions.Independent union initiatives have included the Trade Union Solidarity Committee (founded in 1989) and the New Trade Union Initiative, which had roots in meetings in the 1990s before becoming a network of independent formal and informal sector unions in 2001, and a national federation five years later. It works with informal sector workers on issues relating to both reproduction-related access to social security and production-related wages and working conditions. Levels of organisation of informal workers have increased both in party-affiliated and independent unions,[12] and Agarwala's (2013:8) claim that nine million informal sector workers are unionised (under 3 per cent of informal sector workers and unevenly spread, with, for example, less than half as many unionised construction workers as *bidi* workers) is probably an underestimate by now. Nevertheless over 90 per cent of informal workers remain unorganised.

Beyond formal organisations, there are also localised episodes of collective labouring class action. Lerche (1999) refers to wage-related strikes in eastern Uttar Pradesh, in villages where the dominant class was relatively divided along caste lines, while Kapadia (1993) reveals how relative labour scarcity and caste unity among agricultural labourers in a particular village led to partially successful collective demands for wage increases. Towards the other end of the scale are an episode of high-profile industrial action in the car manufacturing sector in Gurgaon (Monaco 2015) and signs of heightened networking between unionists in different sites (Miyamura, forthcoming). These examples do not mean that there has been a widespread reversion to workplace-based action. Smaller-scale, more indirect state-oriented forms of class struggle remain more prominent.[13]

The latter type of organisation tends to focus its attention on LGIs and their implementation of key government programmes such as the National Rural Employment Guarantee Scheme (NREGS), the National Rural Health Mission and the Public Distribution System (PDS). These small social movements in the Indian countryside, such as the Mazdoor Kisan Shakti Sanghathan (MKSS) in Rajasthan, the Grameen Coolie Karmikara Sanghathan (GCKS) (Village Workers Association) and Jagruthi Mahela Sanghathan (JMS) in Karnataka (the latter is discussed in detail in Chapter 8), are often part of networks such as the recent and ongoing campaigns for the Right to Food, Education, Employment, Education and Health, which lobby the national government to pass and implement pro-labour legislation.[14] Such networks, which include academics and left parties, have played an important role in realising pro-labouring class measures such as the National Rural Employment Guarantee Act in 2005, the National Rural Health Mission of 2005 and the Unorganised Workers Social Security Act (UWSSA) of 2008. Members of the MKSS have sat on the now defunct National Advisory Committee within the central government, while members of the GCKS and the JMS have lobbied state-level officials within the Government of Karnataka.

Do small-scale organisations contribute to a redistribution of power and resources as part of a longer process of pro-labouring class social change, or do they underpin the status quo by not directly threatening the distribution of productive assets or processes of accumulation and exploitation? While some sense a new basis for social transformation among more atomised patterns of collective action (Sanyal and Bhattacharya 2009), others emphasise the need to fold small-scale labouring class political activities into broader mass-based organisations centred on left parties and unions, and to push for 'workers' rights' rather than 'citizen rights' (Bardhan 2011; Bhowmik 2008).

RoyChowdhury (2003) contests the view that small-scale organisations contribute to broader change. She gives the example that the according of land titles to some slum dwellers 'does not address the broader issue of urban land development as a function of the interests of real estate speculators, multinational corporations and state agencies' (2003:5283–5284). The underlying structures that drive processes of exploitation and primitive accumulation, and (re)produce labouring class conditions, remain untouched.

The counter-argument is that it is often the only feasible form of action at this point in time. In the short term, pro-labouring class organisations may have no choice but to soft-pedal in order to avoid a dominant class backlash (see, for example, RoyChowdhury 2005), settling for minor gains (the mitigation of particularly harsh labour regimes in particular sites of production, for example) and slowly preparing the ground for more broad-based labouring class action.

Pro-labouring class organisation that improves circular migrants' access to healthcare while in the city, or that provides them with employment on public works, are significant because they ameliorate their conditions, weaken dependence upon capital and strengthen their ability to make collective demands. Such actions, though, are not without their contradictions – not least in their ability to offer a pressure valve for grievances without threatening structural change in any direct sense.

Lerche (2012:27–28) concludes that India's social policies are more likely to 'manage' poverty than create new social alliances that are capable of pushing through more broad-based improvements in the position of labour. At the same time, he argues that labour's present weakness in relation to capital, and 'the near-impossibility of taking successful action at the workplace', ensures that less direct 'pro-labour government initiatives in areas not directly challenging capital [are] the best way forward', despite their limitations. By this reckoning, indirect strategies of change focused on social policy are an insufficient but significant step, which can both improve material conditions and provide a rallying point for more broad-based labouring class action. On the other hand, they may simply offer a route to minor temporary gains that are vulnerable to push-back from a more aggressively pro-capital state.

A neoliberalisation of civil society?

The state plays an important role in shaping civil society – fostering some forms of CSO, while marginalising or repressing others (Chandhoke 1995, 2003; see also Tarrow 1998 for the related discussion of political opportunity structures). While the Indian government's growing support for civil society can be traced back to the late 1970s and early 1980s,[15] its tenth five-year plan (2000–05) accorded civil society a more important role, arguing that community-based organisations (CBOs) and non-governmental organisations (NGOs) would make local government more 'pro-poor' and more capable of delivering services (GoI PC 2006). Such organisations include Residents' Welfare Associations, Watershed and Sanitation Committees, and NGO-backed village development committees (Chhotray 2011; Coelho and Venkat 2009; Harriss 2006, 2007; Kamath and Vijayabaskar 2009).

Most notable, though, has been the explosion of women's self-help groups (savings and micro-credit groups of around 15–20 women), with millions being set up since 2000 (Pattenden 2010). Such service-delivery organisations, it has been argued in relation to India, pacify 'the poor' and prevent them from 'launching critiques of power structures' (Corbridge *et al.* 2013:225). Along with the decentralisation of government, the proliferation of CSOs has been an integral part of the neoliberal agenda of rolling back the state in India and elsewhere, and has prompted a litera-ture arguing that civil society has been neoliberalised (Arellano-Lopez and Petras 1994; Hearn 2007; Pattenden 2010).

It is worth pointing to the widespread nature of such arguments in the broader literature. In Latin America, Arellano-Lopez and Petras (1994) have contrasted the membership-based grassroots organisations of the 1970s that sought to advance the political and economic position of the labouring class (and the NGOs that provided logistical and polit-ical support), with the increasingly project-oriented local NGOs of the 1980s and beyond, which were focused on securing finance from inter-national NGOs, donors and government departments. Alongside a par-tial retrenchment of the state that included the outsourcing of some of its activities, new patron–client chains emerged as NGOs became clients of donors, international NGOs and government departments; and grass-roots organisations became clients of NGOs.

Civil society in Latin America had become largely oriented towards palliative and fragmented time-bound service delivery, while the struc-tural bases of inequality and impoverishment were increasingly margin-alised from the agenda. Related critiques of civil society have been made in relation to sub-Saharan Africa, with references to a proliferation of contract-oriented 'briefcase' NGO businesses (often headed by former bureaucrats and members of the middle class) that helped to underpin neoliberalism by dampening potential restiveness through a scatter-gun allocation of resources (Hearn 2007).

Similar claims are made about NGOs in India. It is claimed that they have become increasingly concerned with service delivery and driv-ing 'an ineffective micro-level transformation process in which most of the money goes to those who run [them]', in contrast to 'working-class movements and dalit movements' that are concerned with changing the balance of class and caste power (Judge 2011:21; see also Chandhoke 2012). Detailed studies of civil society in particular locations bear out these claims. In Chennai, one of India's largest cities, it has been found that politically oriented labouring class organisations were more likely to have been formed in the 1970s and 1980s, while service-oriented and advocacy NGOs and CBOs were more likely to have been formed since then (Harriss 2006; 2007b).

This cannot simply be seen as a proliferation of new types of CSO. As Harriss notes (Corbridge *et al.* 2013:228), 'upper-middle-class NGOs ... present themselves as agents of social development while effectively neutralising political threats from the poor', often 'crowd-ing out' opportunities for more politicised organisations to coalesce. Harriss (2006; 2007b:2721) argues that middle-class Residents' Welfare Associations in Indian cities are populated by 'consumer-citizens' con-cerned with the self-regulating duties of citizenship, partnerships with private corporations and state institutions, influence over public budgeting and a more transparent and accountable public sector.

The middle class has increasingly turned to private provisioning, and are relatively uninterested in the comparatively small-scale public resources flowing through LGIs, which are primarily a concern for classes of labour (Harriss 2006, 2007b). This corresponds with Chatterjee's (2004) division of a predominantly labouring class 'political society' and a largely middle-class civil society, but Harriss argues (in Corbridge et al. 2013:223, 230) that Chatterjee exaggerates the divide between political and civil society, and suggests that the poor are nevertheless often engaged in civil society.

Chatterjee's dichotomy abandons civil society to the middle classes, and confines the labouring class to parochial appeals to the local state, thereby detaching it from the broader social conflict between capital and labour and processes of accumulation and exploitation. This returns the discussion to the critical question as to whether forms of labouring class collective action are concerned with a redistribution of power and resources. Many of the new CSOs are not (as the fieldwork chapters of this book will show), while those that are focused on redistribution are often highly localised. The ability of the latter to contribute to processes of redistribution will be assessed in detail in Chapter 8. The ways in which the former reproduce the status quo will be discussed in Chapter 7.

The state and social policy in India

The Indian state supports its capitalist class in a variety of concrete ways, from helping to hold down the costs of labour by failing to enforce minimum wage legislation, to providing subsidies in a variety of forms (such as cheap electricity, tax breaks and the subsidisation of foodgrains; Corbridge and Harriss 2000; Frankel 2004; Patnaik 1986). Such forms of support enhance Indian capitalists' ability to compete in the global marketplace, and form part of the state's role of supporting processes of capitalist accumulation.[16]

Its propensity to support capital is increased by the fact that the state's legislative bodies (at national and state levels) are dominated by capitalists (see Chapter 5). This, though, does not mean that the political realm is 'the mere reflection of the economic realm' (Miliband 1973b:85). The state has a degree of autonomy from the capitalist class, which varies in extent and form (Miliband 1973b:85), and derives from its commitment both to support capitalist accumulation and to maintain social stability (in part by ensuring that labour can reproduce itself), as well as from governments' desire for re-election. These objectives can bring the state into conflict with the capitalist class as a whole, or particular parts of it.[17]

Labour also seeks to extract resources and policy concessions from the state, but is generally less well placed to do so. It tends to have fewer allies not only in central and state governments, where policy is formed, but also in the LGIs that now play a central role in the implementation of development and poverty reduction policies. The next two chapters of this book show that the distribution of power within LGIs tends to be closely related to everyday class relations at the level of production.

Even at the level of India's central government, there are times when labour is better placed to extract concessions. For example, the erstwhile United Progressive Alliance government was somewhat more dependent on labouring class votes than its main rival, and more inclined to increase the labouring class's share of public resources (while supporting processes of informalisation). The stronger the pro-labour representations at national and state level, and the more organised labour is throughout society down to the level of LGIs where programmes like NREGS and PDS are implemented, the better able it is to extract concessions in order to improve its material conditions and shift socio-political dynamics in its favour. The latter primarily occurs because government-funded employment and subsidised foodgrains (as well as some other programmes) remove part of the process of labouring class reproduction from direct forms of class relations.

The focus in this book is on processes of policy implementation at the level of LGIs. Hence, in the remainder of this chapter prominent strands in the literature on LGIs and social policy are outlined. Two key points emerge. First, the outcomes of social policy vary according to balances of class and caste power, and as a consequence tend to be controlled by the dominant class. Second, the forms taken by social policy have implications for their potential both to improve the poor's material conditions, and to strengthen their socio-political position. It is argued that universal rights-based programmes are best placed to improve the position of classes of labour.

The dominant class and local government institutions

The outcomes of government policy vary according to the balance of class and caste power. In western Tamil Nadu, a relatively industrialised region with significant levels of commuting to towns for work (Carswell and De Neve 2013; Heyer 2012; Vijayabaskar 2010), the state has strengthened the position of classes of labour through its expansion of social programmes. In parts of Telangana, on the other hand, where social structures are more iniquitous, the primary outcome of the expansion of such programmes has been to improve the material and political position of a dominant few (Picherit 2014). Similarly, as was shown in

Chapter 1, varying balances of class and caste power across the fieldwork state of Karnataka have produced uneven policy outcomes.

The dominant class in the Indian countryside reproduces and reinforces its position by exercising influence over and permeating state institutions at different levels in order to secure individual and collective goals. In the 1980s and 1990s, the dominant class in rural Karnataka used the Karnataka Rajya Raitha Sangha (Karnataka State Farmers' Association, or KRRS), one of India's 'New Farmers Movements', in order to secure collective goals.[18] The Green Revolution had bound farmers' livelihoods up with the state as never before, and increased profits carried demands for better terms of trade and greater political representation until accumulation strategies began to diversify, and the basis for collective action declined (Pattenden 2005).

Rural dominant classes' strategies to reproduce their position have become more individualised (Pattenden 2005). Rather than conflict, the relationship between farmers and the state has increasingly been characterised by collaboration. As the process of fiscal decentralisation accelerated in the 2000s, and the share of public resources channelled through gram panchayats (GPs, village councils) rose sharply, many village leaders in key KRRS strongholds (the fieldwork district of Dharwad being notable among them) became part of the local state as 'gatekeepers' manning the state–society interface. They did so as councillors influencing the distributon of government resources, as 'fixers' helping to secure access into the state (for those seeking employment, government resources such as pensions, or documents such as land titles and caste certificates), as managers of higher-placed politicians' political networks and as contractors building local roads and infrastructure (Jeffrey and Lerche 2000; Pattenden 2011a; Ram Reddy and Haragopal 1985). Reflecting their relatively weak socio-political position, members of classes of labour in India have been relatively dependent on these gatekeepers to access the state and its resources at a local level (Houtzager *et al.* 2007; see also Wood 2003 for a similar argument in relation to Bangladesh).

These 'gatekeepers' are cast in a contrasting light by different authors. From a class-relational perspective, they are located among antagonistic processes of accumulation and domination where they mediate transactions between the public and the state for the purposes of private economic gain, or increased political influence or social status (Harriss-White 2003; Jeffrey and Lerche 2000; Khan 2005; Ram Reddy and Haragopal 1985). They do so as part of a broader 'shadow state' that extends across different levels of government. At the lower levels, its protagonists move 'between the official state where they oversee state development policies, revenue collection, elections and anti-poverty programmes, and the shadow state where, in a range of activities that relate to their official roles, they collect bribes and mediate institutional politics and local agrarian and mercantile accumulation' (Harriss-White 2003:88).

In contrast, others suggest that the interface between state and society has become more democratic, with 'new leaders' emerging to jostle among 'new village-based networks of collective action and political mobilization' (Krishna 2003). From this perspective, intermediaries between state and society 'enabl[e] the democratic process and heighten … state responsiveness by linking "the people" to their government' – a role that is particularly important where party organisations and local government institutions are weakly embedded in society (Inbanathan and Gopalappa 2002; Manor 2004, 2007:658).

A related argument is that the politics of the shadow state, gatekeepers and patron–client relations has been supplanted by a 'post-clientilist state' or 'programmatic politics', whereby re-election comes to depend on the effective delivery of public programmes more than on the distribution of appropriated public resources through patron–client networks (Elliot 2011; Manor 2010). In other words, politics passes a tipping point where politicians' subversion of public programmes no longer brings them the greatest political and economic rewards (Elliot 2011; Manor 2010; see also Weber 1978:984). This is particularly the case, it is argued, where programmes are universal rather than targeted, as gatekeepers' role in selecting beneficiaries is reduced. Gatekeeping moves increasingly to higher levels of the interface between state, society and the 'private sector' (Elliot 2011), while lower-level gatekeeping opportunities dwindle through the vigilance of the greater numbers receiving a regular share of public resources. Consequently either fewer are drawn to lower-level gatekeeping, or it draws in less wealthy, less powerful individuals (see, for example, Rutten 2003:41–93).

There is some evidence of a move *towards* programmatic 'post-clientilist' politics in states like Tamil Nadu and Kerala (Carswell and De Neve 2014; Heller *et al.* 2007; Heyer 2012), but there is also evidence of places where little or no such shift has occurred (Pattenden 2011a; Picherit 2012). There is, then, both continuity and change, and ascertaining why requires empirical analysis using a class-relational perspective. Change is neither even nor linear, and this book (along with evidence from elsewhere such as Picherit 2014; Veron *et al.* 2006) suggests that the shadow state continues to play a prominent role in most of the country because the balance of class forces allows it to.

Rather than contributing to the emergence of a post-clientilist state, decentralisation is likely to increase inequality in those areas where the dominant class maintains control over LGIs. Examples include Uttar Pradesh (Kohli 2011; Lieten and Srivastava 1999) and the fieldwork region of North Karnataka (Pattenden 2011a).[19] Conversely, decentralisation's relative success in deepening democracy in Kerala reflects its relative socio-political and socio-economic equity and decades of strong labouring class organisation and state-led redistribution (Heller 1999; Heller *et al.* 2007; but see Suresh 2009:212–213 for an account of *adivasi* marginalisation). Sub-state differences reflect similar political and economic differences (e.g. Corbridge *et al.* 2005; Veron *et al.* 2006).

The outcomes of decentralisation reflect gender and caste dynamics as well as those of class. A twelve-state study, for example, points to the continued marginalisation of women and members of the scheduled castes (Baviskar and Mathew 2009). Examples are given of dominant caste/class men placing relatively pliant labouring class and scheduled caste individuals (including those directly employed by them) onto councils in order to increase their influence, and of male relatives substituting for women councillors in key meetings (Baviskar 2009:28; Chandrashekhar 2009:258; Mohanty 2009:51–61, 63; Thara Bhai 2009:279).

'The most successful cases [of decentralisation]', Crook and Sverrisson have argued (1999:48), 'were the ones where central government not only had an ideological commitment to pro-poor policies, but was prepared to engage actively with local politics ... to challenge local elite resistance.' Pro-labouring class organisations that mobilise to increase access to public resources can contribute to such processes (Goetz and Jenkins 1999).

Pro-labouring class change and types of social policy

What are the implications of continuing widespread dominant class control of LGIs for the argument that social policy represents a significant arena for pro-labouring class action in contemporary India? Social policy is a 'stratification system in its own right' (Esping-Andersen 1990:3–4). Any flow of public resources will, in its final allocation, strengthen the material position of some and weaken the position of others in relative terms. The steeper the social hierarchies, the more contentious social policy becomes, and the harder it is to increase the share of resources accessed by the labouring class. Nevertheless, social policy has the ability to overcome Wood's (2003) 'Faustian bargain' whereby the poor compromise their political 'space' and social rights in exchange for access to patrons' private resources in the form of employment and credit (Djurfeldt *et al.* 2008:51). This reiterates this book's argument that by reducing such forms of dependence, social policy opens up the poor's political 'space'. This is a critical and widely made point, which underlines the interplay between social policy and the material and political conditions of the labouring class.

The possibilities and limitations of such an approach can be conveyed through a brief discussion of three central aspects of public policy in rural India: the NREGS, the PDS and the UWSSA. Taken together, the first two of these programmes would, if properly implemented, have provided labouring households with over one-third of a family of five's poverty-line income in 2011–12.[20] NREGS alone would have provided 23 per cent. Where utilised, the health-oriented provisons of the UWSSA (the RSBY) would push the total amount close to the overall annual income of such a household. This shows the degree to which labouring class dependence would be reduced if such programmes were implemented fully. It also underlines the extent to which wage-based incomes fall below providing the material requirements of tens of millions of Indian households.

NREGS, which is discussed in detail later in this book, is the programme that most clearly supports the argument that organising for gains from the state through poverty reduction programmes can produce gains for classes of labour and might facilitate more broad-based pro-labouring class action. By providing 100 days of work for every household, it theoretically removes a significant part of labouring class reproduction from the sphere of production relations. Where its wage levels are higher than the prevailing rural casual wage rates, it also puts upward pressure on wages. In other words, it threatens to loosen dependence upon capitalist producers and increase their production costs. As the programme is rights-based, it also provides a rallying point around which classes of labour can mobilise.

As will be shown in Chapter 6, NREGS has been widely resisted by the dominant class. The PDS has been resisted to a lesser degree, as although it is ostensibly a subsidy to the poor through its provision of state-subsidised foodgrains at a fraction of open market prices, it is also a subsidy to capital as it enables it to pay lower wages. The UWSSA, on the other hand, has been resisted at the level of policy formation as the implications of draft proposals for legislation arguably had even greater potential for strengthening the position of classes of labour than NREGS. The National Commission on Enterprises in the Unorganised Sector (NCEUS 2007) had called for legislation to provide a universal social floor for all workers, which would include national minimum social security, a national minimum wage and minimum working conditions (Kannan and Jain 2013a:82). Despite these suggestions, the Act was passed in 2008 in a watered-down form because campaigners' proposals would have increased capital's labour costs and thereby undermined Indian capitalists' international competitiveness. The Act included no binding conditions with regard to working conditions and avoided a national minimum wage, which would have provided a significant rallying point for improving the material conditions of the labouring class. Social policy, then, is formed and implemented among class relations (in their specific and general forms) and processes of accumulation on a world scale. This shows the limitations of seeing the state as a key site of class struggle as well as the possibilities for it to strengthen the position of classes of labour.

The way that programmes are designed of course affects the way that they 'sit among' class relations. It has been argued that where programmes are universal (available to all) rather than targeted (available to some), provisioning expands the social coalition supporting the programme, thereby augmenting its chances of becoming embedded for the long term and increasing pressure for effective implementation (Lerche 2012; see also Esping-Andersen 1990). This has been keenly debated within recent discussions on India's Food Security Act. In campaigning for returning the PDS to its earlier universal form, the Right to Food Campaign argued that leakage levels in the PDS were noticeably lower in states with either universal (Tamil Nadu) or near-universal access to foodgrains (Andhra Pradesh and Chhattisgarh) (Himanshu and Sen 2011:41).

Discussions about targeting have also been prominent in worldwide debates on social protection. The widespread popularity of cash transfers with policy-makers and some academics (e.g. O'Hanlon *et al.* 2010) has recently spread to India with the running of pilot cash-transfer programmes (Standing 2012), and the launching of the Direct Benefit Transfer programme in January 2013. While the World Bank (2011) emphasises cash transfers' greater efficiency and fiscal flexibility, Standing (2012) regards them as a way of sidestepping 'elite capture' of LGIs.

Ghosh (2011) has raised a number of problems with this approach. First, she argues that they provide a means of avoiding increased state expenditure on essential goods and services by facilitating the purchase of private sector services instead (Ghosh 2011a:853). Another issue with cash transfers is that if they are not index-linked to inflation then classes of labour will be less well-off than they would be under universal public provisioning. Cash transfers, moreover, leave issues around working conditions untouched – at least in direct terms. Finally, by sidestepping conflict within LGIs over the distribution of public resources, cash transfers preclude a gradual wresting of control over such institutions *from* the dominant class through political struggles led by classes of labour and focused on increasing their share of public resources. The hypothesis that emerges is that rather than direct transfers, *rights* to employment and foodgrains generate labouring class mobilisation that has the capacity to affect more durable and broad-based changes in local power dynamics. Cash transfers avoid a political process and provide a more technical 'solution', which may increase labouring class incomes more rapidly but with fewer implications for its relations with other sections of society. Its logic, in other words, is more 'residual' than 'relational'.

In contrast to social protection's early-1990s roots in safety nets and discretionary transfers, arguments for a rights-based approach that is better resourced and embedded in state policy have become more widespread over the last decade or so (Koehler 2011:101; Sabates-Wheeler and Devereux 2008). 'Social protection', Devereux *et al.* suggest (2011:1), 'should be fundamentally interested in realising economic and social rights for all ... [and] ... grounded in social justice'. Meanwhile Koehler (2011:101), in reference to labour rights, redistribution of productive assets (including land), the creation of 'decent work' and progressive fiscal policy, has underlined the 'much broader policy architecture' that is required to make social protection 'genuinely transformative'.

The redistribution of productive assets is seen as reducing dependence and facilitating sustainable livelihoods (Devereux and Sabates-Wheeler 2007:24), and is linked to 'strategies to integrate individuals equally into society and enable the excluded and marginalised groups to claim their rights' (Koehler 2011:100). Social protection's transformative potential rests upon the extent to which rights can be claimed, which is 'driven by legislation proper, as well as by transparency and accessibility of information, freedom of the press, and an independent and vibrant civil society and genuine citizens' voice in party politics ... and other political institutions' (Koehler 2011:101).

While forms of representation are of course significant, focusing on 'rights' in the absence of a discussion of exploitation, and referring to the labouring class as 'excluded' rather than 'exploited', reawakens elements of the Weber/Marx divide discussed in the previous chapter. Koehler (2011) indicates that the labouring class needs sufficient economic independence to be able to act politically, but focuses on rights and representation more than on relations of production and concrete forms of exploitation. Assessment of whether or not rights-based entitlements can be used to shift the balance of power towards the labouring class requires analysis of actual processes and dynamics of exploitation, domination and accumulation – something that the next chapters attempt to do.

Conclusion

This chapter has argued that classes of labour in rural India have become increasingly fragmented and informalised. Casualisation of labour relations has been partial and uneven, and unfreedom persists in varying degrees. As the concrete forms of production relations are modified, the dominant class finds ways to expand accumulation and reproduce its control over labour – not least through the LGIs that they tend to control (along with other parts of the state).

Classes of labour can, though, increase their influence over LGIs and their share of public resources through collective class-based action, which can be galvanised by clear points of contention set by rights-based universal poverty reduction programmes. Whether or not such organisations of classes of labour can be scaled up to more broad-based forms of action remains to be seen. The book returns to this question in Chapter 8. Before that it analyses forms of exploitation, domination and accumulation in particular villages and districts in South India, and the concrete ways in which class relations are mediated by the state.

Notes

1 The term 'structural power' draws on Wright (2000) and Silver (2003).
2 This figure is taken from the World Bank, online: http://data.worldbank.org/indicator/AG.LND.IRIG.AG.ZS (accessed 10 September 2014).
3 Estimates of the annual number of days of agricultural labour cluster between 90 and 180 (Himanshu 2011:48).
4 Within the services sector, the high-profile IT sector provided 4.5 per cent of GDP by the mid-2000s, but only contributed 0.21 per cent of aggregated employment (Chandrasekhar 2007).
5 Figures rounded to the nearest million.
6 While the formal (or 'organised') and informal (or 'unorganised') sectors are, of course, highly interrelated, it is analytically useful to distinguish between them.
7 The absence of safety measures is commonplace in India's informal sector, while the number of workplace accidents is relatively high (NCEUS 2007:33–37).
8 It will be applied to electrified units with twenty or more workers and non-electrified units with forty or more workers, as opposed to the earlier thresholds of ten and twenty workers respectively.
9 See, among others, Bhalla (1999); Breman (1974, 1985, 1996, 2007); Da Corta and Venkateshwarlu (1999); De Neve (2005); Djurfeldt *et al.* (2008); Gooptu and Harriss-White (2001); Guérin *et al.* (2009, 2012); Harriss (1982, 1992, 2013); Harriss *et al.* (2010); Harriss-White (1996, 2003, 2008); Heyer (2012); Jha (2004); Jodhka (1994); Kapadia (1993, 1995); Lerche (1995, 1999, 2007); Picherit (2012, 2014); Ramachandran (1990); Rawal (2006); Rodgers and Rodgers (2011); Srivastava (1989); Wilson (1999).
10 Further back in the early decades of the nineteenth century, collective bondage was not uncommon (Menon 1983 cited in Ramachandran 1990:173).
11 The quotation was taken by Banaji from the 1940 Government of Bengal Report of the Land Commission Bengal, Vols. 3–4, Landholders Replies to the Questionnaire issued by the Land Revenue Commission and their Oral Evidence.
12 Personal communication, Satoshi Miyamura, 14 April 2014.
13 The prominence of smaller-scale forms of organisation based in living spaces and oriented towards the state does not, of course, mean that resistance is restricted to that alone. Larger-scale social movements still exist in parts of the country (Kunnath 2009; Nilsen 2010; Shah 2010, 2013). At the other end of the scale, labourers circulating between locations and employers has been seen as a form of resistance among 'footloose' and landless labourers (Breman

1996:155–156, 1999:423–424), which is reflected in evidence of the growing cultural and political assertiveness of returning migrants (Picherit 2012).

14 Likewise in urban Karnataka, the relatively small-scale Karnataka Kolageri Nivasigala Samyuktha Sanghathana, which campaigns for improved services and slumdwellers' land rights (which pits it against slumlords, real-estate mafia and associated bureaucrats and politicians), has links to a broader network of informal sector workers, such as the National Centre for Labour (NCL), which campaigns and lobbies state and national governments (RoyChowdhury 2003:5282; http://nationalcentreforlabour.org/about_us.html (accessed 29 October 2012); see also Harriss 2007b for a discussion of similar organisations in Tamil Nadu).

15 In the 1970s, disillusionment with the state's poverty reduction record and frustration with its lack of capacity fostered the growth of NGOs. The 'Emergency' of the mid-1970s ratcheted up calls for the formation of non-party political organisations (Kamat 2002:10). After the Emergency the government began funding NGOs through public bodies like the Centre for the Advancement of Participatory Action and Rural Technology (Kamat 2002:12).

16 The arguments in this paragraph draw on a number of sources on the nature of the state in India (Bardhan 1998; Chibber 2003; Corbridge and Harriss 2000; Frankel 2004; Harriss-White 2003; Heller 1999; Kohli 1987; 2011; Rudolph and Rudolph 1987) and more generally (Amsden 1989; Evans 1995; Evans et al. 1985:350–351), as well as from a Marxist perspective (Miliband 1973a; Poulantzas 1976).

17 The tensions between agrarian and industrial capital are perhaps the best-known (with the latter tending to seek lower prices for foodgrains in order to hold down the cost of labour-power, while the former seek higher profits by pushing up agricultural prices). For example, in Victorian Britain legislative change to improve working conditions in the 1840s edged forward among tensions between industrial and agrarian capital (Marx 1976). The Factory Acts that emerged did not appear to be in the short term interests of capital, although arguably they were in their long-term interests.

18 The KRRS had a strong social base in one of this book's fieldwork villages in the early 1990s. Scheduled caste men referred to it as an organisation of the rich and said that they had been told to attend rallies. Organisationally it was controlled by dominant caste (Panchamsali Lingayat) large farmers, although small farmers actively supported the organisation (see Pattenden 2005 for further details).

19 Case studies from Indonesia, the Philippines and China (part of an eleven-country study across three continents) similarly point to an expansion of patronage and little evidence of heightened labouring class access to resources or decision-making (Crook and Sverrisson 1999; Nordholdt 2004; Sidel 1996; So 2007).

20 This is based on the per capita poverty-line figure of 902 rupees per month for rural Karnataka, as set by the Tendulkar poverty-line methodology for the given year (GoI PC 2014a:28). For the NREGS wage figures, see The Hindu (2013).

4

Changing dynamics of exploitation in rural South India

The city of Bengaluru harbours a floating population that runs into the hundreds of thousands. Most are unskilled labourers from the neighbouring states of Andhra Pradesh and Tamil Nadu, the north of India and the north-east of Karnataka. Some of these circular migrants only stay for a month or two during the slack season in agriculture. Many stay for several years.

Members of most of the scheduled caste households in this book's Raichur fieldwork area have circulated through the construction sites of Bengaluru at some point in the last decade. They have built offices for IBM, Philips, ANZ and Indian biotech company BIOCON, and comfortable homes for their employees[1] – most frequently for a developer that calls itself 'the foremost creator of gated communities in Bengaluru'.[2]

While labourers from the more remote Raichur fieldwork villages travel almost 500 kilometres to Bengaluru's construction sites because they live beyond daily reach of urban labour markets, their counterparts in the Dharwad fieldwork villages commute to nearby cities. Across both districts over 80 per cent of more than 600 labouring class households surveyed in 2013–14 primarily made a living through informal wage-labour in agriculture, construction and industry.[3] They are, though, integrated into non-agricultural labour markets in markedly different ways. The rural capitalists, with whom they share their villages, also accumulate in different ways, which has implications for how and where labour works and lives, and the forms of control it endures.

A number of other variables including caste and political dynamics are interwoven with these patterns of accumulation and labouring class reproduction to form the broader patterns of class relations at a local level with which 'everyday' relations at the level of production are co-constituted. This chapter's analysis of control within the production process and its immediate 'local' contexts sheds some light not only on differences in material conditions, but also on how poverty reduction programmes play out in particular places in practice (see Chapters 5 and 6), and how organisations of the labouring class might be formed and strengthened (Chapter 8). Put another way, broader class relations cannot be understood without analysing concrete forms of domination and exploitation in particular places.

Village characteristics

The extent to which accumulation is agriculture-oriented reflects differences in levels of irrigation and soil type, and therefore of productivity. While the Raichur fieldwork villages are all canal-irrigated to some degree, the Dharwad villages are dryland villages with a greater share of less productive red soils. In the village where agriculture is least profitable (in Dharwad) capitalist accumulation is more closely related to the local state, while in the village where agriculture is most profitable (in Raichur) surpluses have been invested in agribusiness and securing formal sector city-based employment for the next generation (see Table 4.1).

Levels of landlessness also vary, with the most irrigated village having the most polarised landholdings (see Figure 3). Caste dynamics differ between villages that have a strong dominant caste, and those where power is more evenly spread across castes. Some of the villages' dominant castes exercise considerable influence over politics in the district, while others are politically marginal at that level.

A final significant difference bears reiteration here: poverty levels are higher and social development indicators lower in the Raichur villages (UNDP 2005), which have a greater number of *kachha* (mud) houses, a greater number of child labourers, a greater proportion of households reporting food shortages and a higher chance of family members not being 'shown' to a doctor when sick (reliable public healthcare is largely absent).[4] Social policy (with regard to the major National Rural Employment Guarantee Scheme (NREGS), Public Distribution System (PDS) and housing programmes) is less effectively implemented in the Raichur villages. The most irrigated village, Shiva Camp, has the lowest levels of implementation (NREGS works have not taken place for five years). The more politically connected village of Panchnagaram in Dharwad meanwhile has slightly better levels of implementation than is the case even in neighbouring villages.

A survey of all 901 households in four villages (two in each district) was carried out in 2013–14 (along with semi-structured interviews with around 10 per cent of the households). This chapter focuses primarily on these four villages, but also draws on an earlier survey of over 200 scheduled caste households in four Raichur villages carried out in 2010

Table 4.1 Characteristics of fieldwork villages surveyed, 2013–14

	Shiva Camp (Raichur)	Jagalwara (Raichur)	Kamlapur (Dharwad)	Panchnagaram (Dharwad)
Distance from district headquarters (km)	90	75	12	12
Distance from main road (km)	12	7	10	7
Distance from New Industrial Zone (km)	n/a	n/a	20	9
Land value	Third	Lowest	Second	Highest
Level (%) and type of irrigation	96 (canal)	52 (canal/ river)	18 (borewell)	12 (borewell)
Soil type	> 95% black	> 90% black	Mostly black	Mostly red
Main form of non-agricultural employment	Circular migration	Circular migration	Commuting	Commuting
Main source of non-agricultural work	Construction	Construction	Construction	Industry
Average number of oxen (the main draught animal) per household (proxy for mechanisation)	0.15	0.4	0.5	0.5
Agricultural productivity:[a] 1 = most, 4 = least	1	2	3	4
Main bases of accumulation	Agriculture, agribusiness, formal employment	Agriculture	Agriculture	Agriculture, state-related business

[a] Based on levels of irrigation, soil type, level of mechanisation and cotton yields.

Source: fieldwork data.

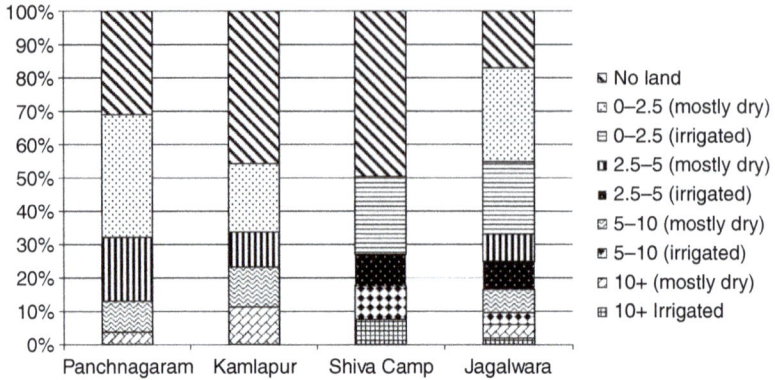

Figure 3 Land distribution in four fieldwork villages (source: fieldwork data)

and 2011 (two of the same villages and two additional villages), and several hundred interviews carried out over a protracted period in a number of villages across the districts. Additional interviews took place in the camps of circular migrants in Bengaluru in 2010.

Dominant class accumulation strategies are more diversified in Panchnagaram and Shiva Camp (one village from each district) than in Jagalwara and Kamlapur. In the latter villages a higher percentage of individuals in dominant class households work in agriculture. Of the former villages, accumulation strategies in Panchnagaram are more oriented towards the state. It has the highest level of public sector employment, the highest number of contractors (most of whom work informally) and the greatest influence over local government institutions (see Chapter 5 for a more detailed discussion).

Accumulation strategies in Shiva Camp are more focused on agribusiness and formal sector employment. Levels of agribusiness exceed those of the other three villages combined, reflecting the greater agricultural surpluses in a village with over 90 per cent canal irrigation. The larger the farmer, the more likely he is to be diversifying into business activities. Having farmed all of his land until 2006, the largest landowner in the village was now leasing out forty of his fifty acres because, as he put it, he was now 'more interested in business than agriculture'. He and his brother have an agricultural inputs shop, and funnel paddy via warehouses and their lorry into the rice mill that they part-own in the sub-district headquarters. Five other grain warehouses had been built since the mid-2000s, an inter-state paddy trading operation had been launched,[5] another agricultural inputs shop opened and six combine harvesters purchased.

Accumulation was being further diversified into white-collar formal employment in the cities. Most of the larger (ten-acre or more) farmers had at least one child employed in the formal sector in Bengaluru, Hyderabad or Chennai. Among medium-sized (5–10 acre) farming families, who are more agriculture-focused and lease in the greatest quantities of land in the four villages, most have somebody either in formal employment in the city or in regular employment in a petty business in a town – as often as not those owned by relatives.

Unlike Panchnagaram in Dharwad (see Chapter 5), state-linked forms of accumulation were almost non-existent in Shiva Camp. Its Telugu-speaking dominant castes hailed from a neighbouring state (see below) and wielded relatively little influence in local government institutions. Although they held the largest number of seats in their nine-village gram panchayat (GP),[6] their members were scattered across a number of villages. The primary power base was among a group of Koruba ('other backward caste' Kannada-speaking) farmers in the village where the GP office was located.

In the next section, changing forms of domination and exploitation in agriculture in Shiva Camp and the Raichur villages are discussed in some detail. The following sections turn their attention to forms of domination and exploitation among circulating and commuting labourers in Bengaluru and Dharwad. The final section considers the socio-political dynamics of change (something that is taken up again in later chapters). The following chapter focuses on forms of domination in the Dharwad villages where state-linked forms of accumulation play a more prominent role.

Changing forms of control over agricultural labour

Non-agricultural employment, which has been significant in the Dharwad villages since the late 1980s, has only recently become widespread in the Raichur villages. In the early 2000s, mechanisation of paddy harvesting was followed by a prolonged period of drought. Demand for agricultural labour fell, the decline of traditional forms of bondage accelerated and a steady trickle of circular migration became a torrent. By the mid-2000s, most labouring class households in the fieldwork villages had migrated to Bengaluru's construction sites.

Somewhat fewer labouring class households had migrated from Shiva Camp, which is almost entirely canal-irrigated and has the most unequal land distribution of the four fieldwork villages (see Figure 3). It is a 'camp' rather than a historical village, meaning that Reddy and Kamma farmers from Andhra Pradesh settled there in the 1960s and 1970s to avail themselves of relatively cheap canal-irrigated land. Labourers and marginal farmers (mostly from the scheduled castes) moved there from nearby villages and neighbouring sub-districts. The large landowners are all

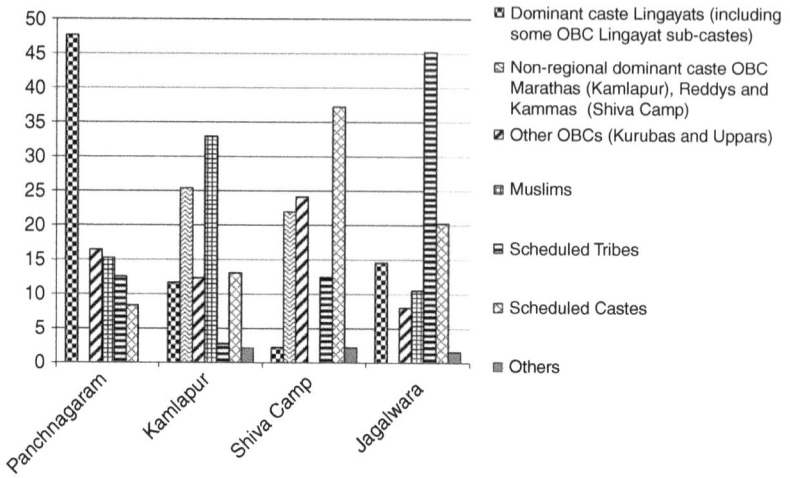

Figure 4 Caste distribution in four fieldwork villages (source: fieldwork data)

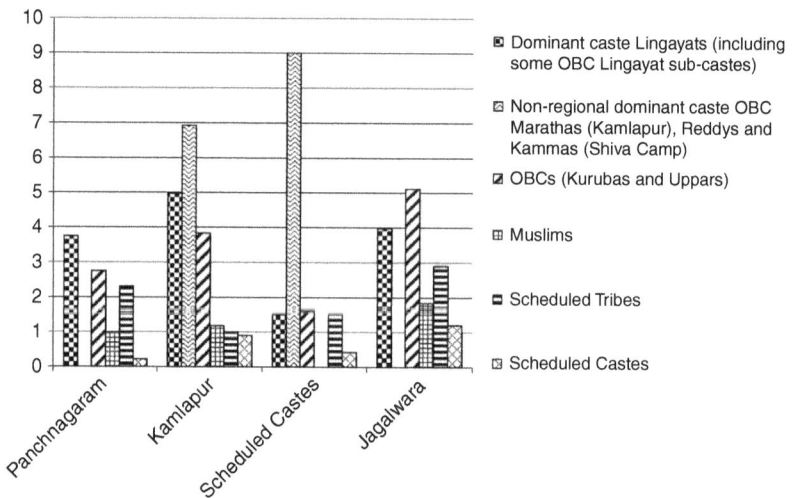

Figure 5 Land distribution by caste (source: fieldwork data)

Kammas and Reddys who have average landholdings of around nine irrigated acres and own close to two-thirds of the land (see Figure 5). Around 20 per cent of the land is owned by two pairs of brothers (one Reddy, one Kamma). On the other hand, around half of the households are landless, and 73 per cent (the highest percentage of the four villages) own less than 2.5 acres (the cut-off point in this village below which households are categorised as belonging to classes of labour) (see Figure 3).[7] The three

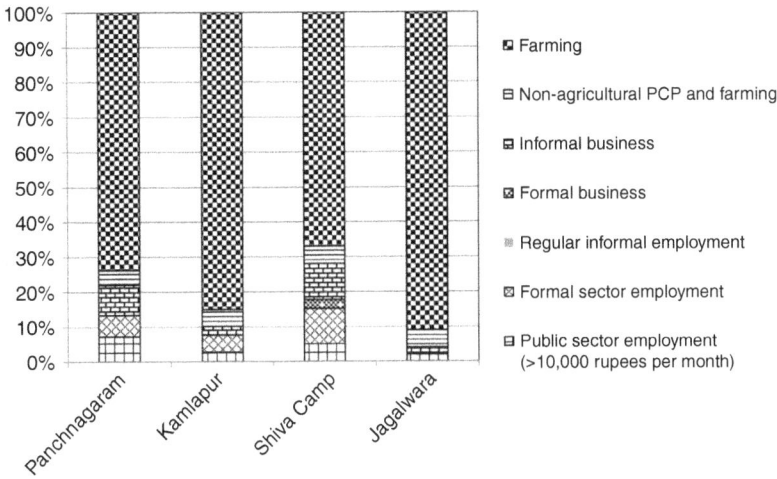

Figure 6 Primary bases of accumulation (among surplus-producing households) (source: fieldwork data)

scheduled castes (former 'untouchables') present in the village own less than half-an-acre on average. The 'middle castes' (mostly Uppars and scheduled tribe Nayaks in the context of this village) own an average of just over an acre-and-a-half.

As well as diversifying into agribusiness and formal employment, farmers in Shiva Camp have pursued a number of strategies in order to reduce their dependence on village labourers as circular migration has increased (see Figures 6 and 7). They have mechanised faster than their counterparts in the other fieldwork villages, have cut back on the amount of cattle that they keep (with the exception of the two or three larger farmers who still have bonded labourers), and have shifted from more labour-intensive crops like cotton and groundnut to less labour-intensive paddy.[8] They have also begun to hire in paddy transplantation gangs from other areas.

Labour bondage has declined to just three cases. This is the most extreme and direct form of controlling labour. Tied to a particular farmer, bonded labourers' wages are considerably lower and they work for long hours seven days a week. In 2010–11, two bonded labourers in Shiva Camp were paid Rs. 30,000 and Rs. 35,000 respectively per year. They were paid in two equal instalments after six and twelve months. In practice, smaller amounts were 'advanced' for consumption or health purposes so that by the end of the year no payment was made, and the labourer in question, although theoretically able to exit, was drawn back into another one-year agreement. For the latter this had been an ongoing cycle since he was a child. The former complained of working 'day and night for ninety rupees', which was less than a third of the wage of casual

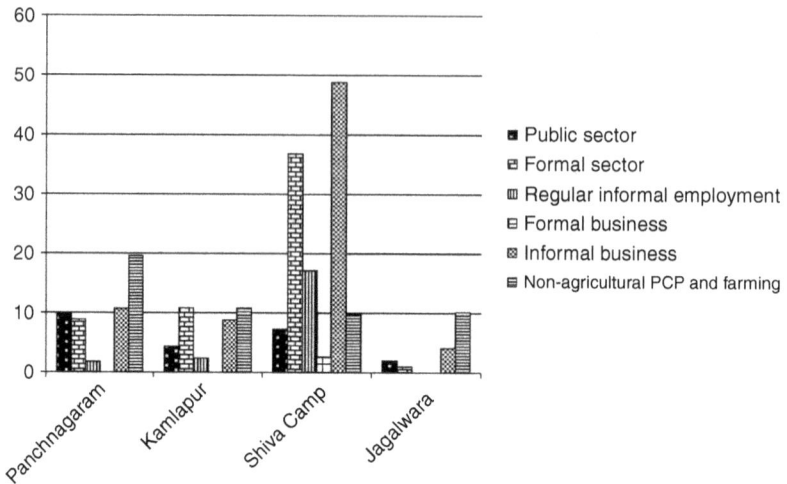

Figure 7 Individuals involved in non-agricultural activities as percentage of total households (source: fieldwork data)

male labourers when calculated on an hourly basis. As well as working 12–14-hour days, when irrigation work required it they worked nights as well.

Excluding those away on construction sites in Bengaluru, around half of labouring class households 'lease in' land. Of these, a minority either pay a cash rent or a share of the crop without any additional ties while the majority are controlled through a variety of interlocking strategies. 'Sharecropping' arrangements are central to these, and generally involve households receiving inputs 'on credit' from a landowner that they are already 'indebted' to, and then transferring the harvest to the same individual. Rent in kind is around one-third of the yield.[9] When added to the 'interest' on input loans, close to half of the harvest accrues to the landowners – over three times more than the five bags received by the labourers. The latter also had to provide the landowner with the right of first refusal over the labour-power of one household member for four hours every morning at 25 per cent less than the going rate (see also Lerche 1999).[10]

In effect the sharecropping arrangements amounted to disguised forms of piece-rated wage-labour with additional ties that extend and intensify the exploitation of labour across the household (see also Rawal 2006). While labour bondage has declined in recent years, such 'sharecropping' arrangements have increased as capitalist farmers seek to offload risks and free up time while retaining tight control over labour. Related arrangements extend into casual employment. Some 'sharecroppers' always work for the same landowner either as 'sharecroppers' or for a daily wage. Others usually work for the same landowner when they work for a daily wage, and while others still do not 'sharecrop' they 'borrow' from the large farmers that they usually work for. There are critical differences at play in terms of the number of days of work accessed by households that (i) circulate (often to repay debts 'owed' to large farmers), (ii) lease land 'independently' as well as working as daily wage-labourers, (iii) 'borrow' and work as daily wage-labourers, and (iv) 'borrow' money, 'sharecrop' and work as daily wage-labourers. Those who do not work for the largest landowners tend to get fewer days of work in the year, which is one of the reasons why labourers say that they prefer to work for them, along with prompter payment of wages and easier access to 'loans'. Larger farmers, for their part, have tended to prefer landless workers due to their greater availability and their higher levels of dependence (and therefore weaker bargaining power). Across the annual cycle, dependence is further rein-forced during slack periods when employment dwindles to a trickle and access to work becomes more uneven and competitive.

The bewildering mix of interlocking labour, land, credit and commod-ity markets is nothing new (Bharadwaj 1985; Lerche 1999; Srivastava 1989), but it has become much less common in contemporary India. Such forms of exploitation are indicative of a situation where the balance of class forces is particularly skewed towards capital, which allows it to increase the rate of exploitation, as helps it to subvert pro-labour elem-ents of social policy.[11]

In 2011, when casual rural wages were rising in real terms across the state (see Chapter 1), wages in the nearby roadside village of Badarapur were 50 per cent higher for men and 75 per cent higher for women than in more remote and tightly controlled Shiva Camp. The rates had con-verged to a considerable degree by 2014, but the initial discrepancy is indicative of the more adverse balance of class forces in Shiva Camp.

In semi-irrigated nearby Jagalwara, labourers were more likely to work outside of their village in nearby more irrigated 'camps' (and where the greater amount of fallow land meant that goat-rearing was a more prominent aspect of labouring class livelihoods). Here, semi-tied forms of labour relations were more likely to be debt-related only. Debt-related ties, as indicated in the previous chapter, are often preferred by farmers where access to alternative forms of employment is greater (Brass 1990; Guérin 2013; Hart 1986), while forms of sharecropping may be preferred in a more closed (local agriculture-dependent) labour market as a means of creating hierarchies among workers (as well as transferring risks, free-ing up time and maintaining control) (Rawal 2006).

This, though, does not mean that rates of exploitation are necessar-ily lower. The wages of a tied elderly labourer in Jagalwara were found to be around one-quarter of regular male wage rates in 2011, while a disabled individual in the same village appeared not to be being paid at all in 2014. In all cases of semi-tied labour, wage rates were less than the prevailing casual rate, but hours of work were usually more akin to those of a casual rather than a bonded labourer. The poorest labouring households were forced to ask for work, and had the least bargaining power. They were often working for wage rates well below the average, and at times they were even overlooked due to their frequent need for prompt payment of wages. The degree and number of variations in the terms of wage-labour reflect labour's high levels of segmentation, and also underline why crude distinctions between free and unfree labour do not hold.

Paddy transplantation and piece-rate wage-labour

Major agricultural tasks for men include spraying fertilisers and pesticides, *bunding*[12] and portering, as well as some sowing and harvesting activities (the former where bullocks are used rather than seeds being directly placed in the earth, which tends to be done by women). For women, the major tasks include weeding, cotton-picking, some harvesting work (although this has been reduced by the mechanisation of paddy harvesting) and the most significant task of all, which is transplanting paddy.[13]

Paddy transplantation in the Raichur villages was done on a piece-rate basis, as were many harvesting operations and a growing share of weeding – tasks predominantly carried out by women. Fewer of these operations had been mechanised, and absolute surplus-value extraction was therefore more marked than in male tasks.

Relatively subtle but significant forms of control were at play within piece-rate arrangements. The daily wage increases according to the area covered, which prompts labour to be self-disciplining and increase the intensity of the labour process itself. With wage levels dependent upon the intensity of work, older women and some younger, more inexperienced labourers were excluded, while stragglers were pressurised by the *maistry* (gang leader) of the transplantation gang and other stronger, faster workers. Lunchbreaks are shorter than in daily casual work. Workers who encourage one another to take their time and 'eat and get strength' when working for daily wages exhort one another to 'hurry and finish food' during transplantation work'.

The preference that female labourers expressed for piece-rate over casual work was almost always qualified. Wages are higher and direct supervision absent, but the work is more intensive and the hours longer (particularly when travelling to other villages).[14] Wages may 'extinguish every trace of the division of the working day into necessary and surplus labour, into paid and unpaid labour' (Marx 1976:680), but at the level of the concrete they do so in different ways.

Piece-rate transplantation work provides over one-third of female agricultural labourers' annual income, and is linked to casual daily work. The transplantation gangs often first complete the work of larger landowners for whom some gang members work as casual daily wage-labourers (and/ or sharecroppers in the case of villages like Shiva Camp in particular). Transplantation's higher daily wages, and the timing of the main transplantation season at the end of the summer slack season when levels of underemployment are pronounced, heighten larger farmers' bargaining power. Smaller farmers generally have to wait, and their land is often located further from the canal distributary anyway (which means that the water arrives there later) (Mollinga 2003).

The extent of piece-rate employment varies across districts and villages, and according to the size of the farmer. Cotton-picking was more likely to be done on a more expensive piece-rate basis in the Dharwad villages than in Jagalwara, and more likely to be done by larger farmers. Smaller farmers generally still opt for daily wage-labourers and employ some older workers.

Relations between maistries, farmers and labourers

Piece-rate work is primarily organised by gang leaders (maistries) who mediate relations between farmers and ordinary gang members. They secure work, negotiate rates, play a leading role in deciding who is included in the gang, collect and distribute wages and influence the pace of work. They often work with trusted lieutenants, and access work through long-term relationships with individual farmers. The relationships between farmers and maistries vary, as do those between maistries and fellow labourers, and the bargaining power each of them has.

In the fieldwork villages, there had been a notable shift from male to female maistries. Of the predominantly scheduled caste gangs in the fieldwork villages, the one in Shiva Camp had been led by a female maistry for twenty years, while the main gangs in the other villages had shifted from male to female maistries in the 2000s.[15]

Gender and class relations are meshed together in complex ways in the interactions between farmers and female maistries. Social spaces are highly gendered, and consequently men can interact with farmers in a greater number of locations than women – including teashops and other places that are conducive to negotiation. Interactions with women are generally restricted to public spaces, which can increase their visibility to other gang members.

In short, the gendered nature of the work process and the gendered nature of social space tend to foster closer relationships between male maistries and farmers within the farmer–maistry–labourer chain. The complaint made against former male maistries was that they had been taking commission from farmers, and in some cases that they drank rather than worked. Women were trusted more.

There is, though, somewhat more than this going on in the shift to female maistries. Male maistries carry saplings but do not transplant and so do not work alongside women in the same way, cannot lead by example (although they can do so indirectly through female relatives), and are more likely to be absent from the worksite. Hence, it is generally easier for female maistries to increase the intensity of work as they are integral to the core labour process.

Farmers have a greater amount of control over labour where they can exert influence over the maistry. For example, farmers in Shiva Camp were rumoured (by the maistry's lieutenant, among others) to be giving the long-term female maistry small additional payments in exchange for agreement to cultivate an area of land that was 5 to 10 per cent greater than it was said to be. In effect, then, farmers were using their influence over the maistry to hold down wage levels.

In Jagalwara, meanwhile, the main scheduled caste maistry received loans from one of the largest farmers. Her husband worked for the same farmer as a semi-tied labourer, and had recently been elected as a GP member after defeating a former male maistry who lived a few doors up in the scheduled caste hamlet. His successful candidacy had been backed by certain larger landowners including his principal employer. Forms of control over labour are intertwined in complex ways, and larger farmers are particularly well placed to work things to their advantage. Even when they do not exercise strong influence over the maistry, their larger contiguous areas of land make it easier for them to manipulate wage rates by underestimating the area to be transplanted.

The conflict between capital and labour in piece-rate work (*gutige*), then, is not limited to the length and intensity of the working day. Claims of a regularised rate for transplanting an acre of paddy in the fieldwork area conceal contests over the actual rate paid by farmers and the distribution of wages among workers. In practice, wages varied by as much as 25 per cent across the 450 km^2 fieldwork area, and farmers were increasingly bringing in outside labour gangs to hold wages down.

The farmer–maistry (–labourer) relation is, of course, not independent of the maistry–labourer relation. In some villages, workers had greater influence over maistries – illustrated in part by a more rapid turnover of maistries. Some labourers claimed that their gangs had become more democratic, and that rather than maistries scolding co-workers, as used to be the case, they were now more likely to scold maistries. Labourers were slowly becoming more likely to keep a record of the wages due to them (enabled by the growing levels of literacy and numeracy), although many remained unclear.

Relations between maistries and other workers relate in part to maistries' socio-economic position. In Shiva Camp, where farmers appeared to exercise considerable influence over the maistry, both she and her lieutenant were from somewhat better-off households. Where labourers' influence within groups was reputed to be higher, the maistries were from less well-off households and were in a similar socio-economic position to most of their co-workers. The implication is that labourers as well as farmers strategise to increase their influence over maistries.

In spite of increased levels of circular outmigration from the fieldwork area, then, farmers found different ways to maintain control over labour. They were helped in the Raichur villages by the distance from urban labour markets, the relatively steep social hierarchies and the weakness of social policy, which meant that class relations were barely mediated by the state at all. Labour relations in these villages had been casualised to a degree, but less than might initially appear to be the case. Although generally shorter-lived than in the past, various forms of ties persisted.

Circular migration through boomtown Bengaluru

Levels of irrigation, and to some extent connectivity (to main roads and towns), correlate with levels of circulation. Some 90 per cent of scheduled caste households in semi-irrigated Jagalwara (in Raichur district) had migrated (in whole or in part) at some point in the 2000s, as opposed to around two-thirds in fully irrigated Shiva Camp. The latter also began migrating somewhat later. With more labourers migrating and for longer, a greater number of migrants from Jagalwara had become semi-skilled workers (who earned 50 per cent more) and construction maistries responsible for recruiting and managing labour (and who play a somewhat different role to the agriculture maistries discussed above and tend to be more distant from labourers).[16] Most labourers from Jagalwara worked for these maistries in Bengaluru. This made access to work more secure, but because as maistries built up relationships with employers in Bengaluru they were entrusted with money to provide labourers with advances, in some cases it also led to labour being more tightly contolled (see also Guérin *et al.* 2009a).

Construction capital controls labour through the use of intermediaries, by segmenting labour and by largely sidestepping labour legislation. By using maistries to hire and manage labour, it maintains high levels of 'remote control' over labour, reduces its costs and increases flexibility. As recruiters, maistries tend to gather workers from their home area, which cuts capital's costs while augmenting its control because labourers

cannot easily disappear, and anyway are unlikely to foot-drag or sour relations with their most likely 'source' of construction work in the future.
The maistry is the primary gatekeeper to wage-labour in the city, just as
the larger landowners are in the village.

Maistries also act as a pressure valve for grievances, helping to undercut potential bases for collective action by filtering demands and periodically seeking concessions. They must strike the right balance between
not making what capital might see as excessive demands, and making
sure that levels of discontent among workers do not jeopardise productivity, although capital can always turn to the reserve army of underemployed labour lurking in the country's rural hinterlands.

Drawn from various locations onto the larger construction sites,
migrant labourers arrive with ready-made segmentations, such as language, caste, age and gender, which capital can manipulate. These are
cross-cut by uneven wage levels – masons earn 50 per cent more than
unskilled workers, while women earn 50 per cent less and are almost
invariably bound to the ranks of unskilled labour. As well as being driven
by the dynamic of competitive accumulation that develops the forces of
production and increases labour's mobility, the tendency towards the segmentation of labour under capitalism, then, is also a conscious strategy.

Control over labour is further compounded by people's reticence to
assert themselves in unfamiliar territory, and, as well as the various forms
of segmentation already highlighted, construction work is divided across
a dizzying array of subcontractors whose gangs complete particular
tasks such as decorating, barbending or concreting. Local labourers, settled in Bengaluru, are less pliable, which perhaps explains why they are
more likely to be hired for short-term jobs that command higher wages.
Migrant labourers, on the other hand, are located on worksites within
easy reach of on-site managers. Collective action is unlikely – compromised by the maistry's links to home villages, by advances and by the
relative absence of social moorings and connections beyond the immediate work gang and those occupying neighbouring sheds (who will often
be from other districts or even from other states).

It is scarcely surprising, then, that collective action to challenge poor
living and working conditions was almost non-existent among these construction labourers. The only time that they bargained over wages was
when they were called on at short notice by managers of other building
sites during slack periods on the larger projects (generally in the rainy
season). They were, however, sometimes physically restrained from
working elsewhere by security guards.

Most migrants from the fieldwork areas (particularly longer-term
ones) worked for large-scale construction capital on big residential and
commercial projects. Wages were lower than on small projects (30 per
cent lower in October 2010 – Rs. 260 per working couple as opposed to

Rs. 340), but work was more regular, and tents (or 'sheds') were located on relatively secure sites with access to drinking water. In other words, large-scale capital's investment in services and security facilitated lower wages. Shorter-term seasonal migrants tended to work on smaller projects where wages were higher but tents were generally located on less secure public ground. For all circular migrants, poor living conditions, increased health problems, heightened risks of violence against women and additional burdens of household labour and childcare on women and girl children appear to be the norm (Breman 1990, 1996; Iyer 2004:85; Mobiles Crèches 2008: Mosse *et al.* 2005:3025–3027).

The sidestepping of labour legislation was facilitated by the use of maistries and subcontracting chains, and through the exertion of influence over state institutions. With one or two exceptions, where workers had died or been injured on site, access to state-backed social security was non-existent. Most notable in their absence were the health-related provisions of the 2008 Unorganised Workers and Social Security Act (primarily the Rashtriya Swasthya Bima Yojana (RSBY), which, at the time of fieldwork, was supposed to provide each household with Rs. 30,000 to cover medical costs every year) and the 1996 Buildings and Other Construction Workers Act (BOCWA). The latter legislates for the disbursement of assistance for medical and other costs (including births, funerals and permanent injury) on all but the smallest sites (GoK n.d.:92; 2010). Even if workers reached the point of applying for benefits, procedural issues stymied implementation because workers required written proof that they had worked in the sector during three of the previous twelve months (GoK n.d.:92, 94). In most cases there was no written record even in the form of a payslip. In some cases the subcontractors for whom labourers worked were themselves unregistered, making access to public resources even more difficult. In effect capital was sheltering behind opaque structures of employment, and at the expense of working and living conditions and, in many cases, minimum wages.

Meanwhile, hampered by a lack of capacity, the labour department had only spent *0.12* per cent of the $120 million that it had collected as a cess for the purposes of the Buildings and Other Construction Workers Welfare Fund between 2007 and June 2010 (an amount that had been collected despite reported widespread private sector evasion).[17] A senior official in the Labour Department stated that they were unable to go after companies that failed to implement safety measures, or comply with any other regulations because they lacked the means, and instead sought to persuade them to comply.[18]

Capital did not always fail to implement safety measures (or social security measures or set up crèches), but this was the general pattern (see also Iyer 2004:86, 90; Mobile Crèches 2008:3–4; Prosperi 2009:5; Shivakumar *et al.* 1991:M31; Van der Loop 1996:79, 183; Virk 2004:162).

Partial compliance with state regulation can barely even be seen as a minor concession to a threadbare and widely compromised state,[19] because it allows capital to claim compliance while using fragmented and flexible forms of labour management to mask the extent of their failure to provide 'decent' working and living conditions. This helps it augment the rate of exploitation while undermining workers' access to healthcare and social security and ensuring that those from the Raichur villages (among others) who have built the offices of major transnational corporations have done so while living on mud floors under blue plastic sheets.

While some have described it as 'the dominant form of economic mobility for the poor' (Deshingkar and Akter 2009:1), others characterise it as a survival strategy, a means of managing debt and a process through which poverty is reproduced and inequalities amplified (Breman 1990, 1996; Mobiles Crèches 2008; Mosse *et al.* 2002:60–71, 2005:3026–3028; Shivakumar *et al.*, 1991; Van der Loop 1996). These views are not necessarily at odds: distress and survival-oriented circulation may also be the dominant form of economic mobility for classes of labour, as the next sub-section indicates.

The outcomes of circulation

In June 2010, average wages for unskilled labourers were 48 per cent higher than in agriculture (40 per cent higher for women, 55 per cent higher for men), and levels of employment among interviewees were 50 per cent higher (Pattenden 2012:172). Circulation for four months of the year increased annual household incomes by 50 per cent, while those migrating for longer periods saw incomes rise even more.

Socio-economic gains were, though, highly uneven. While there was not a single case of either unskilled or semi-skilled workers purchasing new assets, almost all maistries had done so (mostly buying land, but also in one case an auto rickshaw). Most maistries had already owned some land prior to migration (which provides security for loans and wages channelled through them), most were literate and numerate and were promoted between their mid-twenties and mid-forties after several years in Bengaluru. Some had previously worked as agricultural maistries, and most came from households with a relatively large number of male adults. While maistries invested in new assets, most investments in existing assets were made by better-paid semi-skilled workers (who accounted for around 20 per cent of the sample).[20] Overall, 62 per cent of migrant households were found to have experienced minor socio-economic gains. These included investments in education, house improvements, operations on chronic health problems, paying off debts, the levelling of land to facilitate cultivation, leasing larger amounts of agricultural land, buying small amounts of gold, paying for marriages and, in one case, funding a campaign for a seat on the gram panchayat. One individual even became a moneylender, underlining the contradictory aspects of change.

Around one-third of households had seen their socio-economic situation deteriorate during circulation. All such cases involved unskilled labourers, and in each case it had occurred as a result of health issues including death, on-site injuries and road accidents. The poorest households had taken advances from maistries. One such example was a household of seven – parents, four daughters and one son-in-law, of whom all bar one were illiterate. Six other children had not made it past infancy, and the mother had a long-term gynaecological problem as a result of poor maternal care and was barely able to work. The father, who had been a bonded labourer for most of his life, had sustained an injury while working as an agricultural labourer. His maistry nephew had given them an advance that cut into their earnings in Bengaluru, and when they experienced a series of minor health problems, they were forced to return home worse off than when they had left. Initial socio-economic conditions were, then, an important factor in shaping migration outcomes, along with the ability to make the transition to more skilled work and the avoidance of health problems.

The last of these relates to the absence of decent working and living conditions, and to a lack of access to state-backed social security. Had the provisions of RSBY and BOCWA (see above) been implemented, all but one of the households who had experienced a deterioration in their socio-economic position would have seen their position improve instead. Failure to implement government policy was, then, critical to the material outcomes of circulation, and symptomatic both of migrant labourers' political marginalisation in relation to both capital and the state, and also of capital's ability to sidestep government regulations.

Construction capital, then, maintains a high level of control over labour while lowering costs, offloading risks (such as quality control or labour reliability), maximising flexibility and minimising the chances of collective action. All of this points not only to a lack of state will to regulate the sector, but also the construction sector's influence over it. Senior Labour Department officials met with the representatives of capital more frequently than with those of labour (interview, 5 October 2010). It is not just that capital lobbies government for a regulatory environment that increases returns to capital through bodies such as the Builders Association of India, which represents 30,000 construction companies; it also actively resists and sidesteps implementation (see also Breman 1990, 1996:182–185, 198). As Srivastava (2012) has put it, flexibilisation and the 'extraction of surplus value through lengthening of working hours, poor conditions, denial of social security, even where it is due under legislation, is part of capital's growing strategy and portrays its increased assertiveness'.

Commuting in Dharwad

In the Dharwad villages, 300 kilometres to the west, bonded labour had declined earlier – the best part of two decades before it had done in Raichur. The odd case remained,[21] as did forms of sharecropping, albeit with fewer interlinkages with capitalist farmers than there were in the more remote Raichur villages. Unlike the latter, the Dharwad villages were situated within commutable distance of nearby cities. The number of commuters ebbed and flowed with the rainfall. In late 2013, after a good monsoon, most male labourers were working in the villages as agricultural labourers, whereas in 2012 the reverse had been the case. Almost all female labourers, meanwhile, worked in agriculture regardless of the monsoon.

Levels of commuting varied between the two main fieldwork villages (see Table 4.1). In Kamlapur, where levels of landlessness were higher, a majority of labouring class households made a living primarily through commuting to the city. In Panchnagaram, where levels of landlessness were lower, classes of labour were more likely to mix agricultural labour and farming. In this village, only around a third of households primarily made a living in the city. Levels of non-agricultural petty commodity production were also higher, with clusters of basket-weavers and carpenters being particularly prominent.[22] The village's greater numbers of marginal landholdings translated into more complex and somewhat more village-oriented livelihoods.

Labourers from the two villages were, then, integrated into non-agricultural labour markets to different degrees. They were also integrated in different ways (see Figure 8). Besides a handful in each village who were regularly employed in small businesses, and a clutch of market porters, most non-agricultural employment in the villages was either in construction or formal sector industry. In Kamlapur, casual employment in the construction sector was by far the most common activity, while in Panchnagaram industrial work was more widespread, and had increased substantially over the previous decade due to the development of a new industrial area.

Almost 90 per cent who worked in the industrial area did so as unskilled labourers, and a similar proportion were employed informally despite the fact that most were paying out part of their wages for PF/ESI (social security) payments – particularly those working for joint ventures between the well-known Indian Tata industrial house and Brazilian and South Korean capital. Access to social security required 240 days

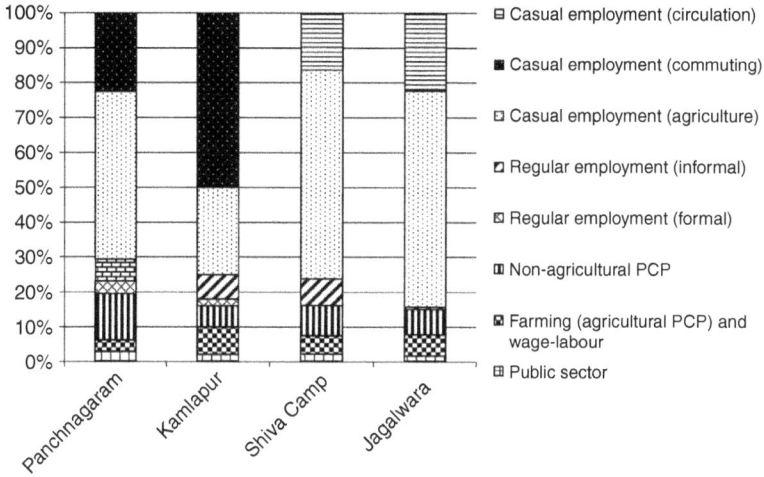

Legend (right of chart):
- ⊟ Casual employment (circulation)
- ■ Casual employment (commuting)
- ▢ Casual employment (agriculture)
- ◪ Regular employment (informal)
- ⊠ Regular employment (formal)
- ⯂ Non-agricultural PCP
- ◙ Farming (agricultural PCP) and wage-labour
- ⊞ Public sector

Chart x-axis labels: Panchnagaram, Kamlapur, Shiva Camp, Jagalwara

Figure 8 Primary bases of reproduction of labouring class households

continuous work, and most workers from Panchnagaram either worked seasonally (as they also had land) or were employed through a maistry for periods of less than six months. Even those who did work regularly for sustained periods were sometimes denied access to payments through bureaucratic foot-dragging. This combination of temporary redundancies, subcontracting and foot-dragging meant that less than 10 per cent of industrial workers received social security payments. Even those working in the formal sector for Tata, then, mostly worked informally, which corresponds with the broader national trend of increasing numbers of informal workers in the formal sector (discussed in Chapter 3). As was the case in the construction sector, maistries and processes of subcontracting played a significant role in facilitating processes of informalisation and remote-control.

As well as differences *between* how villages were integrated into non-agricultural labour markets, there were also differences *within* them. Semi-skilled workers with regular access to casual labour in the city were the most tightly integrated. They rarely worked in their villages and had seen their dependence on village landowners decline the most. Female labourers' dependence had declined the least as only a handful worked outside of their villages – mostly as kitchen hands in large industries.

The decline of dependence on village landowners for wage-labour also varied across streets. The landless, as already noted, were more likely to work in the city, but given the uneven patterns of landownership across castes, and given the role that both kinship and community played in accessing work, levels of commuting across streets varied significantly. In Panchnagaram, the largely landless scheduled castes worked in the city more than some other communities and were more likely to be critical of the dominant. Muslims in this village were more likely to have marginal landholdings, were more closely entwined with the village economy, and were less likely to be critical of the dominant.

Other factors played a role in the way that different communities talked about the dominant. For example, the scheduled castes lived together in a hamlet on the edge of the village, while Muslim households were scattered around the village. Positive discrimination by the government also appeared to play some role. One of the scheduled caste men had benefited from reservations in education and had gone on to take up a political position. There was also relatively widespread awareness that caste-based discrimination was against the law – even though it still persisted in various guises such as the continuing use of separate cups in teashops. Such differences in class relations across different communities within the same village had implications for the way that social policy was implemented (see Chapter 6).

Socio-political change

The ways in which labour is integrated into non-agricultural labour markets has implications for the extent to which it is able to challenge hierarchies at home, as well as working conditions and wage levels in cities. The socio-political gains of circular migration tend to be confined to home villages, and are more likely to be discursive and episodic than embedded or sustained. On their return home many labourers express a greater assertiveness, emboldened by experiences elsewhere and a reduced dependence on dominant class farmers at home. This may be expressed through cultural events (see also Picherit 2012), or by running for a seat on the gram panchayat. Socio-political gains are, though, dissipated by the ongoing process of circulation, which scatters workers between the countryside and the city, making any collective impetus for change unlikely (even putting aside the containment and counter-strategies of agrarian capital). Spatial segmentation, in other words, forestalls the coalescence of factors that might modify class relations, and socio-political gains are marginal and often symbolic rather than substantive (Picherit 2012).

Despite slight gains with regard to agrarian capital in home villages, labour's bargaining power with regard to construction capital in Bengaluru is almost non-existent. Living and working conditions are poor, social security provisions generally unfulfilled and government regulations, insofar as they exist, routinely flouted. The implication is that labour would be better served by an expansion of employment opportunities in its home region, as has been the case in Dharwad, as well as by improved access to social security and better implementation of labour laws both there and in Bengaluru.

The outcomes of circular migration varied to some degree between the dryer village with greater and more established circuits of migration, and the more irrigated village where circulation was a somewhat more recent phenomenon. The former village (Jagalwara) had a greater proportion of semi-skilled workers and maistries, which was indicative of greater socio-economic gains. In the latter village (Shiva Camp), socio-economic gains were marginally lower and socio-political gains were forestalled by the widespread interlinking of different forms of control over labour.

The proportion of public resources reaching classes of labour through poverty reduction programmes was at its lowest in this relatively remote and iniquitous village. As already noted, NREGS had not functioned for several years (see Chapter 6), a number of mud houses remained, a sizeable minority did not have access to PDS and there was very little access to public healthcare. The GP office was located some distance away in another village, and there was a general reluctance to make direct claims of GP members.[23] Eighteen kilometres away in the roadside village of Badarapur, where circular migration was more established, respondents were considerably less deferential to their GP and classes of labour received a marginally greater share of public resources.[24] Minor differences in the concrete forms of class relations, then, can make significant differences to classes of labour's ability to strengthen their socio-political position.

In the Dharwad villages, conversely, the socio-political gains accruing from reduced dependence (particularly male dependence) upon dominant village households were not dissipated by ongoing circulation, and were apparent in discussions with both farmers and labourers. A leading Niwar landowner lamented the tightening of labour markets, and the fact that there was now less scope to 'pick and choose the best workers'. Although elements of dependence remained (for work and credit in the village, and upon dominant panchayat members and labour intermediaries), labourers' qualitatively different attitude to village employers due largely to their more ready access to alternative forms of work indicated some shift in socio-political dynamics. It was in those communities (castes or religious groups) with the highest levels of commuting that criticisms of the dominant class in the village were most pronounced, and a desire not to work for village landowners most clearly articulated. In other words, the less marked spatial segmentation of labour appeared to have generated greater socio-political gains than was the case for circulating labourers, although, as will be shown in the later chapters of this book, classes of labour in these villages lacked the organisational basis required to turn largely symbolic gains into more concrete material ones by, for example, strengthening their influence over local government institutions.

While in the city, commuters are spread over a greater number of worksites and sectors than their circulating counterparts. As well as segmentation across sites, sectors and skill levels, informality (even in the formal sector) weakens their position. Access to non-agricultural employment was also segmented along lines of caste and religious community (see also Harriss-White 2010:156). For example, two-thirds of masons from Kamlapur were Muslims, and painters in Panchnagaram and Neeralbhavi were likely to be from the same community. In addition, some dominant class contractors preferred to employ workers from their caste, or from communities that tended to support the same political party.

Access to non-agricultural employment was also highly gendered – more so than was the case with circulating labour (around one-third of whom were women). With only a handful of women working in industries, and only one or two commuting to the city to engage in various forms of petty trading, labouring class women in the Dharwad villages remained highly dependent on agricultural labour (particularly in households with no skilled labourers).

Female control over higher non-agricultural incomes was often very low. Where men working outside consumed a relatively high share of their city-based wages on themselves, the other members of the household may have seen a decline in consumption in spite of a net increase in household income. Two conclusions can be drawn. First, commuting and circulating impact on socio-political dynamics in different ways, and second, these shifts are highly gendered, and more so in the case of commuting.

The differences between circulation and commuting were minimal with regard to wage levels, but considerable with regard to living conditions – most of those circulating live under blue plastic sheets in 'sheds', whereas all bar a handful of commuting households lived in concrete houses (often government-built ones). Commuting afforded significantly better access to government poverty reduction programmes. Almost all commuting labouring class households had access to PDS foodgrains, and most unskilled labouring households had accessed employment under NREGS (see Chapter 6).

The significance of government programmes and non-agricultural employment as a means of reducing labouring class dependence on the dominant class and changing socio-political dynamics is brought home by farmers' perceptions about the causes of their reduced ability to command labour, and maintain or increase the intensity of the labour process. In a partially canal-irrigated village that was beyond commutable distance (around thirty kilometres) from Dharwad city, farmers made no reference to non-agricultural employment, but pointed the finger very firmly at 'bogus' government schemes – by which they primarily meant the recently expanded PDS, and to a lesser degree various forms of social insurance and NREGS. Prominent GP members were more than happy to admit (during a public discussion in the gram panchayat office) that the latter remained largely unimplemented.

In Kamlapur, the emphasis was also primarily on government schemes, and the PDS in particular. There were also complaints about labour shortages at times of peak demand. In Panchnagaram, on the other hand, large farmers saw the growth of industrial employment as the primary 'problem', and a significantly greater one than NREGS. In Raichur, meanwhile, it was Bengaluru rather than either industry or government schemes that loomed large in farmers' discourse. These perceptions of the dominant underline the importance of labour markets and social policy as sites of class struggle.

Although non-agricultural employment had brought slight economic and socio-political gains, classes of labour remained segmented and unorganised. Collective action was largely limited to cooperation over accessing employment (often on a kin and/or caste basis); to self-help group membership that undermined labouring class organisation and preserved the status quo behind a facade of expanded 'participation' (see Chapter 7); and to a smattering of trade union membership that (as yet) carried little weight. By contrast, the dominant class has been much better able to project its interests – not least through the local government institutions that gave them an opportunity to create new forms of dependence, and dampen down the potential for greater labouring class assertiveness (the subject of the next chapter).

Conclusion

Strategies for controlling labour vary across sectors and locations. Construction capital makes use of labour's many segmentations, maistries and the porousness of government regulations to exert 'remote control' and keep labour costs down. Even industrial capital operating in the formal sector finds ways to informalise labour relations, leaving workers unprotected by the state. Labour relations in agriculture, meanwhile, continue to be marked by a variety of forms of unfreedom. Where agriculture is more profitable (as in the canal-irrigated village of Shiva Camp), control over labour is more marked. Where state-linked forms of accumulation are more prominent (as in Panchnagaram village) the role played by predominantly dominant class/caste men in channelling access to public resources is arguably more significant, as the next chapter will make clear. In overall terms, greater levels of organisation are necessary in order to improve labour's position, but given its weak bargaining position (particularly in certain locations such as among circular migrants and agricultural labourers in villages like Shiva Camp) strengthening access to the provisions of Acts like BOCWA and UWSSA are a significant part of pro-labouring class strategy in the short-term.[25]

Notes

1 Most of the migrants from the Raichur villages have worked on large projects in one of four areas: Devarabeesanahalli and Ramagondanahalli (where high-end residential projects such as Palm Retreat have been constructed); and Manyata Embassy Business Park Special Economic Zone and Electronic City (both home to the offices of major Indian and transnational companies). A minority of migrants have worked on smaller (mostly residential) projects.
2 Construction capital has strong links to the state's politicians – some of whom have primarily accumulated through real estate, or have added to existing wealth through real estate once in office (see Chapter 5).
3 A minority are regularly employed in informal businesses or as skilled labourers in formal sector industries. A small number are low-paid government employees (doing such things as crèche work).
4 Based on interviews and survey data.
5 As an example, *Sona Masoori* (monsoon) paddy purchased around December 2012 at Rs. 1,400 per bag had been traded to Tamil Nadu three months later for Rs. 1,900, indicating considerable profits.
6 In the 2010–15 Gram Panchayat.
7 In the other three villages, the numbers with less than 2.5 acres was slightly under 70 per cent. Across the four villages, just over two-thirds of households were categorised as being part of classes of labour based on net buying/selling of labour-power and landholdings.
8 Since the mechanisation of harvesting in the early 2000s, paddy requires less than half the labour of cotton, which still depends on four rounds of hand-picking, and is now only cultivated by those with greater amounts of household labour at their disposal. Around 80 per cent of the cropped area is under paddy in the early 2010s – a significant increase on the 1990s when cultivation of cotton, pulses, groundnut and chilli was more common.
9 The number of bags of paddy varies from 10 to 15, but clusters around 12 depending in part on how close the land is to the canal distributary.
10 This was the discrepancy in 2011.
11 The rationale for emphasising discussion of relatively exploitative labour relations in one of the more iniquitous of the fieldwork villages is that this exposes a wider array of capitalist strategies of control and expands understanding of the types of tactics required to strengthen the position of labour.
12 Bunds being earthen divisions between parcels of land that demarcate ownership and channel irrigation flows.
13 These lists are not exhaustive. For example, women also sow cotton seeds.

14 The exact relative wage is hard to pin down. Wages are slightly higher on an hourly basis but so is the intensity of work.

15 Scheduled caste gangs were more likely to have female maistries and also to be larger. The latter is the case because of their greater concentration of labourers, while the former may relate in part to intra-household gender dynamics. See Kapadia (1995) for an explanation of why scheduled caste women may have greater influence within the household than is the case with some other castes.

16 Maistries play different roles in different contexts. Maistries in agriculture (particularly female ones) tend to be close to other labourers and work alongside them. In other words, they are labourers themselves. Construction maistries (always male), on the other hand, tend to focus on management and recruitment rather than taking part in the labour process. They act primarily as intermediaries between capital and labour, and in some cases can be seen as small capitalists. Please note that this section draws in part on an article published in volume 3 of the Global Labor Journal.

17 Official records of the Karnataka Buildings and Other Construction Workers Welfare Board (accessed on 14 June 2010).

18 Interviews with senior Labour Department Official, 14 June and 5 October 2010.

19 This statement is based in part on interviews in the Department of Labour in Bangalore in 2010 (see also Breman 2007a).

20 Of the 129 migrant households surveyed in 2010, detailed information on household-level outcomes was collected through two rounds of interviews with 34 households in three different villages (Kumdini Cross, Badarapur and Jagalwara).

21 In late 2013, one worker in Kamlapur was on wages of Rs. 50,000 ($800) and two bags of grain for fifty-two 80-hour weeks.

22 The only statistically significant concentration of 'pure' petty commodity producers in any of the fieldwork villages (see Chapter 2 for definitions of terms).

23 Although some referred to approaching the erstwhile SC Ward member (who now has one of the largest houses in the hamlet).

24 This also relates to levels of collective action. See Chapter 8.

25 There was some degree of organising among construction workers in Bengaluru, but the vast majority of circular migrants were as yet untouched by such processes.

5

Dynamics of domination in rural South India: class relations at the state–society interface

On an April night in 2007 the west-bound carriageway of National Highway 63 was at a standstill. Lorry after lorry parked bumper to bumper for mile after mile, waiting to transport iron ore from Karnataka's Bellary and Koppal districts to Belikeri and other west-coast ports. From there much of it was shipped to China, where demand for the metal had grown in the run-up to the Beijing Olympics of 2008.

Between 2006 and 2010, illegally mined iron ore worth slightly over $3 billion was illicitly exported from the area centred on Bellary (Government of Karnataka Lokayukta 2011:22).[1] Buoyed by their increased wealth, the group of BJP Members of the Legislative Assembly (MLAs) who dominated this illegal mining scene increased their number of seats at the 2008 Assembly election (a few weeks before the Olympics). In the days following the election in which the BJP won 110 out of 224 seats, they are alleged to have bought their party an outright majority by paying opposition MLAs to change sides. Ministerial positions followed and their power grew until a government report on illegal mining in 2011 led to the imprisonment of one of four men popularly regarded as the fulcrum of the mining business, State Tourism Minister Janardhan Reddy, and contributed to the dethroning of Chief Minister Yeddyurappa. As well as allegedly receiving payments from the Bellary group, the chief minister was also caught up in a Bengaluru land scam along with three close relatives and another minister.

By the time of Yeddyurappa's arrest in October 2011, Industry Minister Katta Subramanya was already in prison after allegedly receiving millions of dollars for acting as a gatekeeper in a major land deal relating to the Karnataka Industrial Areas Development Board. Both the Bellary mining mafia and Yeddyurappa subsequently formed breakaway parties (the Badavara Shramikara Raitha Congress and the Karnataka Janata Party), dividing the right-wing vote and paving the way for Congress's return to power in 2013. Although there were signs that the Congress state government tried to improve the implementation of public programmes (Athrady 2013; *Deccan Herald* 2013a, 2013b), fieldwork in rural North Karnataka a year later (in 2014) showed that significant subversion of such programmes remained widespread.

Rather than accumulation by dispossession and headline-grabbing mining and real estate 'scams', this chapter is concerned with the more mundane everyday workings of the state at local level and how they are linked to class relations and the less dramatic process of accumulation by exploitation. It discusses in detail how dominant class men at village level shape government poverty reduction programmes for their own political and economic ends. Their ability to do so depends upon class and caste dynamics and the distribution of power and resources in society. Instead of the surface phenomenon of 'corruption', these processes are understood as part of broader processes of accumulation and domination. Local government institutions (LGIs) are not 'corrupt' in and of themselves, but through the class relations that shape their practices.

As discussed in Chapter 3, the examples of Kerala (Heller 1999), parts of Tamil Nadu (Heyer 2012), and even to some degree the more iniquitous social terrain of North Karnataka (see Chapters 6 and 8), show that LGIs can contribute to pro-labouring class change. Drawing primarily on evidence from the implementation of the predecessor of the National Rural Employment Guarantee Scheme (NREGS), the Sampoorna Grameena Rozgar Yojana (SGRY or 'Complete Village Employment Scheme'), this chapter shows why they tend not to do so.

While the later chapters are concerned with how LGIs may become sites of pro-labouring class change, this chapter's central argument is that LGIs have become an increasingly important basis of rural dominant class control over the labouring class, with heightened significance for contemporary patterns of rural accumulation and domination. The political implications for classes of labour are clear in that their political position continues to be primarily defined not horizontally through their relations with each other, but vertically through their relations with politically active members of the dominant class.

The chapter begins by briefly contextualising the fieldwork material in Karnataka's recent political history. Following that it outlines the scale of appropriation of public resources at the level of the two fieldwork gram panchayats (GPs) in Dharwad district, which between them cover eight villages. It then proceeds to analyse the role of gatekeepers – those who man the interface between state and society (see Chapter 3). Gatekeeping is stratified in order to show its uneven role in patterns of accumulation and the fact that the bulk of gatekeeping incomes flow to members of the dominant class (gatekeeping-as-accumulation). It then shows how the inclusion of farmers with smaller surpluses[2] and labouring class individuals on the periphery of the gatekeeping system both underpins the existing gatekeeping system and helps to reproduce the existing distribution of power (gatekeeping-as-domination). Finally, the chapter follows gatekeeping practices into the state as a whole, linking everyday forms of domination among class relations at GP level to broader patterns of accumulation among the state's leading politicians.

Up until the final section, the chapter is mostly based on fieldwork data collected in the late 2000s (2006–08), and focuses on evidence relating to three poverty reduction programmes including the SGRY, which was the forerunner of the NREGS. Chapter 6, which focuses on NREGS, updates the story. Its data is drawn from the period from 2008 to 2014, and shows the potential for rights-based universal programmes to galvanise contestation of dominant class control of LGIs.

Political contexts

Following independence, the Lingayats and Vokkaligas (the dominant castes in the northern and southern interior of the state, respectively) assumed a leading position in Karnataka's politics. Although only 26.1 per cent of the population, they were the main landowners and exercised considerable influence over village affairs in most of the state (Epstein 1973; Srinivas 1963).

In the 1970s and 1980s control over state politics was broadened beyond the dominant Linagayat and Vokkaliga castes (Raghavan and Manor 2009:2). This process, which built on earlier policies of political accommodation by the rulers of the princely state of Mysore (Raghavan and Manor 2009; see also Bandyopadhyay 2002; Crook and Manor 1998; Kadekodi *et al.* 2007), was achieved in part by increasing levels of decentralisation in 1983. This followed Devraj Urs's 'rainbow coalition' state government of the 1970s, which had drawn in less dominant sections of the dominant castes and a number of hitherto politically marginalised castes.

Urs was careful to ensure that the MLAs in his party ran effective patronage systems in their constituencies by placing (or 'developing') close allies in the all-important posts of Block Development Officer, Executive Engineer and Sub-Inspector of Police (Raghavan and Manor 2009; see also Brass 1997; Jeffrey 2000; Pattenden 2011a). In other words, by the 1980s Karnataka had fine-tuned a relatively stable and broad-based system of patron–client politics, which was then deepened through processes of decentralisation in the 1980s, 1990s and 2000s.

Processes of 'accommodation' have, then, been extended into LGIs, with the state providing relatively 'fertile' ground for 'fixers' (gatekeepers), with enough gaps in the party political system to allow them to prosper, and enough flexibility in its accommodative politics to allow them to survive changes in government (Manor 2004).

While for some democracy in Karnataka had reached 'robust maturity' by the 1990s, this chapter suggests that classes of labour have continued to be marginalised from it in a variety of respects, while the dominant class has continued to expand its political influence, social status and wealth in much of the state.

This chapter, like the book as a whole, links class and caste relations, and relates political processes to the social relations of production and particular forms of domination and accumulation. Similarly to Chapter 3's discussion of the state in India as a whole, it argues that members of the dominant class largely control both LGIs and the state government of Karnataka. As was argued in the more general discussion of the state, this does not mean that the state in Karnataka is a simple reflection of dominant class interests. It also seeks stable conditions for accumulation, and its governments seek re-election. Such concerns have prompted the implementation of substantial poverty reduction programmes (alongside the porous state regulation of labour markets that assists processes of accumulation; see Chapter 4). While these poverty reduction programmes offer the possibility of pro-labouring class change (see Chapter 6), they also feed the patron–client networks (populated, among others, by party political workers, neighbourhood organisers and officials) that hold together politicians' power bases and the processes of dominant class accumulation with which they are entwined.

Where the last chapter focused on more direct aspects of class relations between classes of labour and the dominant class, this chapter and those that follow analyse how class relations are reproduced or contested through institutions of state and civil society. Class relations are, of course, not restricted to production relations alone, but reverberate through local and national state institutions. By allocating greater resources to LGIs, fiscal decentralisation has increased the significance of the state–society interface to class relations.

Domination and the rise of gatekeeping

The 'blurred boundaries' between state and society have been widely studied in recent years in India and elsewhere (Berenschot 2011:10; Chatterjee 2004; Corbridge *et al.* 2005; Fuller and Harriss 2001; Gupta 1998; Harriss 2005, 2006, 2007; Migdal 2001; Nordholt 2004; Sidel 1996; Veron *et al.* 2006). The influence of more traditional local institutions such as the *pol panches* and guilds (*mahajans*) of Ahmedabad has faded (Ananthpur 2007; Berenschot 2011:47, 48), albeit unevenly given that patriarchal casteist Jat *khaps* (caste panchayats) still wield influence in rural areas close to Delhi, and a variety of often caste-based economic institutions continue to regulate swathes of the economy (Harriss-White

2003). Nevertheless, the growth of state functions has been consolidated at the local level (without a commensurate growth in capacity) through widespread processes of administrative and fiscal decentralisation – particularly since the 73rd and 74th constitutional amendments of the early 1990s.

The amount of resources channelled through LGIs has never been greater. Between 2003–04 and 2006–07, following an amendment to the Karnataka Panchayat Raj Act, the amount of funds flowing through Karnataka's village councils quintupled, while those to LGIs as a whole almost trebled. A number of high-profile state schemes like Suvarna Karnataka and World Bank-funded watershed and drinking water programmes further increased GP budgets, while the implementation of NREGS (since 2008 in Dharwad) had expanded GP budgets to over Rs. five million by the 2010s – around ten times what they had been a decade before.

The institutionalisation of fully elected GPs in 2000 added over 50,000 GP members to the ranks of the gatekeepers 'manning' the interface between state and society. The numbers swell with every round of council elections, as many GP members maintain gatekeeping roles after they relinquish their seats. A number of recent studies view Karnataka's decentralisation process in positive terms, arguing that it has reduced levels of corruption to as little as 5 to 10 per cent (Manor 2007:658), democratised the state–society interface (Ananthpur 2007; Crook and Manor 1998; Inabanathan and Gopalappa 2002; Manor 2007), increased levels of awareness among the population (Manor 2007), improved the accountability of local institutions, made service delivery more effective (Ananthpur 2007; see also Besley *et al.* 2007) and acted in synergy with recent high growth rates to produce 'the Karnataka model of development' (Kadekodi *et al.* 2007).

The evidence presented in this chapter, which draws on fieldwork in the eight villages of two gram panchayats in Lingayat-dominated Dharwad district (which lies on the main Mumbai–Bengaluru highway around 300 kilometres west of Raichur), cuts against arguments about the emergence of a post-clientilist state (see Chapter 3). This does not mean that the situation is not dynamic, or that things are not moving (unevenly) towards 'post-clientilism', but it does mean that claims about the extent of change may have been overstated.

The eight fieldwork villages lie between eight and seventeen kilometres from the city of Dharwad in the GPs of Panchnagaram and Kamlapur.[3] As indicated in Chapter 4, these villages are dryland villages, with lower levels of productivity than the canal-irrigated villages in Raichur. With the lowest levels of irrigation and poorest soils in its panchayat, the village of Panchnagaram had the highest levels of gatekeeping and the greatest number of contractors. The role played here by state-related forms of accumulation were, then, relatively high, and this had implications for the ways in which the dominant class reproduced its position and exerted control over classes of labour.

Panchamsali Lingayats dominated Panchnagaram Gram Panchayat. In 2005–10 they, along with other Lingayats, held ten of fifteen seats.[4] In the 2010–15 GP, this number had fallen to six, but the Panchamsalis remained dominant. They exercised considerable influence over the selection of works and the allocation of resources, and controlled both contract distribution and the figurehead GP President who was an elderly illiterate man from the Lingayat florist sub-caste.

In Kamlapur Gram Panchayat, on the other hand, political power was more finely balanced across the Lingayats, Muslims and Other Backward Caste (OBC) Marathas.[5] In the 2005–10 GP, the Lingayats and Muslims occupied nine of fifteen GP seats (and monopolised the GP presidency), while the Marathas only had three. The 2010–15 GP had an almost identical distribution of power, although the GP President for the first half of this period was a Maratha.

Interviews were conducted with forty-five gatekeepers in the eight villages, and an additional twenty-six officials and councillors across the district, on between one and a dozen occasions over the course of a decade.[6] Interviews took place in government offices, village streets, houses, fields and teashops. Among other things, questions covered the surpluses generated by agricultural land and other productive assets, and recent acquisitions and major expenditures. These were contextualised by a survey of economic assets and activities, and access to government development schemes in over one-third of households in Panchnagaram and Kamlapur. In addition, official documents were scrutinised (including the divisional link document, district level plans and district/taluk/gram/village and works-wise documentation of spending), and works relating to the three main schemes at the time of fieldwork were directly observed. These were the SGRY, the SGY (*Swachh Grama Yojana* or 'Clean Village Scheme') and the main state and national housing schemes (*Ashraya Yojana* and *Indira Awaas Yojana*). Additional interviews were conducted with those living adjacent to recent public works. Works-wise data had glaring inaccuracies that became clear when triangulated through direct observation of public works and bystanders' accounts of their scale and duration. There were also cases of duplication across different schemes. The estimates of gatekeeping incomes that emerged from these methods provide an indication of the scale of appropriation of public resources.

Estimates of the share of public resources that were appropriated averaged at 40 per cent, although the level of appropriation in road and gutter work was generally substantially higher. Appropriation levels in the SGRY were found to be as high as 90 per cent (primarily through the listing of 'ghost' workers to enable the exaggeration of the number of workdays). Official records for SGY were less detailed, and estimates of levels of appropriation of funds (50 per cent) were more conservative. Ten per cent was routinely appropriated from the construction costs of each housing unit, while the listing of 'ghost' houses on government documents meant that overall leakage levels were in the vicinity of 33 per cent.[7]

A conservative estimate is that village gatekeepers in the two GPs appropriated Rs. 2.192 million ($54,800) in 2006–07.[8] These funds were distributed according to a relatively organised system (see also Wade 1982:293). Although the initial series of payments followed a similar pattern (with a regular percentage going to the engineer, councillors (primarily the GP President) and officials (primarily the GP Secretary but more recently the Panchayat Development Officer (PDO) as well)),[9] it was harder to pin down how much of the payments some of these individuals kept because of onward payments in the direction of more senior politicians and officials, such as the Executive Officers of the sub-district councils and the local MLA. The latter received payments from multiple sources including contractors.[10]

The caste dynamics of the district influence gatekeeping hierarchies. Kamlapur's leading gatekeepers were either Panchamsalis (the district's dominant caste) or Muslims (a key votebank of the then sitting MLA), and none of the three villages in Kamlapur GP where OBC Marathas were the dominant caste had leading gatekeepers. All bar one of Panchnagaram GP's leading gatekeepers were Panchamsalis (the dominant caste in each of those villages as well as in the district) – the exception being the brother of a former farmers' leader.[11] The allocation of seats on local councils, party tickets to stand for a particular seat (particularly prominent at MLA level) and contracts for road, gutter and other works was often highly contested. Arguments over the allocation of contracts generally involved the more influential members of the GP, and included more senior politicians as the size of the contract increased.[12] Caste, class, kinship and party political allegiance all played a role.

The number of contractors had slowly grown during the 2000s along with levels of funding to LGIs. Control over contracts, initially centred on the most politicised villages, had been partially diffused across the GPs. A two-tier contracting system was at play with a handful of licensed contractors, who handled larger jobs and work outside their GP, and around three times as many unlicensed contractors (working off others' licences) who did smaller jobs in their own GPs. The latter were mostly close relatives or associates of current or former leading councillors, and in some cases GP members themselves.

The distribution of resources between villages and GPs was affected by the location of leading gatekeepers. In each GP the village with the highest levels of gatekeeping had a sitting district or sub-district councillor, and one or more individuals with strong links to sitting or recent MLAs. Official records accessed in 2007 showed that disproportionate amounts from certain schemes flowed into district councillors' constituencies, which boosts their popularity and enables them to strengthen their network of political workers (Pattenden 2011a). The distribution of resources and contracts (formal and informal) related, then, to the more general distribution of political power, which is in turn linked to the gatekeeping histories of particular villages. The latter is shaped by the broader patterns of accumulation, which, as already indicated, are linked to irrigation levels, soil quality and proximity to urban centres.

Over time, certain villages (or rather clusters of gatekeepers within them) became more prominent. Patterns of distribution were modified after elections, particularly if an opposing party took control of a GP. Some new individuals entered the fray, while others switched political allegiance to maintain their position, and others still were somewhat marginalised – perhaps waiting for the party political dynamic to turn full circle, at which point they would be rewarded for their loyalty. When the BJP won a majority in Panchnagaram GP in 2010, the numbers of contracts awarded to its supporters increased. This triggered a row with the pro-Congress relative of a former GP President, which was resolved through a compromise brokered by the GP's most senior political figure (a district councillor).

Gatekeeping-as-accumulation

Levels and types of gatekeeping: class relations at the state–society interface

In late March and early April, the driveways of government engineering offices were congested with the motorbikes of village gatekeepers. This was the height of the gatekeeping season – the frenzied days when most contracts were allocated before the monies were returned unspent to the state or union governments at the end of the tax year.

Five different types of gatekeeper were identified in the fieldwork villages (although some gatekeepers perform more than one role). The first category are the councillors (at village (*gram*), sub-district (*taluk*) and district (*zilla*) level) who distribute and appropriate the government funds allocated to their respective councils for the purposes of development and poverty reduction. The second category, political workers, work for councillors (and at higher levels for MLAs and MPs), and carry out a range of tasks intended to maintain and advance their position from canvassing for support at election time to providing 'muscle' to intimidate rivals. They may also be deployed to increase levels of accumulation outside of politics: for example, by helping to secure preferential access to rice mills. In return they expect financial or political rewards (see also Berenschot 2011 for a similar analysis in an urban setting, and Rutten 2003:69 for similar patterns in the private sector). They are differentiated by the amount of work they do, the influence of their patron and their proximity to him. They have to be carefully managed, as they may usurp their patron's position if they become influential – as happened in Dharwad in the run-up to the 2004 state Assembly elections.[13]

The third category, fixers (or 'social workers', as they sometimes call themselves), complete a range of bureaucratic tasks (such as accessing a caste certificate or a pension) on behalf of others in exchange for status and income. Fixers often have a specialisation, such as police work or revenue department work, and when fieldwork was conducted between 2006 and 2008 'fixing' was widespread in the fieldwork villages. With the gradual computerisation of such tasks, and the introduction of the Aadhaar scheme of identity card-based direct transfers for a number of programmes, there is evidence that fixing is on the wane (see Elliot 2011:69). Nevertheless, with the Aadhaar scheme in its infancy in North Karnataka in late 2013, labouring class respondents mostly stated that fixing remained significant, while others indicated that it was less prominent than it had been. Fixers are mostly current and former GP members, and are differentiated by the quality and quantity of their connections.

The fourth category of village-level gatekeepers are the officials who generally live in the GPs in which they work – primarily GP clerks and assistants to the Village Accountant. GP Secretaries, PDOs and Village Accountants tend to live in nearby towns. Above them are the district- and sub-district-level gatekeepers such as the Executive Officer of the sub-district council, Line Department officials and the Chief Executive Officer of the District Council.

The fifth category are the contractors who negotiate with other gatekeepers for public works contracts. In the late 2000s, licences were required for all works of over Rs. 100,000 ($2500). Class 3 contractors were entitled to take on works of up to one million rupees, and Class 2 up to four million rupees. Smaller contractors usually focus on contacts in the local GP, while larger ones cultivate connections with sub-district and district councillors and engineers. Opportunities for newcomers are shaped by the distribution of licensed and informal contractors. One village in each of the two fieldwork GPs had significantly more contractors.

Gatekeeping incomes were far from evenly distributed by class, caste and gender. From the sample of forty-five gatekeepers, over 90 per cent was found to flow to members of the dominant class, significantly more flowed to men than women, and around three-quarters accrued to members of the dominant caste. Gatekeeping has been divided here into three levels, which correspond to levels of gatekeeping income and influence.

Table 5.1 Class and caste breakdown in Panchnagaram and Kamlapur villages

	Percentage of population
Surplus-producing farmers (mostly dominant class)	34.5
Labouring class	65.5
Brahmins	0.5
Lingayats	32
OBCs	28.5
Muslims	21.5
Scheduled castes and tribes	17.5

Source: fieldwork data.

Level 1 gatekeeping contributes to capital accumulation and wealth creation, and in the late 2000s was estimated to be providing incomes of between Rs. 80,000 and Rs. 800,000 per annum ($2,000 to $20,000). This facilitates upward mobility through investment in existing and new assets, and boosts status by funding lavish weddings, bigger houses and larger vehicles. Level 2 gatekeeping contributed to a degree of wealth creation through annual incomes that were between Rs. 25,000 and Rs. 80,000 in the late 2000s ($1.70 to $5.50 per household per day), thereby boosting consumption and political status but without – besides rare exceptions – clear implications for upward economic mobility. Level 3 gatekeeping provides marginal and temporary increases in income (up to Rs. 25,000 per annum in the late 2000s), but does not provide the basis for either upward economic mobility or greater political status.

Level 1 gatekeepers

Fifteen Level 1 gatekeepers were identified in the eight villages. Most were from the dominant caste, all were from the dominant class, and they had average landholdings of twenty-eight acres. Four were current or former district or sub-district councillors, seven current or former GP Presidents or Vice-Presidents, seven were contractors and two were Fair Price Shop Licensees (the father of one had also been a licensee and had played a prominent role in the local cooperative bank). Only two were from the lower reaches of the dominant class.

The routes taken by these individuals to gatekeeping's upper reaches had certain patterns – particularly among the four most prominent gatekeepers, who between them appropriated over one-third of all gatekeeping incomes. All four were or had been prominent local contractors, and of these one had become a sub-district councillor and another had become a district councillor.[14] Another narrowly missed a seat on the district council in 2010 when he stood in the name of his mother.

All bar one had been to university, where significant political connections were forged. All had strong connections with the sitting or previous MLA. For two Level 1 gatekeepers, including the most successful in the eight villages as a whole, the Fair Price Shop licence was a significant part of the upward journey. This conferred responsibility for allocating heavily subsidised foodgrains under the Public Distribution System (PDS) to all below-poverty-line households, which provided considerable influence as the foodgrains made a significant difference to household consumption levels. Good relations with the licensee could increase the amount a household received, and poorer households lived in fear of losing their card. Even when higher gatekeeping positions had been secured, licences were often kept in the family to help maintain popularity by dispensing favours.[15] Among the other Level 1 gatekeepers, two had risen up the gatekeeping ranks through a combination of fixing and petty business, and another through smaller informal contracts.

Although there were similarities between how individuals became Level 1 gatekeepers, there were also subtle differences reflecting their different socio-economic starting points. Those who came from a wealthier and traditionally more powerful household had shorter routes to the upper reaches of gatekeeping. The two coming from the strongest socio-economic and socio-political position were university graduates who had accessed lucrative contracting roles through personal connections to contractors and politicians at GP and district level. Before the rise of SHGs reduced business, one of them had been the main moneylender in his village. Another came from lower down the socio-economic ladder and had reached the role of political worker for the MLA and contractor by developing a small dairy business (the same line of business as the MLA, who became a close ally).

On average it was found that Level 1 gatekeepers secured an estimated 37 per cent of their income through gatekeeping (some of which was passed on to others). Although partially eclipsed by the gatekeeping season, agriculture still remained slightly ahead of gatekeeping as the primary basis of accumulation – accounting for 46 per cent of income. All Level 1 gatekeepers drew sufficient income from gatekeeping to enable investment in new assets. In Panchnagaram, they were more likely to invest in property, make symbolic investments on lavish weddings and cars or save funds for political purposes.

Across all the villages, there was little evidence of investment outside of agriculture beyond urban property, higher education, a smattering of formal sector jobs, one or two small businesses and further investments in politics. Over six years as a contractor and councillor, the leading gate-keeper in the eight villages had invested in four acres of land, property in the city and a warehouse, which acted as a source of patronage as it allowed farmers to store grains until prices rose. There were some indica-tions of constraints. For example, the brother of one of the leading gate-keepers had obtained a government subsidy with a view to setting up an oil-milling facility, but had decided it was not viable given the strength of existing competition.

Leading gatekeepers with large landholdings often expressed frustra-tion at the unpredictability of agriculture's returns, were relatively slow to take up high-value crops and had significantly lower profits per acre than others with similar landholdings. In other words, they saw gatekeeping as a more lucrative (and more interesting) occupation than farming. In some villages, leading gatekeepers had not reduced their focus on agri-culture – in part because they were less prominent gatekeepers, and in part because, with better soils and higher levels of irrigation, agriculture offered better returns.

Gatekeeping-as-domination

Level 1 gatekeepers' position as the dominant individuals at the inter-face of state and society is about more than accumulation: it also helps them to maintain their political dominance at a time of increased non-agricultural employment (see Chapter 4). It is necessary, then, to go beyond the narrow observation that appropriation of public resources can form a significant part of the overall accumulation of leading gate-keepers. Rather, Level 1 gatekeeping needs to be seen in the broader context of the production and reproduction of *class relations* in contem-porary rural India.

Dependence upon village gatekeepers for access to public resources is, of course, not new. Access to the PDS through local gatekeepers stretches back to the 1960s, while they have long played a critical role in allocating houses or low-interest loans and grants (such as through the Integrated Rural Development Programme of the 1970s). Recent processes of administrative devolution and fiscal decentralisation have, though, increased village-level gatekeepers' influence. On the other hand, the more recent implementation of universal schemes such as NREGS should reduce dependence on intermediaries, although gatekeeping is not necessarily diminishing so much as changing its forms, as analysed further in Chapter 6.

Table 5.2 Distribution of gatekeepers in Panchnagaram and Kamlapur
Gram Panchayats

	Level 1	Level 2	Level 3
Number of individuals	15	20	10
Dominant class (%)	100	90	10
Labouring class (%)	0	10	90
Landholdings (acres)	28	8.6	1.5*
Dominant caste (%)	80	60	
Estimated average daily gatekeeping income per household member (Rs.)	120	18	6
Accumulating through gatekeeping	100	In some cases in the long term	0

Source: fieldwork data.

While growing levels of non-agricultural employment erode dominant
class control over labour, the heightened significance of village-level gatekeeping increases it. Classes of labour, with fewer connections in the state
and less leverage over it, are more dependent on gatekeepers to access the
state and its flows of public resources (Berenschot 2011:11, 17, 54; Harriss
2005). This is especially so for female labourers given that many labouring
class men from the Dharwad villages work in the city. Some actively cultivate connections to gatekeepers, while the most marginalised may even do
unpaid work or work longer hours in the hope of gains from government
programmes.

Level 3 gatekeepers

Level 3 gatekeepers were almost all illiterate labouring class women. All
bar one were labouring class, all bar one were women and all bar two were

illiterate. Their average landholding was 1.5 acres,[16] and all of the two GPs' scheduled caste and scheduled tribe gatekeepers belonged to this category – mostly employees and debtors of dominant class gatekeepers. Across all of the villages, no scheduled caste or scheduled tribe councillors exercised any degree of political influence outside their wards. The same, with one exception (the sister-in-law of a sub-district councillor), was true of women members.

Level 3 gatekeepers do not accumulate. Those occupying council seats between 2005 and 2010 had paid Rs. 20,000–25,000 to secure their seat (generally on credit), and received between Rs. 5,000 and Rs. 25,000 per annum in gatekeeping income. Even at the very top of this scale, this barely represented Rs. 100,000 over a five-year term – equivalent to $1.37 per day and insufficient to facilitate upward mobility. Most received considerably less, and had borrowed the initial amount from employers-cum-creditors, who placed them onto the council to increase their own influence and reduce the number of active councillors pressing for significant portions of public finance. In addition, it helped to reinforce their control over labour.

In one case a scheduled tribe female GP member, who played no gatekeeping role at all, appeared to have been elected 'without her consent'. She worked for her village's two leading gatekeepers, with whom she had long-term debts. She had been told to stand and was lent the requisite amount of money by one of her employers. She derived no benefits from her role, and her patron may have been appropriating 'her share' of gatekeeping income, setting it off against the compound interest her household had long been paying him.

Level 3 gatekeepers are marginalised within gatekeeping processes. They attend formal GP meetings, but generally play no active role either in them or in the informal meetings that precede them, during which key decisions tend to be made. Their gatekeeping role is largely restricted to their wards, where they allocate houses and supervise public works and toilet construction. It is not unusual for Level 3 gatekeepers to have small public works (paving stones and drains) located close to their homes. They also tend to receive preferential access to government schemes – such as increased access to subsidised foodgrains and housing grants. They were also approached by neighbours seeking access to public resources, but like the small financial gains, these increases in influence tended to dissipate once they left office.

Level 3 gatekeeping plays a specific role in shoring up the gatekeeping system as a whole. Limited material gains ensure loyalty to the gatekeeping system, and encourage other members of the labouring class to aspire to a future share of public resources. This helps to foster 'acceptance' both of the gatekeeping system and broader relations with the dominant class since labouring class dependence is reinforced by the need to access public resources as well as wage-labour through the dominant class.

The preponderance of female Level 3 gatekeepers was particularly useful given that agricultural labour was predominantly carried out by women. The inclusion of a few labouring-class gatekeepers on the fringes of the system helped to support a systemised process of accumulation and domination by the dominant class. A steady and visible downward trickle of public resources acted as a constant reminder of potential 'rewards' and disciplined classes of labour, enhancing the power of gate-keepers and fostering vertical over horizontal forms of politics. In order to succeed, though, the gatekeeping system needed more than the acqui-escence of the labouring class. It also needed to keep the lower reaches of the dominant class in the fold.

Level 2 gatekeepers

Level 2 gatekeepers, a slight majority of whom are dominant caste, are mostly drawn from the lower reaches of the dominant class. Their aver-age landholding was 8.6 acres – in many cases (particularly in the less irri-gated villages) insufficient to generate adequate surpluses for productive investments. Thirteen were current or former GP members, three were officials, three were political workers and one was a full-time fixer.

Level 2 incomes varied between Rs. 25,000 and Rs. 80,000 per annum in the late 2000s ($625 to $2,000 per annum, or less than $1 per house-hold member per day), which had been insufficient to lead to any investment in new assets in the two-and-a-half years prior to the main fieldwork, unless combined with income from agriculture. Many enjoyed heightened levels of social status and political influence – something that continued after their time as councillors for those who maintained their role as fixers. For most, Level 2 gatekeeping provided increased levels of consumption, and in many cases it was primarily the gatekeeper himself who increased his consumption while hanging around in teashops and bars in town with other gatekeepers (often a prominent part of the gate-keeping process).

Level 2 gatekeepers, who generally required the support of more influ-ential villagers to establish themselves, took up such positions in order to increase incomes to meet major life-cycle expenditures such as wed-dings, and in the hope of rising up the gatekeeping ranks or being able to expand their assets. Gatekeeping helped to assuage feelings of playing second fiddle, and offered them the *possibility* of individual and collect-ive upward mobility and increased status, and a semi-urban way of life.

Level 2 gatekeepers were most prominent in more peripheral villages, where, as well as fixing, they acted as political workers for more senior politicians. Routes to more prominent Level 2 gatekeeping positions had less clear patterns than in the case of Level 1 gatekeepers. Examples included a surplus-producing farming household with shops in the village and the city and close links to their village's former sub-district councillor; and a former bus conductor and long-term fixer-turned-GP member, who was also the MLA's key political worker in his village. Level 2 gatekeepers in more marginal villages were the primary contact points for contractors, and were central to the allocation of informal payments to their village's other GP members. Most of the remaining Level 2 gatekeepers were less influential GP members who did fixing work and supervised public works in their neighbourhoods in exchange for a small cut. They also worked for more prominent gatekeepers by monitoring street and household politics, or helping to shore up support by directing resources to supporters.

Level 2 gatekeeping, then, has little direct bearing upon patterns of accumulation, but reproduces the status quo by reinforcing the position of those at the lower end of the dominant class, and preventing divisions within it by dampening down frustrations about small surpluses and limited influence. In addition, as was the case with Level 3 gatekeepers, by providing some with gatekeeping incomes, it made others aspire to similar positions and dissuaded them from contesting the system.

The dominant class, then, exercise a disproportionate influence over LGIs and the resources that flow from them. They use that influence not only to accumulate but to reproduce their dominance, expand their political influence and, when appropriate, create divisions. More generally, the perpetuation of vertical forms of politics helps to maintain political and economic hierarchies. Gatekeeping also helps to compensate for the erosion of dominant class control of labour by generating new forms of dependence, which assists the broader process of accumulation. In other words, it ensures that the ways in which the 'local state' mediates class relations tends to strengthen the position of the dominant.

Accumulation and gatekeeping at state level

The local gatekeeping dynamics flow into the broader political arenas of state and national politics. State politics are 'fed by the tributaries of political activity in … districts and … constituencies', which are fed in their turn by the 'springs and rivulets' of the many villages (Bailey 1963:2; see also Rutten 2003:41–93 for an account of how rural capitalists shift their focus from LGIs to central state institutions as they scale up their levels of accumulation). In other words, the interface between the local state and society, which influences patterns of accumulation and domination at the local level, also moulds broader political and economic dynamics, which turn back on the local via processes of policy formation and implementation.

While leading GP members influence the allocation of GP seats, sub-district and district councillors often influence the selection of GP Presidents, and MLAs and district Party Presidents play a role in the selection of district and sub-district councillors (interview with key informant and close relative of leading mid-level district politician, June 2011). These chains of influence extend into the Line Departments (such as the Departments for Women and Child Development, Watershed Development, Agriculture and Horticulture). MLAs often involve themselves in the process of selecting *anganwadi* (government crèche) workers, who sometimes help to manage votebanks and act as conduits of patronage – not least due to their widespread access to self-help groups (interview with Child Development Protection Officer, November 2006). MLAs also influence the appointment of engineers and influential officials within their constituency, such as the Executive Officer of the sub-district council.[17] They receive payments from those accessing posts – money that will percolate upwards to more senior politicians and downwards to support networks.

Senior engineers play a prominent role within the upper tiers of gatekeeping at district level. Their team have the power to pass works off as of adequate quality or demand further amendments. In other words, they regulate the profit margins of contractors, allowing some to lower quality and increase profits, while driving down or cancelling the profits of contractors linked to political opponents by insisting on higher quality levels (see Wade 1982:294–295 for an outline of how engineers have controlled contractors in Andhra Pradesh). Similar patterns are at play in the awarding of contracts to NGOs (see Chapter 7).

Most of those who clamber up from gatekeeping's 'trenches' to its 'commanding heights' (state and national assemblies and the ministerial berths of government) do so from starting points in the dominant class. As well as gatekeeping incomes, those who rise to the position of MLA tend to also have significant bases of accumulation that are at least partially independent of politics. These alternative bases of accumulation may fund political activities and vice versa. All of Dharwad's district councillors in 2005–10 were from the dominant class, as were all of the sub-district councillors interviewed during fieldwork and all of its MLAs.

An analysis of elected Members of the Legislative Assembly in Karnataka reveals much about the class nature of the state and the role it plays in the accumulation of individuals and specific sectors of the economy. The purpose is not to speculate about the sources of politicians' wealth, but to indicate possible relationships between 'legal' and 'illegal' forms of accumulation (profits from illegal forms are invested in legal forms and vice versa), and to show that most MLAs emerge from dominant class backgrounds. The remainder of this section outlines the socio-economic position of Karnataka's MLAs through a summary of their own official declarations, and then outlines their primary bases of accumulation, some of the strategies they use to establish themselves as politicians and some of the ways in which they have diversified their economic activities over time. Understanding routes to formal power, and the interplay between state politics and forms of accumulation and domination in society, is of some use for assessing how classes of labour might increase their leverage over the state.

The vast majority of MLAs are drawn from the dominant class. Some 93 per cent of MLAs officially declared assets of one crore (10 million) rupees ($160,000) or more prior to the 2013 Assembly elections (through affidavits submitted with nomination papers),[18] 56 per cent of more than four crore rupees ($640,000), 20 per cent of more than 20 crore rupees ($3.2 million) and 12 of more than 100 crore rupees ($16 million) (ADR 2013:26–35). One declared assets of more than 900 crore rupees ($144 million) (ADR 2013:26). The 92 MLAs who were re-elected in 2013 had seen their average assets rise by an average of $2 million (72 per cent) since the previous election in 2008 (ADR 2013:2, 24). The average asset growth of all 224 MLAs over the same period was 135 per cent.

Asset accumulation is driven by legal forms of accumulation (such as hotel chains, air cargo operations and franchised car dealerships), and through (sometimes) illegal forms of accumulation by dispossession (through real-estate deals, for example), as well as the less dramatic process of accumulation by exploitation. It is also linked to the gatekeeping processes discussed above. It has been argued that these need to be understood as being shaped by, and constitutive of, broader processes of accumulation, domination and exploitation. Such processes, though, are often obscured by treatments of 'corruption' that disembed the appropriation of public resources from its social, political and material contexts.

Information was collected about 85 current MLAs (38 per cent) out of the 224 in Karnataka (of whom 98 per cent are men), and eight MLAs who had lost their seats in the 2013 assembly elections. Discussions were held with key informants with direct links to district and higher levels of politics in the state. Additional information was gathered from 100 hours of online searches of MLAs' economic activities through such sources as their company websites, and major national English-language newspapers such as *The Hindu* during 2012, 2013 and 2014.

The sample is heavily biased towards the north of the state, and in particular to Bombay Karnataka where the author has lived. Of the current 85 MLAs (as well as five former MLAs) about whom information was collected, 49 were from the north of the state and 36 were from Bombay

Karnataka. The remainder were from Bengaluru (18), the south (12) and the coastal districts (5). This means that most MLAs from the north-west and Bengaluru are included in the sample, as opposed to slightly less than a quarter of the MLAs from the other areas.

Information collected from newspapers and online sources has been treated with considerable caution, and only used where there is strong evidence for a particular activity (such as the government report on mining). Wherever possible, the testimony of key informants has been cross-referenced with media and official sources, and vice versa.

Tentative conclusions can be drawn about MLAs' primary bases of accumulation in the three main clusters of MLAs in the sample. Agribusiness was the most common basis of accumulation among MLAs in the north-west (36 of the 85 in the sample). Seven in the north-west owned sugar factories (this is the area with the highest concentration of sugar mills – 39 in the three districts of Belgaum, Bijapur and Bagalkote), while other forms of agribusiness (mostly trading and processing, but also inputs like irrigation pipelines) accounted for a further eight. Away from the irrigated sugar-cane belt, forms of agribusiness-related accumulation among MLAs in dryland areas of North-West Karnataka included cotton ginning, groundnut milling (a former MLA), agricultural input and out-put trading and dairy production.

Real estate was the most prominent basis of accumulation among Bengaluru's MLAs, while in Bellary it was mining. Seven in the sample had made their way primarily through real estate (mostly MLAs in Bengaluru), while most of the eleven in the sample for whom mining was the primary basis of accumulation were from down NH 63 and past the trail of parked lorries in the Bellary area. Most recent MLAs and MPs in this area are linked to mining, which has long been a prominent basis of political power around India.

Other prominent bases of accumulation among the MLAs in the sample included contract work (seven), stone quarrying (two), trans-port and services (five), cooperative banking (three), the media/acting (three) and large landholdings (eight). Over a dozen came from political families (in most cases their father had been an MLA or chief minis-ter),[19] while up to nine appear to have primarily worked their way up through the ranks as party activists. Four were either doctors or law-yers. Others in the sample had primarily accumulated through higher education establishments (primarily medical and engineering colleges), the trading of fish-feed and canned fish, shipping and (allegedly) timber smuggling. Some had started out as moneylenders, small contractors or local liquor producers, and worked their way onto council seats. Two had been labour contractors.

As patterns of accumulation are modified over time, so too is the provenance of politicians. Hence while agrarian capital's role in national policy was on the rise in the 1970s in the wake of the Green Revolution (Varshney 1995), more recently accumulation through the real-estate sector has become an increasingly prominent basis of politicians' accumulation. The scale of wealth creation through real estate makes the procession of Hero Honda motorbikes down (recently resurfaced) country roads in the 2000s, and then of Tata Sumos in the 2010s, seem relatively insignificant. The two levels are, though, intricately linked, as this chapter has shown.

As well as the prominent bases of accumulation, patterns emerged in discussions with key informants about strategies used by emerging politicians. Some lead demonstrations on issues of significance to their core constituents, such as irrigation or the agricultural terms of trade. Several BJP politicians had become more influential in the aftermath of the communal tensions that arose over the use of the Igdah Maiden in Hubli in the 1990s. Another MLA had played a central role in the formation of 800 women's self-help groups, whose households could deliver upwards of 20,000 votes. As well as educational and social welfare programmes, she was also involved in a milk cooperative, which linked her to another aspect of consituents' livelihoods.

Another MLA from the north-west had started out as a moneylender (far from the only case where this played a significant role in the initial expansion of influence and income). Over time he and his family built up their landholdings and began to play a prominent role in the cooperative banking sector. He boosted his popularity by leading farmers' agitations for better terms of trade, and established strong relations with senior politicians. More recently, he is one of several MLAs alleged to have secured a pledge for investment in one of his businesses at a Global Investors Meet in the North Karnataka region – one of a number of memoranda of understanding signed relating mostly to pharmaceuticals, sugar, food processing, cold storage, engineering and cars (*Times of India*, 22 December 2010).

Two of the wealthiest twenty MLAs provide contrasting examples of accumulation (ADR 2013:26). The first of these 'came up' through agri-business, starting out as an input trader in the the 1960s. By 1972, his company was one of the largest fertiliser traders in the state. In the 1990s he diversified into the trading of tractors, watches and Sony electrical goods. Further diversification led to the trading of motorbikes, wind turbines and cars. By the time a second car dealership came on line, a new line of business had been opened in construction and real estate.[20] The second individual, whose assets were valued at 186 crore rupees in 2013 (around $30 million), expanded his family business of mining and trading iron ore, and then diversified into the manufacture of pig iron (VSL Steels), information technology, real estate, engineering and building (Balaji Builders), Air Cargo, movie and TV production, and online entertainment portals and clubs. A substantial dairy facility and sugar factory were at the planning stage at the time of writing.[21]

Over time many MLAs have diversified their economic activities, with some investing in real estate (ownership and trading of land and commercial and residential property, but also construction), while others have moved into media (for example, a minister who owns a sugar factory now also owns a Kannada news channel). Others in the sugar industry have diversified into cement and steel production, which has also been taken up by some of those involved in mining iron ore. Others still have diversified into advertising, or have bought up shares in large businesses, or invested in healthcare, resorts or online entertainment portals.

In line with Krishna's (2003) argument about a democratisation of the state–society interface, a large landowner (from a household of historical landlords and tax collectors) lamented the fact that it was easier for people to rise up the political ranks than it once had been. It seems, though, that the routes up are largely populated by members of the dominant class. The point here has not been to argue that the types of accumulation referred to are dependent on being in a prominent political position, but to point both to the class nature of the state and also the interplay between accumulation in general, accumulation that is state-facilitated and accumulation that involves the private appropriation of public resources. Put simply, state formation and class relations are mutually constitutive.

Bureaucrats of course play a critical role. The distribution of power between elected representatives and officials varies across districts and even GPs. Although most officials are complicit in the gatekeeping system, they often have little choice. More than one Indian Administrative Service (IAS) officer interviewed in Karnataka since 2006 has said that they (and others) are constrained in their ability to challenge the appropriation of public funds. If too many feathers are ruffled or payments are not made, then local political leaders (often the MLA) may ask ministers to have the official in question transferred (see also Wade 1982:307, 311–312). The shadow state has its own regulatory norms, and those who fall foul of it by appropriating too much or too little may be moved on.

There are also gaps in staffing levels. For almost a year between the departure of one IAS officer and the arrival of the next, the important post of Raichur District Chief Executive Officer (who oversees development programmes in the district, which includes gram panchayats with some of the lowest levels of implementation of poverty reduction programmes in the state) was occupied first by someone from the Karnataka Administrative Service who did not want the post and was often absent, and then by an official from the Indian Forestry Service who was largely unfamiliar with the requirements of the job. Administrative posts in relatively affluent areas are more popular, and tend to be secured through higher informal payments.[22]

It is also worth noting that the physical gap between villages and officials at sub-district level and above is often quite large. Such officials rarely venture into the field, and when they do it is usually for a well-planned and stage-managed occasion. One particular district-level official became quite agitated on the way to a village for the purposes of data collection for this book because he had not been there before and nobody was expecting him. Officials' reticence to step into the field in part reflects issues of state capacity, and in part a perceived divide between urban middle class and rural India.

The ways in which the economic and political spheres co-constitute one another, though, is not beholden to a linear course (like everything else). Forms of accumulation and their links to political power reach crises for a variety of reasons from overproduction to party political competition. Illegal mining was a key basis of the 2008–13 BJP government's outright majority, but it was also a primary cause of its subsequent defeat. The mining lobby had become the object of national political calculations as well as the cause of the wrath of a vocal minority in civil society. The dynamics of accumulation can create competition and division as readily as building seemingly unassailable political fronts.

Machinations of accumulation and power trigger counter-moves and division at all levels of the Indian polity from GP wards to the constituencies of the national parliamentary seats. As political parties come and go from government in Karnataka, down at village level the money channels change course somewhat. Some new gatekeepers emerge while others fade away. There are some changes in the pecking order, but little fundamental change in gatekeeping's overall implications: the state–society interface continues to primarily serve the dominant class, particularly in the relatively iniquitous districts of North Karnataka.[23]

It is not improbable that the lower levels of gatekeeping may recede in importance in the coming years, while the higher levels grow in scale (Elliot 2011). As HBO's carefully researched fictional TV series *The Wire* showed by illustrating the links between drugs money, human trafficking, intelligence agencies, real estate and politicians, the boundaries between legal and illegal accumulation, between lawbreakers and lawmakers and between public and private are as blurred as the somewhat more prosaic distinction between state and society (see Harriss-White 2003; Roy 1996). For the time being the shadow state remains prominent in most of India, and continues to strengthen the position of the dominant class. At village level it does so by reproducing the power of the dominant as gatekeepers of public resources. Universal rights-based programmes do, though, offer greater possibilities for classes of labour to increase their influence over LGIs, and modify class relations in their favour. Their expansion, amidst heightened levels of labouring class organising, could accelerate poverty reduction whilst weakening the position of dominant class gatekeepers.

Notes

1 Assuming a conversion rate of 40 rupees to the dollar, which was prevalent during the early years of this period.
2 They are located at the 'lower end' of the dominant class, but include one or two households whose lands are primarily worked by household members.
3 In five of the villages, the Panchamsalis (a farming sub-caste of the Lingayats), were the dominant caste in terms of landownership, while in the other three the OBC Marathas were. The 'dominant caste' is numerically dominant, owns most of the land and wields a disproportionate amount of power (Srinivas 1963). Please note that the middle part of this chapter draws on an article published in volume 11 of the Journal of Agrarian Change.
4 The Lingayats and the dominant caste in southern rural Karnataka (Vokkaligas) have tended to secure a disproportionate number of seats in LGIs (Crook and Manor 1998).
5 OBCs occupy a middling position in terms of caste hierarchies in the fieldwork area.
6 Twenty-nine current and five former district, sub-district and village councillors, three of whom had been major contractors, three of whom had brothers or sons who were actual contractors, most of whom were engaged in 'fixing', and many of whom either had acted as political workers or continued to do so, one full-time fixer who had never been a councillor, two low-level political workers and two high-level political workers who have never been councillors, two GP clerks and two GP secretaries. Three officials in the Department of Women and Child Development, one from the Watershed Department, eight low-level taluk (sub-district) and zilla (district) panchayat officials, and seven senior taluk and district-level officials, including the taluk executive officer, the district chief planning officer, the district chief executive officer and two district collectors.
7 The same figure was put forward by Reddy and Acharya (2007) for the state as a whole.
8 See Pattenden (2011a:176) for a detailed breakdown across the GP President, other councillors, contractors, fixers and others.
9 PDOs are a relatively new rank of officials intended to improve GP administrative capacity but largely integrated into the gatekeeping system.
10 Reliable figures on these payments proved particularly elusive as they were often buried in clandestine negotiations between powerful gatekeepers.
11 Similar concentrations of power were identified in Raichur's GPs. In one of the fieldwork GPs (that of Shiva Camp), which had twenty-five members (2010–15 GP), the Reddys were the most numerous group, followed by Korubas (OBCs). The former were scattered across five different villages (camps) and primarily influential at that level. Four of the five Korubas, on the other hand, came from the village where the GP was headquartered, and

exercised considerable influence over it. They were helped by the GP's disparate nature (spread across nine different villages and camps and, in some cases, poorly connected by mud roads), and by the fact that one of them owned eighty acres of irrigated land. The Reddys and Kammas were relatively marginal to the GP beyond joining hands with caste fellows to protect access to water. As noted in Chapter 4, their accumulation strategies focused on agriculture, agribusiness and formal employment in the private sector, and had very little to do with the state. The GP was relatively polarised in socio-economic terms, which also contributed to it having the highest levels of appropriation of public resources of any of the seven GPs encountered during fieldwork (see discussion of this in relation to Shiva Camp in Chapter 4 and Saraswati Camp in Chapter 8).

12 There have also been disagreements between different levels of government over the distribution of resources. In the mid to late 2000s, for example, councillors and officials from sub-district councils resisted cuts in their share of local government money.

13 In the following state election, the earlier incumbent is alleged to have played a significant role in de-seating his successor (still from the same party), by distributing money in certain pockets of the constituency and encouraging two or three minor candidates to stand in order to take some votes from the sitting MLA. Similar strategies were reported in Raichur, with a prominent Congress politician undermining a rival by encouraging others to stand against him – actions reputedly driven in part by his intention to free up an election ticket for his son. During the last state elections in Dharwad district in 2013 it is alleged that an influential MLA saw off threats from a former MLA by dispatching his 'chamchas' (political workers) to physically restrain those of his rival. Disputes continue further up the chain over ministerial berths and who should be chief minister, with rivals undermining one another and sometimes threatening their party's interests in order to have their way.

14 They were mostly Grade 2 contractors. In the early 2000s, one was doing fifteen to twenty jobs annually of between Rs. 500,000 and Rs. 2 million across Dharwad district (interview, 6 July 2008).

15 At another level, small and large-scale industrialists forge similar links to the state. See, for example, Rutten (2003:74) and Damodaran (2008).

16 Excluding the one dominant class ST woman from a relatively marginal village.

17 Wade (1982:305) argues that initial payments for posts depend to some degree on the applicant's influence – i.e. on his ability to command a sizeable informal income and distribute shares upwards. If the applicant is well connected, a lower initial payment may be accepted.

18 The conversion rates used in this book vary according to the year that is being referred to. By late 2013, prevailing exchange rates had risen to around 60 rupees to the dollar.

19 Although the bulk of such cases were captured, it is possible that some were missed. While some are widely known (the sons of HD Deve Gowda and Dharam Singh, for example), others are less well known (for example, the fact that Jagdeesh Shettar's uncle was elected as a Jan Sangh MLA in 1967).

20 The primary source is Belladandcompany.com (accessed 15 June 2012).

21 The primary source is sladgroup.com (accessed 21 October 2014).
22 Hence in Belgaum district, for example, more irrigated areas like Nippani, Chikkodi and Athani, which have higher levels of accumulation, are in more demand than largely dryland areas like Saundatti. Parts of North Karnataka have seen an expansion of irrigation with the Upper Krishna Project playing a major role. Bagalkote is one of several districts to have benefited. The now bifurcated Gulbarga district has also benefited, as have parts of northern and western Raichur district.
23 Additional research visits to the south of the state, and in particular to a GP in Maddur taluk in Mandya district, where interviews were conducted with GP officeholders and a caste/class-wise sample of constituents, showed a more equitable distribution of power and resources than in the north (although the scheduled caste minority were relatively marginalised). In addition, see Carswell and De Neve (2014), Heller *et al.* (2007) or Heyer (2012).

6

Social policy and class relations: the case of the National Rural Employment Guarantee Scheme

The National Rural Employment Guarantee Scheme (NREGS) is a universal rights-based programme, and as such it is argued here that it provides possibilities for classes of labour to challenge existing distributions of power within local government institutions (LGIs), and even to modify class relations in their favour. In operation since 2006, NREGS guarantees 100 days of employment on government-funded works for every household in rural India. It also entitles those waiting for work for more than two weeks to unemployment benefits.

In 2011–12 in the fieldwork state of Karnataka, 100 days of NREGS work would have provided each household with Rs. 12,500, or 23 per cent of the poverty-line income for a family of five.[1] The implications of this are considerable, and particularly so in Karnataka, which has seen its rate of poverty reduction fall behind almost all other states (see Table 1.3), and where NREGS has been shown to be performing relatively poorly up until this point (Usami and Rawal 2012).[2]

As NREGS is one of India's largest poverty reduction programmes, analysis of the programme is critical to assessing whether such interventions are pro-labouring class in practice. As well as improving economic conditions, NREGS could disentangle a substantial proportion of labouring class livelihoods from direct relations with dominant class employers. By increasing its economic independence, NREGS stands to modify the balance of socio-political power in labour's favour, and increase its political 'space' (as was argued in Chapter 3). Moreover, it potentially provides classes of labour with a common agenda – something that its many forms of segmentation undermine (see Chapter 4). As well as threatening the dominant class's ability to control labour, it also threatens its profit levels by putting upward pressure on wages wherever NREGS wages are higher than the prevailing male or female casual wage rate. Given that this is most likely to be the case where prevailing poverty rates are higher (see

Table 6.1), NREGS is particularly contentious where the conditions of classes of labour are at their worst.

Conversely, although employment programmes are often seen as threatening control over labour and the cost and intensity of labour-power, they can also be understood as a means not only of subsidising the costs of labour's reproduction (Ghosh 2011; Herring and Edwards 1983), but also of maintaining social stability, reworking forms of domination (through dominant class control of the programme) and reproducing exploitative social relations. As has been argued throughout this book, the role of the state is both contradictory and contested.

This chapter shows why, where, when and how NREGS either contributes to pro-labouring class change or to reproducing the position of the dominant class. It proceeds in four parts. The first provides a brief overview of how the implementation of NREGS has been contested across India as a whole, and outlines how NREGS's uneven performance relates to distributions of power and resources. The following sections analyse longitudinal fieldwork data from Dharwad and Raichur to show how NREGS outcomes vary across time and place. These sections illustrate how initially high levels of implementation in Dharwad have declined due to increased (but uneven) dominant class control over the scheme, and how the initial subversion of the scheme in Raichur has been partially challenged by collective labouring class action. In the conclusion, NREGS is located in the broader context of social policy, underlining how poverty reduction programmes vary in the extent to which they challenge the existing balance of class forces, and pointing both to their limitations and their capacity to contribute to pro-labouring class change. The chapter is based on research conducted in Raichur in 2008, 2011 and 2014, and in Dharwad in 2011 and 2013 (the scheme was first implemented in Raichur in 2006 and in Dharwad in 2008). Interviews on NREGS were conducted in a total of nineteen villages, which were selected on the basis of irrigation levels, proximity to urban labour markets and class and caste dynamics.

NREGS in India: contestation and uneven outcomes

There is evidence of both the dominant class and classes of labour making gains through NREGS, which underlines how state mediation of class relations is contested. Case studies show that NREGS has improved the material conditions of classes of labour, with studies pointing to reduced levels of malnutrition, reduced levels of migration and gains for scheduled castes and the elderly (Carswell and De Neve 2014; Drèze and Khera 2011:44; Gill *et al.* 2013:479–493; Jankimow 2014:264; Khera and Nayak

Table 6.1 Rural casual wages (male and female) relative to NREGS wages in 2007–08 and 2010–11 (selected major states)

	2007–08 male wages compared to NREGS wages	2007–08 female wages compared to NREGS wages	2010–11 male wages compared to NREGS wages	2010–11 female wages compared to NREGS wages
Kerala	Higher	Lower	Higher	Higher
Punjab	Higher	Lower	Higher	Higher (marginal)[a]
Karnataka	Lower	Lower	Higher	Lower
Andhra Pradesh	Higher (marginal)	Lower	Higher	Lower
Tamil Nadu	Higher	Lower	Higher	Lower
Maharashtra	Lower	Lower	Higher	Lower
Rajasthan	Higher	Lower	Higher	Lower (marginal)
Odisha	Lower	Lower	Lower (marginal)	Lower
Uttar Pradesh	Lower	Lower	Higher	Lower
Bihar	Lower	Lower	Higher	Lower
Madhya Pradesh	Lower	Lower	Lower	Lower

[a] Marginal means by less than two rupees in 2007–08 and by less than five rupees in 2010–11.

Sources: GoI LB (2010:162, 2013:101); www.nrega.nic.in/wages.pdf; www.nrega.nic.in/nerega_statewise.pdf (accessed 19 February 2015).

2011; NCEUS 2009:220; Pellissery and Kumar Jalan 2011; Narasimha Reddy 2013:77, 148).[3] Studies also point to NREGS heightening labour's bargaining power and contributing to better treatment by employers, such as shorter working hours and reduced levels of harassment of women (Gill et al. 2013:479; Jankimow 2014:272; Narasimha Reddy 2013:145). The harassment of women declines as they have to ask dominant class male farmers for work somewhat less frequently,[4] and have to collect wages from them less often, which lowers the frequency of personalised and sometimes protracted power-laden interactions that are especially likely to be difficult for single women (Khera and Nayak 2008:51–52).

Table 6.2 NREGS wages, rural casual wages, agricultural wages and inflation (all figures for Karnataka)

	NREGS wages (from 1 April of each year)	Male rural casual wages (NSS)	Female rural casual wages (Karnataka) (NSS)	Rate of inflation (rise in CPIAL compared to previous year)	CPIAL Base 100 = 86/7
2005–06	n/a	55.3	33.9		341
2006–07	69			26	367
2007–08	74	68.5	44.9	39	406
2008–09	82			52	458
2009–10	82	96.9	62.8	77	535
2010–11	100			60	595
2011–12	125	162.9	99.9	70	665

Sources: GoI NSS (2007, 2009, 2011:95, 2013:101); GoI MOSPI (n.d.); Reserve Bank of India (various).

There is also widespread evidence of NREGS putting upward pressure on wages from case studies and large multi-state datasets (Berg *et al.* 2012; Carswell and De Neve 2014:1). Unsurprisingly, given that women's agricultural wages are more likely than men's to be lower than NREGS wage levels (see Table 6.1), upward pressure on female agricultural wages has been found to be greater (Azam 2012; Gill *et al.* 2013:479, 485; Narasimha Reddy 2013:158). Weight is added to such arguments by the fact that casual rural wages in Karnataka rose almost three times as fast between 2009–10 and 2011–12 (when NREGS wages also saw their fastest growth) as they had done between 2005–06 and 2007–08 when NREGS had just started and was only operational in a minority of districts (see Table 6.2).[5]

Capitalist farmers seeking to protect their ability to accumulate and control labour have responded to NREGS in a variety of ways ranging from the militant and direct to the subtle and indirect. They do so not just by trying to minimise threats to their interests, but by using NREGS to increase control over labour, boost the profitability of landholdings and heighten their influence over LGIs. Control over the state–society interface is at stake, as well as class relations at the level of production.

Dominant class resistance to NREGS has encompassed disincentivising participation by delaying wage payments, intensifying NREGS work to make it less appealing, and delaying or blocking implementation

(Gill *et al.* 2013; Kumbhar 2013). More militant responses have included refusing to employ labourers who sought greater implementation of the programme or denying them access to other forms of social policy (see below; Jankimow 2014:276), and even in some cases (in several states including Jharkhand and Odisha) killing pro-NREGS activists (Anon. 2009; Hard News n.d.).

Less direct strategies include those discussed in Chapter 4 as broader responses to the growth of non-agricultural labour, such as reducing the need for labour-power by mechanising production, shifting to less labour-intensive cropping patterns, bringing in labour from other areas or disciplining it by reinforcing debt-related ties.

Less antagonistic ways of protecting control over labour include timing NREGS works during the agricultural slack season, or restricting them to mornings so that labourers are available for agricultural work in the afternoons (Narasimha Reddy 2013:144–145). By increasing the total amount of work in villages, NREGS can deter labour from commuting or migrating, and subsidise both its reproduction and the labour costs of capitalist farmers (Herring and Edwards 1983).

NREGS has the capacity to generate cross-class gains by regenerating (or creating new) public assets, and by enhancing the productivity of farm land (Ghosh 2011; Gill *et al.* 2013:489). Although there are cases where land upgradation has focused on marginal farmers (Narasimha Reddy 2013:129), studies point to the disproportionate amounts of work being carried out on larger farmers' land (Shah and Mehta 2008:21; see also Herring and Edwards 1983).

The dominant class also uses state institutions to turn NREGS to its advantage – both in direct ways by using its influence over LGIs (see below), and less directly by pressing state and central governments not to increase NREGS wage rates (e.g. Gill *et al.* 2013:468).

NREGS wages have increased less steeply since 2012, a trend that is continuing under the recently elected more obviously pro-capital BJP-led national government. National Sample Survey (NSS) wage data show that NREGS wages have increasingly fallen below average rural casual wages across the country (see Table 6.1), which can be seen as part of government attempts to rein in rural wage growth in order to hold down wages and stem inflation (GoI LB n.d.(a)).

Attempts to shape national policy in favour of rural capital are resisted in their turn by the coalition of pro-NREGS social activists, academics and left parties who pressed for the National Rural Employment Guarantee Act to be passed in the first place (Chopra 2011, 2014:91).[6] They have continued to campaign for effective implementation – both for increased technical capacity (Ambasta *et al.* 2008) and timely consumer price index-linked wage rises (Sivakumar 2010:11). Pro-NREGS strategies have included lobbying (such as through the now dissolved National Advisory Committee, which involved face-to-face meetings with members of the central government), and more local-level organisations focused on improving implementation (Khera and Nayak 2008; Pankaj and Thanka 2010:48; Narasimha Reddy 2013; see also Chapter 8).

Uneven outcomes

This chapter argues that variations in NREGS performance at district and village level relate to distributions of power and resources. The extent to which the dominant class controls LGIs is significant, along with the patterns of relationships between a village and its LGIs (in other words, the distribution of power beyond village level), the organisational strength of both classes of labour and the dominant class (reflective of intra- as well as inter-class relations), and whether labourers in a particular village are within commutable distance of urban labour markets or are dependent on selling their labour-power to members of the dominant class in their village, which restricts the capacity to organise. Finally, as well as the patterns of labouring class reproduction, those of dominant class accumulation (and the extent to which they buy labour-power in the village) also have a bearing on the outcomes of the scheme. In other words, the outcomes of an intervention like NREGS, as was shown to be the case with labour relations (in Chapter 4), relate closely to particular forms of class relations in specific locations as well as to broader distributions of power and resources.

These variations are reflected in the broader patterns of NREGS's performance across India, which spans locations with no NREGS work at all to others where households have received more than 100 days (Gill *et al.* 2013:475, 494; Narasimha Reddy 2013:122, 143; see also Pellissery and Kumar Jalan 2011:285). NREGS has been found to perform worse in states with greater degrees of inequality and poverty, such as Uttar Pradesh, Jharkhand and Odisha (Bhatia and Drèze 2006; Kumbhar 2013; NCEUS 2009:217), than in those where the overall balance of power has shifted towards classes of labour in recent decades. The latter includes parts of Tamil Nadu, where relatively dispersed processes of industrialisation have increased access to non-agricultural employment and diffused dependence on the dominant class (Carswell and De Neve 2014; Djurfeldt *et al.* 2008; Harriss *et al.* 2010; Heyer 2012), and Kerala, where contemporary village-level women's organisations have been able to build upon the labouring class's historically rooted socio-political strength and the state's relative socio-economic equity (Heller 1999; Kannan and Jagajeevan 2013). The relatively strong NREGS performance in Andhra Pradesh and Rajasthan, meanwhile, has been attributed respectively to effective bureaucrats and prominent pro-labouring class civil society organisations (Aakella and Kidambi 2007; Narasimha Reddy 2013:134).

NREGS in North Karnataka

The implementation of NREGS in the fieldwork districts of Dharwad and Raichur has followed contrasting routes. In 2010–11, two years after implementation began, the average annual number of workdays per household in five Dharwad villages was 107. In Raichur, the average across eleven villages in the scheme's third year was less than ten, reflecting more obvious forms of dominant class opposition (see Table 6.3).[7] By late 2013 and early 2014, the situation had changed. In Dharwad, the number of workdays received had halved. In Raichur, the number of days, though still significantly lower than Dharwad, had more than doubled.

In the Raichur villages, widespread subversion in the initial stages gave way to slight (and uneven) improvements, in part due to higher levels of labouring class organisation – primarily in the form of an association of labouring class Madiga women called the Jagruthi Mahela Sanghathan (discussed in detail in Chapter 8), which has consistently pressed certain GPs to improve implementation. In both Dharwad GPs the initially high levels of implementation have declined over time (a trend corroborated at state level by government data; see Usami and Rawal 2012:89), in part due to gatekeepers increasing their control over the programme.

There are a number of major differences between the fieldwork villages, which have been discussed earlier in the book. Dominant class unity in the Dharwad villages is somewhat greater (particularly in Panchnagaram GP) and facilitated by the Lingayats' strength in that district, while in Raichur labouring class unity is somewhat greater, and is facilitated by the considerable numbers of scheduled caste Madiga labourers.[8]

Rather than openly resisting NREGS, Dharwad's dominant class has deployed a variety of strategies to shape it in its interests, while segmenting the labouring class and co-opting elements of it. In Raichur, on the other hand, the dominant class's initial response was to impede implementation. This means that less emphasis was placed on co-opting classes of labour, who were therefore more likely to form a counter-movement. The scenario in Raichur could be characterised as class conflict, while the more complex scenario at play in the Dharwad villages can be seen as a form of dominant class hegemony. As well as broad differences between the districts, there were also significant ones within them, which will also be analysed.[9]

Table 6.3 Estimated number of days of NREGS work per household per annum

	Two–three years after first implementation of NREGS in district[a]	Five years after first implementation	Seven years after implementation
Dharwad	107	50	n/a
Raichur	6	15	25

[a] NREGS started two years earlier in Raichur than in Dharwad. The left-hand column is based on data collected in 2008 in the case of Raichur and mid-2011 in Dharwad. The middle column is based on data collected in 2011 in Raichur, and late 2013 in Dharwad. The right-hand column is based on data collected in 2014.

Source: fieldwork data.

The rise and fall of NREGS in Dharwad, 2011–13

In mid-2011, two years into the programme,[10] there was evidence that NREGS in Dharwad district was generating significantly greater benefits for classes of labour than earlier public works programmes. In the six villages of Panchnagaram and Kamlapur Gram Panchayats (three in each) that were the primary focus of NREGS-related fieldwork in Dharwad, most labouring class respondents who wanted NREGS work were receiving between 70 and 200 workdays.[11] Although skilled workers who commuted to the city had little interest in NREGS due to their higher wages, around 200 workers always took up NREGS work (referred to here as 'regular' NREGS workers). These were mostly unskilled casual labourers who moved between the fields and the city for work. There were also around 300 'irregular' NREGS workers who were doing 20 or 30 days of work, and sometimes leasing their cards to more regular workers. While regular NREGS workers were all labouring class, irregular workers were more likely to be dominant caste and from slightly better-off households.

The 'mates', who were responsible for organising gangs, supervising works and liaising with GP members and officials, were all dominant caste *and* class, with the exception of one scheduled caste man who was removed from his position following squabbles with farmers. Workers in the six villages were organised by mates into thirteen gangs – one gang in each of four villages, and nine in the remaining two.

Access to the programme, then, was relatively broad-based, and whereas contractors had been at the centre of money flows in previous employment programmes, NREGS wages had begun to be paid directly to labourers' bank accounts. NREGA stipulates, moreover, that 60 per cent of spending should be on wages, thereby limiting the amount that can be spent on materials. As a result, gatekeepers' well-established system of controlling programmes and appropriating resources had been loosened.

Gatekeepers in Dharwad initially shaped the scheme to protect their control over labour and restrain upward pressure on wages. They also sought out an effective system for appropriating NREGS funds, while the dominant class more generally looked for ways to use NREGS to enhance agricultural productivity and profitability.

Upward pressure on wages and potential impacts on access to labour-power were initially mitigated in four different ways. First, because women's access to NREGS posed a greater threat to labour supply and wage levels (see Tables 6.1 and 6.2), NREGS work was often channelled through men. For example, mates reduced female access by tending to insist that digging work was done in a pair that included one man (see also Khera and Nayak 2008:54; NCEUS 2009:224; Pellissery and Jalan 2011:287).

Second, work was spaced in two- to three-day blocks once every two weeks, which allowed labourers and marginal farmers to do both agricultural and NREGS work. Third, work was increasingly shifted to the slack summer season when demand for agricultural labour was minimal (but working conditions were more difficult due to the heat). Lastly, NREGS was used to increase control over male labour by augmenting levels of village-based employment and thereby deterring commuting (and later on by selectively allocating access to NREGS work – see below). In 2011, NREGS work was also made more attractive by paying labourers on a piece-rate basis (for each mango pit dug), which enabled them to earn more than the full day's wage of Rs. 125.

Some dominant class farmers were able to use NREGS to increase their land's profitability, as a significant proportion of spending in these villages in the early years of the scheme was on small-scale works on farmland (more than one-third of spending in Panchnagaram GP in 2009–10, for example).[12] Although regulations stipulated that these should be for farmers with less than five acres (most of whom were marginal farmers in these dryland villages, and therefore part of classes of labour), in practice they were relatively unpopular with smaller farmers. This was because in these GPs smaller works usually meant the planting of fruit trees, which were an unattractive proposition to the less well-off as they have a lengthy time lag before yielding. Partially as a consequence of this, in 2012–13 many of the beneficiaries in Panchnagaram village were from the dominant class and two-thirds were from the dominant caste.

When interviewed in 2011 farmers had been quick to point the finger at NREGS for the recent marked increases in wage levels – unsurprising given that this followed a two-year period when inflation had spiked, NREGS wages had increased by just over 50 per cent and male rural casual wages had jumped by 68 per cent (see Table 6.2). Having accelerated from 2009, NREGS wage rises tapered off in 2013–14 and 2014–15. In addition, the *amount* of NREGS work in the Dharwad villages had declined, with most workers complaining of a shortage and receiving less than fifty days.

By late 2013, the threat posed to dominant class interests by NREGS had receded, and it was the nearby industrial area that was now identified by Panchnagaram's farmers as the main threat to their control over labour. Farmers in Kamlapur and the more remote village of Morab, meanwhile, continued to bemoan NREGS and 'bogus' government schemes in general, which they believed made workers 'lazy' and 'uncooperative'. The recently expanded PDS (which now provided rice at one rupee per kilo) was the primary target of their ire.[13]

As the hiatus triggered by NREGS died down, the initial more tentative steps taken by dominant class gatekeepers to weaken NREGS's impact had been superseded by a more sophisticated and decisive gatekeeping process, which reflected gatekeepers' growing control over the process and their ability to use the retreat from general to selective NREGS access to further divide labour.

Gatekeepers, accumulation and control: uneven implementation of NREGS at village-level

Patterns of labouring class reproduction and dominant class accumulation (and of class relations more generally) affected how NREGS was implemented across different villages. Kamlapur's labouring class (as discussed in Chapter 4) was relatively independent of village-level economic activities. Urban employment was the primary basis of material reproduction for 62 per cent of them, as opposed to just 35 per cent of labouring class households in Panchnagaram village.[14] Access to urban labour markets was, though, highly gendered. There was not a single female labourer from Kamlapur working in industry or construction, and only a handful from Panchnagaram worked as unskilled industrial labourers. On the other hand, the majority of agricultural labourers in both villages were female, and the proportion in Kamlapur was higher (58.3 per cent) due to the greater levels of male commuting.[15]

While Kamlapur's labouring class (as a whole) was less dependent on the village economy, its dominant class was more dependent on accumulating through agriculture than its counterparts in Panchnagaram, and hence was somewhat more concerned about control over agricultural labourers. All of the larger (10-acre-plus) landowners in Kamlapur were primarily focused on agriculture, while most of Panchnagaram's larger farmers were primarily focused on other economic activities. It had a greater number of contractors (six as opposed to one), greater influence in district politics and greater influence over its GP (see Chapter 5).

NREGS, then, was more contentious in Kamlapur than Panchnagaram in that it posed more of a threat to dominant class farmers. On the other hand, the potential gains for classes of labour as a whole were greater in Panchnagaram (and for women in both villages), and in this respect was more contentious there. These differences were reflected in the discourses of both farmers and labourers in the two villages. Kamlapur's farmers remained hostile to NREGS in 2013 whereas Panchnagaram's no longer seemed concerned by it. Labourers in Panchnagaram, meanwhile, were more likely to complain about a reduction in NREGS work than those in Kamlapur.

In Panchnagaram, labouring class dependence on the village's dominant households was further augmented by the fact that most of its labour intermediaries were from the dominant class, while all of Kamlapur's were from the labouring class (the former worked in industry and the latter in construction). In addition, Panchnagaram had a number of dominant class road contractors, some of whom took labourers with them to work in other locations. In overall terms, then, Panchnagaram's dominant class maintained tighter control over male labourers than was the case in Kamlapur.

Panchnagaram Gram Panchayat

The dominant class in Panchnagaram had several advantages over its counterparts in Kamlapur. Its accumulation strategies were more diversified, and its control over labour somewhat greater. That dependence was augmented by the dominant class's greater control over the GP and NREGS, which is partially explained by its greater caste-based unity. The Panchamsali Lingayats dominated each village and the GP as a whole (see Chapter 5). In each of the GP's three villages, a dominant caste/class NREGS 'mate' had been carefully chosen by prominent gatekeepers and was firmly under their control. Each of the three was relatively young and had no independent political base.

The economic and political strength of dominant class Panchamsalis was mutually reinforcing. Its control over labour was reinforced by the extent of its control over the GP and the distribution of the public resources that flowed through them. NREGS was no exception. As the availability of NREGS work declined, the dominant class reasserted its role in selective distribution of public resources to further divide a labour force that was already fragmented between the landless and wage-labour-dependent marginal farmers, between regular and casual labour, and between those who worked on a skilled or unskilled basis in the city.

In Panchnagaram village, workers from streets/communities that were more oriented to non-agricultural urban labour markets (in part because they owned less land) saw the most marked decline in access to NREGS work – primarily scheduled caste Madars and those living in a mixed community labouring class hamlet just outside the village. In contrast, the economic activities of the Muslim community were more village and agriculture-oriented – most owned some land (1.75 acres on average), as opposed to only around 10 per cent of the Madars. Although less likely to work outside the village than the Madars, the Muslims were nevertheless more likely to work in construction and included several masons including a maistry (labour organiser) who worked for one of the village's contractors. In other words, Muslim households were both more integrated into village economic activities and more closely linked to the GP (through the contractor), and included skilled construction workers who were useful for NREGS building works. Unsurprisingly, their access to NREGS work remained significantly greater.

Access to NREGS work had become similarly uneven in neighbouring Neeralbhavi village. Members of most households in one particular street (which was home to the scheduled tribe dominant class Vice-President of the GP) still received 100 days of work. Similarly to those with greater access to NREGS work in Panchnagaram, the street was largely labouring class and had a disproportionate number of masons, as well as house-holds that mixed marginal farming with agricultural labour. NREGS, they said, made them more inclined to stay in the village than to look for work outside. In the neighbouring scheduled caste street, the story was quite different and there were complaints about reduced levels of NREGS work. This segmentation of NREGS workers enabled gatekeepers to sta-bilise their network of labouring class allies in the process of implement-ing the scheme.

Although the rule that 60 per cent of expenditure should be on wages was initially adhered to, over time gatekeepers increasingly reverted to less labour-intensive, larger-scale 'concrete works', which are preferred by contractors (officially barred from NREGS works but still widely active in the fieldwork villages) and gatekeepers more broadly (see also Gill *et al*. 2013:476; Kumbhar 2013:414). In Panchnagaram GP a gradual shift from 'mud' to less labour-intensive 'concrete' works (the share of concrete works rose from 64.5 to 80 per cent between 2009-10 and 2012-13 (see

Table 6.4 Distribution of type of works, Panchnagaram GP

Type of works	9–10% of overall NREGS spending	12–13% of overall NREGS spending
Public 'Concrete Works' (guttering, roads, public buildings)	64.6	80
Public 'Mud Works' (primarily tanks)	1.6	10
Private 'Mud Works' (primarily pit-digging/ tree-planting)	33.9	10

Source: data collected from GP officials in 2011 and 2013.

Table 6.4)) further eased the appropriation of resources and reduced the actual number of NREGS workdays that were made available. This reflected both the dominant class's control of the programme and the embedding of a system of appropriation that bore many of the hallmarks of earlier public employment programmes.

A number of respondents in every village, as well as former 'mates', confirmed that the practice of channelling money to gatekeepers through labourers' bank accounts was widespread in the fieldwork villages.[16] Those who complained about falling levels of NREGS work in many cases received small payments in exchange for allowing gatekeepers to empty their accounts of their NREGS 'wages' (for work that they had not done). There had been hitches when NREGS wages began to be paid through bank accounts, with 'mates' reporting that some jobcard-holders had refused to hand over money from their bank accounts. Over time, though, gatekeepers smoothed the money flows by only channelling payments through cooperative cardholders – part of a broader process of gatekeepers reasserting their dominance over the state–society interface.

Perhaps coincidental, it was nevertheless striking that every time the author and his research assistant entered a GP office in late 2013, they stumbled upon discussions between GP officials and contractors about payments, or, in one case, an argument between a current and a former GP President about who should get what cut from a particular construction job. The former GP President had seemed nervous and ill-at-ease shortly after he took up the post two-and-a-half years previously. Now, not long after his tenure had come to an end, he had the assured air of a 'leader'. A junior official who was present on both occasions had made a similar transition. On edge during the earlier visit, he now responded to questions on NREGS in a calm and authoritative manner, referring cheerily to hundreds of pages of official on-line data to support his claims.

Respondents gave a variety of reasons for playing along with processes that the gatekeepers had established for implementing NREGS, all of which point towards the ongoing fragmentation and dependence of labour. As well as the money, they did so in the hope of future work, or simply 'for an easy life' and to avoid threats and harassment. It was reasoned that one individual going against the system would make no difference, and the possibilities for collective action among such a highly segmented workforce were extremely limited anyway. The labouring class still saw the GP as the preserve of the dominant. Challenging the status quo was understood to be both risky and futile.

Classes of labour saw their gains from NREGS dwindle over time, while Panchnagaram GP's united dominant class was able to reaffirm its ability to control and appropriate public resources. This in turn helped the dominant class as a whole to reproduce its control over classes of labour.

Kamlapur Gram Panchayat

In Kamlapur GP, in contrast to Panchnagaram GP, there was no single dominant caste or community – Marathas, Muslims and Lingayats all influenced proceedings, the GP was more physically disparate, party politics more delicately poised and, unlike Panchnagaram, rivalries among gatekeepers sometimes bubbled out of control in the absence of a coherent dominant class. Aspiring gatekeepers could sometimes play on those divisions to establish themselves.

NREGS's decline in villages in Kamlapur GP played out somewhat differently both from Panchnagaram and from each other. In Kamlapur village, farmers' antipathy towards NREGS became apparent when they removed a scheduled caste 'mate' after he pushed 'too hard' for NREGS works to be implemented.[17] Gatekeepers first pressurised him by telling him that payments for works would not be sanctioned (a useful way of being able to rein in 'errant' mates), and subsequently replaced him with a member of a dominant caste farming family. In Kamlapur village, then, the tensions around NREGS were inter-caste and inter-class in nature.

In Niwar, on the other hand, *intra*-class tensions played a significant role. Closer to the city than any of the other villages, the number of days of NREGS work in Niwar declined relatively precipitously between mid-2011 and 2013. Jobcards that showed payments of up to Rs. 10,000 between 2009 and 2011 in some cases showed no payments at all from 2011 to 2013.

A row between GP members and mates had played a significant role in the scheme's decline in Niwar. The two leading gatekeepers were less concerned with subverting NREGS than with their stone-quarrying and city-based banana-trading businesses. The village's three mates domin-ant class stepped into the organisational vacuum, and began to appro-priate what was seen by the more established gatekeepers as being much more than 'their share'. The latter then attempted to reimpose control by replacing the relatively powerful mates with more pliant ones who were less effective at organising the NREGS process. Implementation levels subsequently fell, prompting one labourer to comment that NREGS had been buried in mud (*mannalli muchidaru*).

NREGS, then, played out somewhat differently across the two gram panchayats, which is indicative of variations in the unity of the dominant class, distributions of castes and gatekeepers, and patterns of accumu-lation, exploitation and domination. The retreat from more general to more selective access to NREGS work increased gatekeepers' influence over the process because it further divided an already segmented labour force between those who were partially or entirely excluded and the core group of NREGS workers who still accessed 100 days of work.

Class conflict in Raichur

In the Raichur villages, as already noted, levels of development are lower and poverty levels higher. The villages are also more remote, with very lit-tle access to urban labour markets apart from through long-distance cir-cular migration. When in the countryside, labourers are largely dependent on agricultural labour (unlike those in the Dharwad villages). Levels of dependence on the rural dominant class have declined more slowly than in Dharwad, and only really broke down to any significant degree when circulation to Bengaluru became widespread in the early 2000s.

In contrast to Dharwad, the number of NREGS workdays was ini-tially very low in Raichur (see Table 6.3). One hundred households in eleven Raichur villages had received an average of just six days of work a year between 2006 (when NREGS was initiated in Raichur) and 2008. Follow-up fieldwork in 2010, 2011 and 2014 showed some increase – to a large degree due to the work of the Jagruthi Mahela Sanghathan (JMS), an organisation of female labouring class Madigas (scheduled caste), which campaigned for improved implementation.

The changes, though, were highly uneven. NREGS implementation improved more in villages that were closer to the main road and more closely linked to non-agricultural labour markets, as well as where the JMS had a stronger presence. For example, in one roadside village (Badarapur), which was home to a JMS leader, each scheduled caste household had received around twenty days of work in 2011. Jagalwara, which is a relatively remote and only semi-irrigated village, had seen a slower increase in NREGS days. Even here, though, initial dominant class resistance to NREGS had been eroded to some degree by JMS pressure, and farmers' growing realisation that NREGS could improve groundwater management. There was also strong demand for NREGS work from classes of labour facing relatively severe levels of under-employment, which meant that the dominant class could increase NREGS work without losing control over labour. Increased NREGS work and improved groundwater management could also reduce the village's relatively high levels of circular outmigration. In other words, a pro-NREGS coalition of sorts had been formed. Consequently, in 2013 labouring class households in Jagalwara received more days of NREGS work than in the previous four years (between 15 and 20), and in 2014 the number of workdays increased further (from 20 to 25 days).

In contrast, in the similarly remote village of Shiva Camp, NREGS work, as intimated in Chapter 4, had been non-existent since 2007 when GP officials had taken labourers' jobcards. This remained the case in July 2014 when fieldwork was last conducted, and reflected the broader socio-political dynamics in that village: access to non-agricultural labour markets was lower, control over labour greater, the GP office more remote and the JMS 's presence weaker. The high levels of canal-irrigation meant that farmers had a somewhat greater need for labour-power than in drier villages, and were more likely to complain of 'labour shortages'.

In such a context it is unsurprising that capitalist farmers saw NREGS as a threat. The relative scarcity of access to non-agricultural employ-ment increased the potential for a surge in demand for NREGS – par-ticularly if promptly paid work began to be made generally available. There was also a greater threat of collective action by the labouring class than was the case in Dharwad due to the greater caste-based unity of the labouring class. These differences made NREGS more contentious here than in the Dharwad villages.

There was clear evidence of gatekeepers dragging their feet over NREGS implementation. Tactics included claiming that there was no work to do, withholding wages for long periods so as to dampen demand for further work, non-payment of wages, making working conditions harsher than agricultural labour, the sowing of division and the buying of acquiescence through the provision of payments to some members of the labouring class (without their having worked), the appropriation of wages deposited in bank accounts through the borrowing of bank cards and the compli-city of officials, attempts to buy off JMS activists and threats, issued via a labouring class GP member, to withhold other government programmes such as housing grants from those demanding NREGS work.

While classes of labour in the Raichur villages were more cohesive in caste terms than their counterparts in Dharwad, the reverse was true for the dominant class. Unlike Dharwad, where Lingayats dominate, there is no single dominant caste in the Raichur fieldwork area. The Nayaks (scheduled tribes) are the largest caste and dominate in some villages, the Korubas are also influential in some (but rarely dominate as they are fewer in number), and Lingayats and Reddys have broad-ranging influence, although that of the latter is more restricted to the 'camps' that they had moved to from Andhra Pradesh.

Works on private land were less widespread in the Raichur villages than was the case in Dharwad. Given that these are more likely to generate disagreements than works on shared infrastructure, this may be attributable in part to the absence of a single dominant caste, and indicates that the more divided nature of the dominant class made it harder for it to shape the programme to suit its interests.

Although the level of NREGS works was lower, the level of appropriation of NREGS funds was not. Research conducted in 2008 indicated that gatekeepers in Raichur were appropriating even more of NREGS funds than they were in Dharwad (Pattenden 2011b). Spending on GP seats had risen further in Raichur than Dharwad, and high rates of appropriation provided a further disincentive to effective implementation as the potential 'losses' for gatekeepers were greater.

Widespread non-implementation in the Raichur villages was indicative of their more polarised class relations, but also of a more divided dominant class. Implementation was worse where classes of labour were more dependent on their village's dominant class for their material reproduction (and socio-economic and socio-political hierarchies were steeper), and better where the labouring class was organising collectively through the JMS.

Conclusion

NREGS threatens to loosen labouring class dependence on the dominant class, provide a rallying point for classes of labour and put upward pressure on wages. From the perspective of the dominant class as a whole, it is arguably more contentious than PDS, which subsidises wages more directly (by significantly lowering the cost of foodgrains), but less contentious than the Unorganised Workers Social Security Act would have been had it included measures such as a national minimum wage, which would have more directly affected a larger swathe of the economy.

The contested nature of NREGS's implementation has been shown in concrete forms across a number of villages and gram panchayats in two North Karnataka districts. Where the dominant class was more united (as in Dharwad's Panchamsali Lingayat-dominated Panchnagaram GP), it was able to shape NREGS rather than impede it. Where NREGS sharpened antagonisms between labourers and farmers to a greater degree (as in Shiva Camp, Raichur), it was more likely that the dominant class would obstruct it. Where the labouring class was more organised (as in certain Raichur villages), implementation levels improved to some degree.

Broader NSS data indicating the relatively poor performance of NREGS in Karnataka as a whole has been shown to be particularly applicable to the state's northern interior, where poverty levels tend to be higher, socio-political hierarchies steeper and dominant class control over local government institutions greater. Although the fieldwork findings are more similar to those from Odisha (Kumbhar 2013) than to those from Tamil Nadu (Carswell and De Neve 2014), elements of the latter's analysis also hold in the fieldwork villages. NREGS can alter socio-political dynamics in labour's favour, may put upward pressure on wages and can increase labouring class incomes (as well as levels of dominant class accumulation). Its ability to do so reflects the dominant class's unity and ability to shape state practices, the concrete forms of class relations and the extent of labouring class organisation.

Detailed analysis of class relations throws up variables that require the attention of policy-makers. It matters that the dominant class is more likely to resist the scheme in Kamlapur than in Panchnagaram, and in Shiva Camp than in Jagalwara. It matters that the dominant class in Panchnagaram is able to find ways to divide labour. Awareness of different patterns of class relations and a sense of their geography in a given sub-district should allow those responsible for implementing the scheme at state and district level (where officials tend to be somewhat more independent of the dominant class) to predict the wholesale subversion of the scheme in villages like Shiva Camp, and to find ways to modify implementation practices in such places.

Although the implementation of NREGS in Dharwad had similarities with that of its predecessor (the SGRY), there were significant differences. More money was spent on wages (rather than building materials) than had been the case with SGRY, which meant that more labouring class households that saw an increase in their incomes. NREGS works were much more likely to employ labourers from the same village, which increased labourers' ability to shape the implementation process. Much depended on who organised labour. In Dharwad, the mates were firmly controlled by the dominant class (with one short-lived exception), whereas in Raichur members of an organisation of classes of labour had at times taken responsibility for organising NREGS works.

The chapter has shown that NREGS is better seen as part of the relational forms that (re)produce poverty than purely as a programme intended to reduce poverty. The high levels of appropriation of NREGS funds in evidence in the fieldwork villages underline the extent to which the dominant class controls those LGIs. This, though, is the starting point for analysis rather than its endpoint. The appropriation of resources is a superficial phenomenon that needs to be understood in relation to patterns of accumulation and forms of exploitation and material reproduction – both in particular social settings and more generally.

The high rates of appropriation do not mean that NREGS has failed – simply that classes of labour are not yet strong enough to challenge the dominant class and press for NREGS to be implemented in such a way as to redistribute power and resources in their direction. Stronger organisations of the labouring class are required to do so – a tall order given its degree of fragmentation, particularly where socio-economic and socio-political hierarchies are at their steepest.

Although the state is ultimately pro-capital (more obviously and completely so since the election of the Modi government), and it may primarily have sought to use NREGS to maintain stability, defend (international) competitiveness and facilitate the continuing exploitation of India's labourers, NREGS can still ease the process of labour's material reproduction and provide classes of labour with the breathing space required to organise and mobilise – so long as the inevitable counter-moves and strategies of the dominant class can be negotiated. By foregrounding the antagonistic nature of NREGS (and social policy more generally), a class-relational approach is well placed to explain the unevenness of social policy's intentions and outcomes as dominant and labouring classes unite and divide; as they enter periods of compromise or heightened antagonism with one another; and as processes of accumulation generate different forms and patterns of wage-labour, intra-capitalist competition, domination and labouring class organisation.

The central argument of this chapter has been that detailed analysis of class relations in its particular as well as its more general forms is required to understand where and why government interventions that favour labour more than capital in theory also do so in practice. Collective action has been shown to be an important part of this, and the next two chapters focus on labouring class organisation. Chapter 8 analyses the small labouring class social movement referred to in this chapter, and considers how larger movements might emerge. In the next chapter, though, attention falls on forms of collective action that undermine the organisation of classes of labour.

Notes

1 This is based on the per capita poverty-line figure of Rs. 902 per month for rural Karnataka as set by the Tendulkar poverty-line methodology for the given year (GoI PC 2014:28). For the NREGS wage figures, see *The Hindu* (2013).

2 Recent data indicates a drop-off in levels of implementation. Ministry of Rural Development data (reported by local officials) showed a 36 per cent drop in the number of persondays generated by NREGS between 2010–11 and 2011–12 (Usami and Rawal 2012:89).

3 Counter-evidence emphasises unevenness. For example, a study of *adivasi*-dominated parts of eastern Gujarat, where implementation levels have been low, found no noticeable decline in distress migration (Joshi 2012 cited in Kannan and Jain 2013b:69).

4 Farmers will often call labourers for work, either directly or through inter-mediaries. In the summer season, though, work is scarce and female labour-ers are often obliged to approach farmers for work. If NREGS is implemented during the summer season, then the extent to which it reduces personalised interactions will increase.

5 Real wage increases accelerated substantially (see Table 6.2). Of course, real wage acceleration is not being attributed to NREGS alone. For a more detailed discussion of real wage patterns over the last three decades, see Chavan and Bedamatta (2006), Singh and Srivastava (2005, 2006) and Usami (2011).

6 It has also been in evidence in the press (Drèze 2011:12–13).

7 Precise figures on the number of workdays are unobtainable. The correlation between the actual and officially recorded number of workdays noted on job-cards has become increasingly weak over time. Jobcard-holders who had not worked for several years had jobcards showing 100 workdays in the previ-ous twelve months. Nevertheless estimates of the number of paid workdays can be made by asking each member of the household how many days s/he had actually worked in a particular period. Such responses form the basis of Table 6.3.

8 Raichur district has more than twice as many members of the scheduled castes as Dharwad (Pattenden 2011a; 2011b:478; UNDP 2005).

9 Findings from 19 villages cannot be seen as representative of Karnataka as a whole. Pro-labour outcomes are more likely in the more developed coastal and *ghat* (hilly) belt of the state, and also in the somewhat more developed parts of the inland south (UNDP 2005). It is suggested, though, that the field-work findings are far from unusual in the inland north of the state in particu-lar – a region with a population of 24.6 million people (Government of India Census 2011).

10 Although implementation began in Dharwad in 2008, no works were imple-mented in the fieldwork villages until 2009.

11 Two hundred is double the stipulated maximum for each household. A num-ber of factors may explain this: (i) some households needed considerably more than the 100 days offered in order to meet their material needs; (ii) regulations were loosened (in practice rather than on paper) as there was considerable pressure from the Chief Executive Officer of the district at that time to increase the amount of NREGS persondays completed. She was later awarded for the performance of NREGS in the district.

12 NREGS works either upgrade private land, agriculture-related public assets like tanks, or village infrastructure.

13 Just as an inflationary spike had coincided with the first two years of NREGS, exaggerating its perceived link to rising wages, so an increase in demand for

    agricultural labour after a relatively good 2013 monsoon had exaggerated the impacts of the PDS expansion.

14 In Kamlapur, 44 per cent of households are landless as opposed to 31 per cent in Panchnagaram.

15 These male labourers performed an estimated 38.1 per cent of the total working days based on estimates of the amount of time each individual spent doing agricultural labour in each year. Female agricultural labourers worked on a greater number of days of the year.

16 The situation in some Raichur villages was worse, with some respondents not knowing what their cards had been used for since they had been taken by the GP six years previously.

17 His family had close historical ties to the larger landowning families in the village, and his appointment may have reflected dominant caste assumptions that he could be easily controlled.

7

The neoliberalisation of civil society: community-based organisations, contractor NGOs and class relations

It has been argued in this book (see Chapter 3) that the proliferation of civil society organisations (CSOs) in India since the 1990s represents a neoliberalisation of civil society. This is a general argument in that it relates the proliferation of CSOs to broader neoliberal policy that has sought to 'thicken' civil society while reducing the role of the state, and a more specific argument about its impacts on class relations in particular places. Rather than seeking a redistribution of power and resources towards classes of labour, such organisations tend to reproduce rather than challenge the status quo. According to this argument, non-governmental organisations (NGOs) become increasingly oriented around obtaining contracts from the state, while community-based organisations (CBOs, the most common form of CSO) tend to be organised across class lines, which makes them unlikely to seek redistribution of power and resources between social classes. Instead they tend to replicate neoliberal approaches to development by overlooking the central antagonism in society between capital and labour, and seeking to implement individualised interventions centred on microfinance and petty forms of 'entrepreneurship'. Interventions are usually focused on women who are made to 'feel responsible for their relative poverty, drawing [them] more tightly into patronage networks, and inculcating forms of economic discipline' (Corbridge *et al.* 2013:228).

This chapter analyses fieldwork data from Dharwad district in order to assess these claims. It begins by outlining the distribution of CSOs in the district before assessing NGO activities. It then analyses self-help groups (SHGs, the most common form of CBO) in two particular villages. Fieldwork for this chapter was primarily collected in the second half of the 2000s, but includes information from interactions with SHG members and NGO managers during subsequent field visits (most recently in late 2013). These found high levels of continuity (particularly with regard

Table 7.1 NGO activities, Dharwad

	Activities undertaken by 31 NGOs
Activities by NGOs	Manufacture of organic pesticides; crèche management; centre for victims of violence against women, legal aid for victims of violence against women; resolution of intra-family and inter-neighbour disputes (family counselling centres); homes for older people; child labour schools; training for income generating activities (livestock rearing, candle-making, noodle-making, pickle-making, petty trading, sewing); accountancy/book-keeping training; vermicomposting and organic farming training; adventure camps for youth groups; rainwater harvesting; skills development for the unemployed; signing up households for health insurance; campaign against human trafficking; rehabilitation of trafficked girls/women; selling life insurance; anti-arrack campaigns.
Activities by NGOs and government	SHG formation, microfinance and micro savings; watershed development (irrigation channels, tanks, farm ponds etc.); integrated pest management training; primary healthcare and management of primary health centres, antenatal healthcare, reproductive health programmes and immunisation drives; housing repairs and construction, construction of drinking-water towers and installation of drinking-water bores and taps; education grants for marginalised social groups; programme for elementary education for girls; provision of clothing; construction of toilets, construction of bus shelters; sponsoring IGAs (primarily dairy, animal husbandry); construction of school building; management of common property resources; resettlement and rehabilitation of those displaced by development projects; raising awareness about HIV and other STDs, cleanliness, child trafficking, dowry harassment, child marriages, women and child rights; rehabilitation of child labourers; collecting electricity bills; delivery of drinking water; yoga classes.

Source: fieldwork data.

to NGOs). The only significant change concerned the scale of SHG loans (discussed below). The chapter's focus, as in the book as a whole, is on how power and resources can be redistributed towards classes of labour. The chapter's central argument is that the neoliberalisation of civil society crowds out and undermines pro-labouring class organisation.

The forms taken by civil society vary according to the history of states and their distributions of power and resources. So, for example, Kerala's civil society is relatively politicised due to the historical strength of its labouring class (Heller 1995, 1999). Andhra Pradesh, on the other hand, has the largest number of SHGs of any Indian state and probably the greatest number of CBOs, in part because of the state government's proximity to neoliberal policy-makers in the early 2000s, and in part because of the way that CBOs have been used for party political ends (Chhotray 2011; Johnson *et al.* 2005; personal communication, David Picherit, November 2012). Similar variations are replicated at sub-state level. For example, Dharwad district has somewhat fewer labouring class organisations than parts of the north-east of the state (including Raichur), where there are greater concentrations of scheduled caste labourers (see Chapter 8).

Civil society and contractor NGOs in Dharwad

The district register of CSOs revealed a surge in Dharwad's NGO numbers since the year 2000.[1] Of the district's eighty-nine development-related NGOs,[2] only fourteen had been in operation prior to 1999.[3] Some 90 per cent of CBOs had been set up during the same period. Including CBOs, there were an estimated 6,000 development-related CSOs in Dharwad district among a population of around two million – approximately one for every seventy households. In the sub-district where the two main fieldwork villages are located, there were 1,669. Of these, 1,400 were SHGs, and more than 100 were other CBOs – mostly watershed development committees linked to the World Bank-funded Sujala Programme and Village Development Committees set up by the NGO World Vision. International organisations have contributed directly to CSO proliferation in the fieldwork area. By the early 2000s, the World Bank and Department for International Development had sponsored the formation of more than 4,000 SHGs and other CBOs in Karnataka as a whole, and several hundred in Dharwad district (as well as a dozen NGOs) (UNDP 2005:292).

While NGOs had long been given contracts for specific tasks such as running schools and training centres, and even though the bulk of development finance remained in state hands,[4] in the 2000s the contracting out of government activities to NGOs had gathered pace, partially due to pressures from international donors (interview with BAIF, 3 February 2007). NGOs are delegated such 'soft governance'-related tasks as awareness-raising, SHG formation and training (see Table 7.1), and sit on an array of committees, overseeing a variety of tasks from the allocation of grants to CBOs to monitoring police performance and child marriage.

During an interview with a representative of the Abdul Nazir Sab State Institute of Rural Development (Karnataka's most prominent government think tank on decentralisation) in late 2006, three concerns were raised about 'rural development sanghas' (associations). It was stated that they were dominated by better-off members of villages, that programmes intended to benefit the poor were primarily benefiting middling and wealthier village households and that NGOs were 'disappearing' on completion of their contracts. In other words, those controlling and benefiting from CSOs in rural Karnataka were primarily 'the better-off', while NGOs were becoming 'contractor NGOs'.

Of the fourteen development-related NGOs active in Dharwad in the 1990s, most were primarily focused on livelihood diversification and activities intended to improve the economic position of the poor (fieldwork interviews; see also Kamat 2002). Their logic was usually 'residual' in that they sought to 'fill gaps left by the state' and provide the poor with what they were lacking rather than facilitate more direct challenges to the status quo.

NGOs have since become more oriented towards local government contracts. Integrated Development Services – one of Dharwad's oldest NGOs – is a case in point. In the late 2000s it was primarily financed through local government institutions (LGIs) charged with implementing the World Bank's Sujala watershed programme. As well as growing links between older NGOs and LGIs, interviews with managers of a number of the newer NGOs indicated that they had been formed in order to secure contracts from local government. Prominent 'contractor' NGOs were found to be run by those who had previously operated on the fringes of the 'shadow state' as lower-level gatekeepers, and were now using the contacts they had developed to help them access local government contracts.

While a number of NGO managers were met in their offices and in one of the restaurants frequented by local government officials, a number of NGO offices were found to be locked up, or in some cases there was no longer any trace of the organisation at all. Without funding, these organisations become defunct, and hence a number of 'ghost NGOs' lurk on official records. In Panchnagaram, 'ghost' CBOs were identified that appeared to have been created on paper by officials from the appropriate line department in collaboration with one or two influential village members. For example, most health committee members did not know that their committee existed, and it appeared to have never met (see also Johnson *et al.* 2005: 954).

The number of 'contractor NGOs' (or 'briefcase' NGOs; Hearn 2007; Jenkins 2004) has grown, and now represent a substantial share of the rural development NGOs set up in or since the year 2000. They are distinguished from NGOs (often older organisations) that remain development-related in their outlook even though they are also jostling for government contracts. The latter organisations are labelled here as 'client' NGOs.

Of twenty-seven rural Dharwad NGOs visited in the late 2000s, eight were contractor NGOs and half of these were dormant or defunct. All were led by well-educated members of urban and rural dominant classes, including village gatekeepers. Some were formerly fringe members of the shadow state, and all had used connections to contractors or politicians to obtain contracts. Of the remainder, eleven were 'client' NGOs with strong links to local government, six were mostly funded directly by larger NGOs, and one was trying to defend members of classes of labour whose common property resources were being appropriated and operated in a neighbouring district despite being based in Dharwad.

In order to secure a local government contract, between 10 and 20 per cent of its value was routinely paid to officials including case workers, middle managers and department heads.[5] A failure to pay the correct amount, or to pay supplementary amounts (when further tranches of funding were released), can trigger a similar dynamic to that enacted between engineers and contractors in road-building (see Chapter 5). If there has been a shortfall in informal payments, the official assessing the work is likely to criticise the NGO and increase its costs, sometimes to the point of forcing withdrawal from the contract.[6] Conversely, if informal payments have been made, low-quality work may be endorsed. Members of more established Dharwad NGOs with relative autonomy from local government were highly critical of the process of awarding contracts, alleging that contracts were not awarded to the best NGOs, but to those with the best-placed political connections.[7] NGOs supporting the sitting MLA stood a greater chance of success.

Contracts on more prominent schemes,[8] which were subject to greater public scrutiny, were generally awarded to Dharwad's most respected NGOs.[9] One such NGO was working on the World Bank-funded Sujala watershed development programme in collaboration with the Department of Watershed Development (DWD), and was responsible for monitoring CBOs set up under the programme and for overseeing the selection and implementation of watershed works.

Once works were completed, a technical inspection was conducted by the DWD, following which payments were dispersed to farmers, workers and the NGO. The NGO found itself squeezed between the DWD officials and the dominant village members who tended to control the scheme's CBOs. The NGO met with resistance when it attempted to insist upon a more democratic decision-making process within the CBOs. When it tried to challenge informal moneylending practices in one particular village, influential individuals accused them of being 'Christian proselytisers'. The NGO's fieldworkers stated that there was an in-built procedural bias towards upgrading the land of larger families since it was easier to reach spending targets by working on larger landholdings. It also found that the decision to distribute labourers' wages via farmers resulted in delays and underpayment. Pro-labouring class outcomes were, then, often compromised by the prevailing power dynamics within the villages, and the Sujala programme seemed to be adding to existing inequalities.

NGOs became preoccupied with meeting the guidelines laid down by the government as part of their contracts, triggering claims that a concern with the quality of interventions had been supplanted by a check-list culture. For example, in relation to the microfinance-related Swarnajayanti Gram Swarozgar Yojana (Golden Jubilee Village Self-Employment Scheme, which grew out of the earlier Integrated Rural Development Programme), each NGO received Rs. 10,000 in the mid-2000s for each SHG they formed, which was released in four instalments. The first instalment was released after group formation, the second after the SHG opened a bank account, the third after it undertook income-generating activities (IGAs), and the fourth after IGA-related sales. This had fostered a narrow focus on a handful of members in order to activate disbursements, and had also led to false documentation of IGA activities (such as women posing with borrowed vegetables).

As well as meeting quotas on loan dispersal and forming federations of SHGs, the necessary criteria for accessing tranches of government funding included making statements about hygiene and HIV/AIDS, where the emphasis was on information dispersal rather than information retention. One NGO had stopped coming to Kamlapur village when groups opted not to pay them a service fee. Their only subsequent intervention had been to persuade/cajole two SHG group presidents to join the taluk-level SHG federation (for which the NGO is paid by the government). Both groups' involvement stopped after they had paid a membership fee and attended one meeting.

Rather than assessing impacts on the economic position of the labourers or on patriarchy, district-level Department of Women and Child Development (DWCD) meetings that evaluated SHGs revolved around quantitative concerns such as the numbers of groups formed, loans disbursed, bank linkages set up and buffaloes purchased (see also Goetz and Sen Gupta 1996:47, Kalpana 2005:5401; Sud 2003:4806).[10] NGO assessment criteria were similar, and poverty reduction was equated to mere group existence by most NGO managers as well as district-level government officials.[11]

At the time of the main fieldwork in the late 2000s, many anganwadi (government crèche) and NGO workers were not supervising SHGs because of the low payments they were being offered for doing so. Once group formation was completed, visits were limited to loan disbursement and collection, and to IGA training exercises for which a fee was sometimes charged. In some cases, then, poor villagers were asked to pay for NGO training programmes, meaning that the costs of some reputedly 'pro-poor' interventions had been displaced to the poor themselves. Elsewhere, crèche managers claimed that the NGO that hired them had asked them for an informal payment in order to secure their jobs (interview with crèche workers, March 2007).

While most NGOs in Dharwad have upward links into the state, they access their 'target populations' through village leaders (larger landholders, gram panchayat (GP) members, anganwadi workers and teachers), which may compromise their ability to channel resources to classes of labour. NGO directors said that it was preferable to bring village leaders onside because they facilitate interventions, and without their cooperation they may face obstruction and, at worst, exclusion from a village. One NGO manager claimed that gifts were given to 'the gram panchayat people' so that they could get on and do their work.[12] Similar claims were made by the regional director of a national agency responsible for dispersing funds to NGOs, who stated that NGOs came to 'agreements' with village leaders, as well as with officials responsible for dispersing funds.[13]

A further dimension of NGO interactions with the local state was that they sometimes duplicated each other's work (see Table 7.1). NGOs also appeared to undermine the workings of the local state to some degree. For example, a particular district councillor had plenty to say about construction-related works, but viewed education and social welfare sub-committees as a 'time-pass'. 'We have an NGO who take care of the poor. We do not need to do that. Whatever they need, the NGO will provide.'

Self-help groups and class relations

The chapter now turns to a more detailed analysis of CBOs, whose sheer numbers and presence in every village make them a highly significant form of CSO in contemporary India. In 2006, *The Hindu* newspaper claimed that loans totalling $2.5 billion had been distributed to India's thirty-one million SHG members, allegedly benefiting 50 per cent of the country's poor.[14] Formed by NGOs and anganwadi workers (government-supported village-level women and child development workers), and sponsored by state and national governments and international agencies, SHGs have become an integral part of policy prescriptions for tackling poverty.

Part of the broader international microfinance agenda that has involved tens of millions of people in over 100 countries (Arun and Hulme 2009:1), SHGs have occupied a prominent place in recent Government of India policy documents,[15] as well as those of the World Bank and other international agencies (e.g. UNDP 2005:281). The former viewed SHGs as part of a bottom-up process that, along with other CBOs, NGOs and LGIs, would reach the 'hard-core poor', in part by including them in policy processes (GoI PC 2006:49), thereby complementing the World Bank's (2007) goal of increasing the 'voice' of the poor and promoting public sector transparency and accountability. NGOs would facilitate the poor's access to public resources, and help overcome gender, caste and 'income'-based divisions by 'empowering the voiceless and giving visibility to the invisible' (UNDP 2005:279; see also World Bank 2001:110, 114).

International agencies, meanwhile, have described SHGs as 'the single most significant economic development strategy for women' (UNDP 2005:289–290), and as showing that with 'efforts at mobilisation and empowerment even the poorest women can manage their own resources well and benefit from economic opportunities', thereby promoting rural growth (World Bank 2006:xviii). What is more, such CBOs would be above societal and party politics (GoI PC 2006:44). In sum, SHGs have been widely seen as advancing the goals of economic development and poverty reduction by thickening civil society, expanding the poor's social capital, engendering development and complementing decentralised good governance with empowering participatory processes.

Karnataka has an above-average density of SHGs by national standards.[16] A range of public and private institutions are involved in SHG promotion, including NABARD (the National Bank for Agriculture and Rural Development), DWCD Dharwad, the Department of Agriculture, the World Bank, rural banks and a number of large and small NGOs. Of an estimated 7,200 SHGs in Dharwad district in late 2006, approximately 50 per cent had been formed by NGOs, 20 per cent by banks and 30 per cent by the DWCD.[17]

Detailed evidence from twenty-three state- and NGO-backed SHGs in two villages (Panchnagaram and Kamlapur) will form the core of what follows. Discussions were held with officeholders/members of nineteen groups. All had been formed during or since 1999, and 70 per cent had been formed during or since 2003. Fourteen had been initiated by NGOs and nine by government agencies (mostly the DWCD). By 2007, $29,625 had been disbursed to the groups from private and government sources, mostly from the government's Swarnajayanti Grameena Swarozgar Yojana (Golden Jubilee Village Self-Employment Scheme; henceforth SGSY). In 2007, fifteen of the twenty-three groups were either dormant or defunct.

The core data were collected from five SHGs (three in Kamlapur village and two in Panchnagaram village), which were selected to cover the key variables including NGO- and government-backed groups, the amount of finance groups had received, how long the groups had existed for (between eighteen months and eight years) and different levels of class/caste heterogeneity (one group was predominantly scheduled caste, one was entirely scheduled tribe, one was predominantly Muslim, one was predominantly dominant caste and the other had a broad mix of caste and religious affiliation). Four of the five groups selected for detailed analysis were dormant (a pattern not untypical of the district as a whole).[18]

Interviews, which focused on perceptions of and participation in SHGs, as well as on the use of loans, were conducted with all seventy-five members of the five SHGs in 2007. Around one-third of the respondents were subsequently asked about their participation in SHGs and levels of borrowing in late 2013. Further interviews were conducted with all four city-based NGOs that had sponsored groups in these villages, and eight additional Dharwad NGOs involved in SHG promotion. In the state sector, discussions were held with the hierarchy responsible for forming and supervising state-backed SHGs: the DWCD's Deputy Director and Programmes Director, the sub-district (taluk) level Child Development Project Officer (CDPO), circle supervisors (responsible for SHGs in around seven villages) and village-level anganwadi workers. State and bank officials charged with monitoring the overall progress of SHGs at district level were also interviewed, including the Zilla Panchayat (ZP or district council) officials responsible for implementing SGSY, and members of the panel that selects beneficiary groups.

SHGs, loans and class relations

SHGs' economic impacts will now be briefly outlined before their internal politics and broader political contexts are discussed. Despite claims made by DWCD officials and NGO workers that groups were homogeneous in

Table 7.2 Class profile of five Dharwad SHGs (N = 75)

Village	Sponsor	Dominant class	Labouring class
Kamlapur	DWCD	4	9
Kamlapur	DWCD	3	12
Panchnagaram	DWCD	7	13
Kamlapur	NGO	0	10
Panchnagaram	NGO	4	13
Total as %		24	76

Source: fieldwork data.

socio-economic terms, four of the five groups included members of the dominant class (see Table 7.2). Overall, dominant class women made up just under a quarter of group members.

The labouring class was more likely to take internal loans. Some 80 per cent of them took internal loans, as opposed to only 59 per cent of dominant class members. However, the latter received 75 per cent of the money. The labouring class borrowed smaller amounts, primarily for basic needs such as food, clothing and medicine. Many used small external loans (slightly larger amounts) for basic needs as well, while one or two used the money to pay off informal moneylenders. Dominant class members, on other hand, were more likely to use both internal loans and small external loans for investments in new assets, agricultural inputs and livestock and micro-enterprise. Some used them for marriage, jewellery and religious purposes, and one or two re-loaned their loans at higher rates of interest. While most labouring class households did not see sustained economic gains as a result of small external loans, a majority of dominant class households did (see Pattenden 2010 for a more detailed account).

In other words, SHGs increased inequality rather than diminishing it. This was most immediately apparent in groups with particularly marked internal socio-economic differences. One entirely scheduled tribe group in Panchnagaram included four dominant class households and thirteen labouring class ones. The latter in many cases worked in the fields of the former, and in some cases were indebted to them. When the group's NGO 'sponsor' transferred money intended as a small loan for each household, the dominant class group Vice-President kept the loans of a number of the labouring class members and bought a buffalo.

In 1999 and 2001, an NGO-backed SHG in Kamlapur accessed $6,000 (Rs. 250,000), or up to $600 per head, under the government's SGSY for the purpose of buying buffaloes. Although almost all members saw small to moderate profits in the short term, better-off members of the group were more likely to maintain profits in the longer term because most labouring class group members were unable to keep buffaloes during gaps in lactation as they could not afford to buy them fodder or take time out from wage-labour to graze them. In some cases, moneylenders were appropriating milk in lieu of 'interest' payments. In other words, like the smaller loans already discussed, these government-backed loans exacerbated inequalities.

Women from the poorest households, whose consistent inability to meet basic needs compromised the ability either to save or to repay small loans, were sometimes expelled from groups (see also CIDA 1997; Kalpana 2005:5401; Montgomery and Weiss 2005:6). The poorer the household, the greater were the pressures generated by the requirement to save. For example, Ningawa was a landless labourer with a sick husband, six children under the age of twelve and only one wage-earning child. She was forced out of her group by its President because of her inability to save or repay small loans. In another case, Shantawa, who was from one of the poorest households in Panchnagaram, had borrowed Rs. 4,000 from her own SHG and a further 6,000 from two other SHGs to meet the costs of her fourteen-year-old daughter's marriage – hastily arranged to protect her from her father's drunken assaults. Her husband was largely spending his wages on himself, and her wages as an agricultural labourer were very low. Interest on all three loans was mounting, but in the case of the loans from other groups, caste and kin ties bought her time (and a lower interest rate). In the case of her own group, pressure to repay mounted to an intolerable level. Ridiculed in public by the moneylending dominant class President, she and her husband repaid the amount by borrowing money from unofficial moneylenders at a higher rate of interest.[19] Shantawa was forced to take two of her other children out of school to earn a wage (one of whom was later kidnapped and disappeared following an encounter whilst a circular migrant), and was blamed by her husband for the mounting debts.

The core bases of extreme poverty, which are exploitative labour relations and usurious credit relations, and which are compounded by underemployment, health crises and intra-household inequalities, were reproduced by SHGs rather than challenged by them. As already noted, SHG sponsors appeared to be unconcerned by the unequal outcomes of their interventions. The consequence was the formation of groups with significant internal disparities, which were generally dominated by wealthier and more powerful households who cornered the bulk of material and political benefits.

While SHGs have reduced dependence on informal (and, in some of the fieldwork villages, sometimes violent) moneylenders, they at times operated like moneylenders themselves. Research conducted in late 2013 among a sample of the same households showed that the amounts loaned within groups had grown along with the size of the savings pool. Where in 2007 internal of loans of Rs. 2,000 had been commonplace, loans of between 6,000 and 20,000 had become more widespread. This meant that by late 2013 SHGs had made a more substantial dent in levels of informal moneylending than had been the case earlier. Informal moneylending was, though, still widespread, particularly in relation to larger amounts borrowed to meet the costs of health crises and weddings. As had been the case in 2007, some of the poorest women remained excluded from SHGs, some of the groups that had collapsed by 2007 remained defunct and inequalities remained in loan distribution. In other words, SHGs continued to reproduce or even exacerbate existing inequalities.

By late 2013, the number of SHGs had further increased. They were now significantly more likely to be sponsored by private sector organisations (including NGOs and microfinance institutions (MFIs)) than by the state. A handful of MFIs had become particularly prominent. The way these institutions operated varied markedly, and sometimes differed within the same institution. There were widespread reports of the employees of one particular high-profile MFI charging high interest rates and using intimidatory tactics to recover loans (see also Taylor 2011). In some cases, those working for MFIs and NGOs were increasing interest rates in order to supplement low wages. The NGOs themselves are often located in larger organisational chains, taking contracts from larger organisations to disburse credit and collect repayments.

Intra-SHG politics

As well as the bulk of officeholders (group Presidents and Vice-Presidents) being from better-off households, correlations were found in both villages between the socio-economic composition of groups and the distribution of power within them. In the groups that had greater levels of socio-economic equity, the influence of the group President was restricted, while group officers dominated SHGs with greater levels of internal inequality.

A disproportionate share of internal loans went to the officeholders' caste and kin fellows and party political allies. In a group presided over by a pro-BJP Maratha woman, over three-quarters of loans went to the

President and two of her relatives, and, although only one-third of the group were BJP supporters, in the GP election year 89 per cent of loans had gone to BJP supporters. In another group, 46 per cent of loans in the previous three years (2004–07) had been allocated to the two officeholders. In a third group, which had the largest number of labouring class members, 60 per cent of loans had been allocated to one of its wealthiest members who was trusted to repay promptly.

Officeholders and members of the dominant class were better informed about potential sources of external credit, IGAs and training opportunities due to their greater proximity to SHG sponsors. Only officeholders had invested in 'micro-enterprises' such as trading bangles and making pickle. Another dominant class group President had plans to use expected bank finance for an IGA. Her illiterate labouring class sister-in-law did not know about the expected finance, and it was said that she did not need to know as she would be unable to repay the loan anyway.

The groups were almost exclusively focused on loans. The majority of women stated that their groups had not provided them with information about government poverty reduction programmes, while initiatives to reduce the high illiteracy levels in the groups were for the most part unsustained box-ticking exercises. Issues like violence against women, access to government housing and employment programmes, women's education, reproductive health and (of course, given their multi-class composition) labour relations did not figure in group discussions.

The dominant class has no incentive to contribute to an improvement in the material conditions of the poor, or to arm them with greater knowledge of their rights. Such developments could have negative impacts on their ability to command a cheap labour force, or maintain their socio-political dominance over the village with all the material benefits that that helps to confer.

Gender relations

Iniquitous intra-household relations affect SHG outcomes. Men generally own all productive assets, control most household income, pool a smaller share of their wages for basic household needs than women, dominate official external interactions and enjoy the proximity of lifelong friends and relatives rather than in-laws and newer friends in the case of married women living patrilocally. In short, the socio-economic and socio-political scales tend to be firmly tipped towards men, although the degree to which they are varies. For example, the greater integration of labouring class women into labour markets can contribute to a stronger intra-household position than is the case for their dominant class counterparts, who are more restricted to the domestic sphere by issues of pride and status, as well as a general lack of necessity for them to earn wages. Equally, greater incorporation of women into the labour market increases work pressures, particularly if the division of labour in the domestic sphere remains largely unchanged (Da Corta and Venkateshwarlu 1999; Garikipati 2008, 2009; Kapadia 1995).

There was little evidence of SHGs or their sponsors seeking to challenge patriarchal relations. The deputy director of the DWCD (theoretically the most influential individual with regard to SHGs at district level) argued that patriarchy was challenged simply through the existence of SHGs. SHGs had empowered women, she argued, because women now left their homes, met bank officials and had some sense of financial matters.[20] An NGO director with four groups in Panchnagaram, meanwhile, did not regard patriarchy as an issue for his groups, stating in response to a question about gender-related issues that his organisation treated all people equally regardless of gender, caste or faith.[21]

Evidence from within SHGs indicates that impacts on gender relations have been limited (see also Garikipati 2008:2621–2633; Goetz and Sengupta 1996; Guérin and Palier 2005:345). Women's control over household finance had in most cases not increased. Women usually handed external and internal loans over to their husbands, although in some cases women took internal loans without their husbands' knowledge. In other words, insofar as intra-household financial control had altered, the gains for women were covert rather than overt, reflecting SHGs' limited capacity to 'engender development'. There was also considerable evidence that SHG membership placed new pressures on women – for example, the repayment of SHG loans was seen as the woman's responsibility (see above). This acted as a deterrent to the take-up of IGAs, as in the case of one dominant class respondent who expressed her desire to set up a provisions shop but feared the intra-household fallout should she fail.

Only one person from the five groups (a group President) was aware of a programme to support victims of domestic violence. Neither of the anganwadi workers in the fieldwork villages was clear about its details, although it was their responsibility to spread information about it. The Kamlapur anganwadi worker denied that domestic violence took place in her village,[22] a view that contradicted the testimony of several group members. Iniquitous intra-household control over financial resources and divisions of labour weakened women's ability to contest domestic violence – particularly for women whose capacity to work was restricted by caring for infants.

An NGO responsible for operating a safe-house for victims of violence against women as part of the government's Santhwana programme was not only unable to prosecute cases of violence against
labouring class women by dominant class men, it was unable to locate
such cases as, even if the victim's family knew about the programme
(itself unlikely), they would not dare to report the case for fear of a
backlash against their family.[23] Even in cases within more dominant
sections of the village, patriarchal constraints often came into play. As
a result, in the late 2000s the NGO was taking up an average of four
cases of rape and sexual harassment per year in an area with a population of over one million, underlining how potential linkages between
civil society organisations and women were being mediated by class
and gender relations.

SHGs and party politics

In the five groups where each member was interviewed, personal crises of the group President, in-fighting, and allegations of corruption lev-
elled against officeholders had all played a role in some cases of group
breakdown. Party politics or the interrelations between party politics and
labour relations, though, had played a role in the breakdown of all the
groups.

Kamlapur's most 'successful' SHG (in terms of accessing bank finance)
had been rendered inoperable within six months of the 2005 GP elections. The reason was not because of party political differences within
the group (all bar one were Congress supporters), but because the bulk
of the village's large landowners had supported the right-wing BJP in the
elections. Heavily defeated at the polls, they had decided to flex their
political muscle in the fields by barring Congress-supporting labourers. One of the group members had herself defeated the BJP candidate,
making the group an obvious target for retribution. With daily wages
hit and agreements over who should receive loans no longer possible,
morale plummeted and the group ceased to function. Another group,
which had also supported Congress, escaped retribution as its dominant
members were somewhat better-off and relatively free of village labour
relations.

Despite the rise of free voting (where members of the labouring class
choose whom to vote for rather than voting along the same lines as
their principal employer), labouring class women's continuing dependence on local landowners for wages compromised this socio-political
position. Relationships between SHGs and district-level institutions
were also politically mediated. For example, the wife of a long-standing

GP member (and prominent village gatekeeper) was the president of one of two groups to secure SGSY finance. Both groups were assisted by the then GP Secretary and by the President of the sub-district council, who put his weight behind their applications at the district council in exchange for the group members canvassing on his behalf at election time.

Even the distribution of interest payments within SHGs was influenced by party politics in some cases. In one group that had received SGSY finance, Congress supporters had repaid a greater proportion of their loans. When loan repayments were rescheduled, the group's pro-BJP president decided to charge all members equally for outstanding interest owed by the group as a whole, thereby disproportionately rewarding her political allies.

The extent of links to formal politics varied between the villages. Of eleven groups in Kamlapur, only three had officeholders who were immediate relatives of councillors. In more politicised Panchnagaram (see Chapter 5), six SHGs had officeholders who either had been GP members at the time of group formation, or were immediate relatives of someone who was. Three were immediate relatives of leading district and sub-district councillors.

Party political divisions were more prominent in Panchnagaram. One group, whose membership was characterised by tight caste and kinship homogeneity, had ground to a halt when a leading figure in the Congress party tried to buy the group's support. The group's vice-president was the mother-in-law of a leading figure in the opposing party, and a conflict between money and kinship/caste 'loyalty' broke the group up. Politics and labour relations played a role in SHGs in both villages, although if anything the influence of village-level politics was more pervasive in Panchnagaram.

SHGs are also influenced by district-level politics. Almost all SHG members in the fieldwork villages had been summoned to attend political rallies, mostly in support of the sitting MLA. Resources were also channelled towards SHGs in exchange for votes or active support in state assembly elections. According to one key informant, at the time of the 2004 election the MLA distributed Rs. 20,000–30,000 to Panchnagaram's village leaders and 6,000–7,000 to SHGs,[24] which made them part of a much broader interplay of processes of accumulation and distributions of power (see Chapter 5).

Anganwadi workers, along with others in the DWCD hierarchy and NGO workers, often act as political agents, calling members for rallies and helping politicians to manage their votebanks (see Chapter 5). Unsurprisingly, the selection of anganwadi workers had become a highly politicised process. In 2006, the number of anganwadi workers in Dharwad taluk was increased by 23 per cent. The additional forty-one anganwadi workers were selected by a committee that was dominated by the MLA,[25] who tried to ensure that appointees were sympathetic to his party and that the votebank role of SHGs was tilted in his favour.

The MLA, more generally, was influential in the appointment of senior rural development officials. Although the District Council (ZP) Committee that allocates SGSY funds to SHGs should be made up of ZP officials and NGO representatives, a fourth member was seen to be present on these 'grading' trips in February 2007 – the MLA's fixer in the Taluk Panchayat.[26] Also on the committee was an NGO initially described only two months before by the ZP's *then* new SGSY officer as 'taking government money and doing nothing'.[27] The junior official in question's initial enthusiasm about rural development had given way to a more 'pragmatic' approach and he now worked with the NGO. Shadow state practices were systemic within Dharwad, and it was significantly harder to resist these than to be complicit in them. The view (expressed in government planning documents and referred to above) that CBOs would be insulated from politics (of any description) appears to have been a little optimistic – as most normative liberal assumptions are.

Conclusion

The SHG explosion complements neoliberal discourse by emphasising self-reliance and community action, and fostering entrepreneurship and a low-cost private–public approach to social issues. What emerges are CBOs that maintain the status quo, or exacerbate inequality, and are linked to processes of accumulation – be they village-level lock-outs or district-level shows of strength for sitting or aspiring MLAs.

Like many NGOs in the fieldwork district, SHGs were formed and supervised by individuals focused on winning contracts, meeting targets or releasing 'tranches', and seemingly uninterested in the detail of how their activities impacted on the material and political conditions of the labouring class. That the SHGs emerge from and sit among class relations appears not to be taken into account. SHGs provide low-cost highly visible anti-poverty initiatives that complement the erosion of the state's role in development. They provide a relatively cheap way of managing poverty without affecting any fundamental shift in the distribution of political or economic resources. The latter process would be better served by the proliferation of organisations of the labouring class rather than 'community'-based ones that generally end up in the hands of the dominant. This is the central concern of the final chapter.

Notes

1 Records of the District Registrar, Mini Vidhan Soudha, Dharwad, accessed June–July 2007.
2 Identified using (i) official records, (ii) the snowball method (through which each NGO interviewed is asked to name others that it knows/works with), and (iii) the lists of NGOs under contract with the Zilla Panchayat and the Department of Women and Child Development (DWCD).
3 Development-related NGOs accounted for around one-third of the CSOs registered between 1999 and 2006. The remainder were mostly religious and education societies.
4 For example, the DWCD had allocated between 5 and 10 per cent of its budget to NGOs in 2006–07.
5 The information for this paragraph was provided by key informants who work in NGOs and have made payments to officials.
6 In at least one case (with regard to an NGO running a school for child labourers), the level of informal payments forced the NGO to withdraw.
7 Based on interviews with leading members of three of Dharwad's most established NGOs between March and July 2007.
8 Jala Nirmal Yojana, Sujala and Suvarna Gramodaya.
9 Respected means those NGOs that were consistently named by their peers as 'doing good work'. In Dharwad, this amounted to five NGOs.
10 Interviews with DWCD officials; minutes from district-level CDPOs meeting, May 2007.
11 Interviews with NGO directors.
12 Interview with NGO director, 8 June 2007.
13 Information based on an interview with the regional director of the national agency (CAPART) in June 2007.
14 Based on a conversion rate of Rs. 40 to $1.
15 Report of the Eleventh Plan Working Group on Poverty Elimination Programmes. Please note that this section draws on an article published in volume 37 of the *Journal of Peasant Studies*.
16 Approximately 1 per 160 people in March 2006 (NABARD 2006a:7), while the fieldwork district of Dharwad (with 5,134 bank-linked SHGs in 2006) falls below the state average of 8,331 per district (NABARD 2006a:33).
17 Interview with SH Patil, NABARD representative Dharwad District, 12 January 2007.
18 Based upon visits to ten additional villages in the district.
19 See also Kalpana (2005:5402).
20 Interview with Deputy Director of DWCD, May 2007.
21 Interview with DP, March 2007.
22 This implies that social acceptance of domestic violence is widespread, as the Ministry of Women and Child Development (2006:98) has indicated.
23 Interview with NGO worker, 19 January 2007.
24 Interview, 7 March 2007.
25 Interview with CDPO (sub-district-level DWCD officer), February 2007.

26 The ascription of the term 'fixer' to the individual in question is based on circumstantial evidence noted on twelve visits to the taluk panchayat (sub-district council) office between December 2006 and March 2007.
27 Interviews with junior district council officer in December 2006 and January and March 2007.

8

Organisations of labouring class women

In contrast to the neoliberal civil society organisations (CSOs) of the previous chapter, the focus here is on an organisation of labouring class scheduled caste female agricultural labourers in the fieldwork district of Raichur (Karnataka). The organisation, the Jagruthi Mahela Sanghathan (JMS), is made up of around 550 labouring class Madiga (scheduled caste) female labourers organised in thirty-five village-level associations (sanghas) in twenty-two villages across two sub-districts (Manvi and Sindhanur).

The chapter focuses primarily on three particular village-level associations, and poses three central questions. First, it seeks to understand why the organisation's strength varied across the different villages. This raises issues that have been discussed throughout the book. Variations in village-level class relations and differences in degrees of labouring class dependence on its village's dominant class, the ways in which class relations are mediated by local government institutions (LGIs), and the dynamics within the group and the social movement as a whole all loom large in the analysis.

The second question concerns the JMS's forms of organisation. These have taken three predominant forms: conscientisation, mobilisation and NGO-related livelihood diversification. It is argued here that the last of the three is problematic with regard to the broader goals of movements of the labouring class. JMS mobilisation has focused on gender- and caste-based forms of violence and discrimination, and, increasingly, on improving access to government poverty reduction programmes – most notably the National Rural Employment Guarantee Scheme (NREGS, discussed in Chapter 6), but also the Public Distribution System (PDS) and the National Rural Health Mission. Campaigns oriented around these public programmes are arguably where the JMS most directly takes up class-based issues. More direct contestation was made difficult by the prevailing balance of class forces. In challenging LGIs, the social movement faced a dominant class whose influence was relatively undiminished despite the growth of circular migration out of the area (see Chapter 4).

The JMS, then, is relatively typical of the type of organisation discussed in Chapter 3. It is a small-scale labouring class organisation oriented to a considerable degree around increasing the labouring class's share of public resources, and through that aiming to modify class relations in favour of the labouring class. It is also the only labouring class organisation across the three dozen villages where fieldwork was conducted.[1]

Having asked why organisational strength varies across villages and how the organisation works and in relation to what, the final question concerns the limitations of localised action and the possibilities for scaling up. To what extent has the JMS succeeded in countering gender- and caste-based forms of oppression, and to what extent has it been able to increase labouring class access to public resources and through that modify class relations?

All households in three sanghas were interviewed in 2007 (the three villages concerned are different from those focused on in Chapters 4 and 6). Some were re-interviewed in 2008, and additional field visits took place in 2010. Interviews were conducted with members of six other sanghas, key social movement activists at the organisation's headquarters and with a number of officials at each of the three levels of local government.

The chapter proceeds in three steps. It begins by outlining the story of the JMS during the 2000s. It then sketches the socio-economic and socio-political dynamics in the villages of the three sanghas. Finally, it analyses the experiences of the three sanghas before concluding.

Conscientisation and mobilisation: the emergence of a social movement

The JMS was formed in 2000 by four social activists from outside the district. They, along with five local staff and six sangha members who had become full-time sangha organisers, made up the core group until 2008. Considerable emphasis was placed on processes of conscientisation during this period. Members discussed forms of class-, caste- and gender-based domination and exploitation. There were weekly sangha meetings, monthly meetings of sangha leaders and annual meetings of all 550 sangha members. There were mobilisations against caste-based discrimination and inter-caste rape. In the early 2000s, sangha members marched in response to a rape incident, and in 2006 a large protest concerning the same issue took place in another of the villages where the JMS was organised. Awareness was raised about the provisions of poverty reduction programmes and the procedures for accessing them, and campaigns were organised to improve access to them. The JMS also organised training sessions focusing on methods for increasing soil fertility and agricultural productivity, and workshops on livelihood diversification activities such as jewellery-making.

By 2008 the four activists who had set up the JMS had moved back to the cities. The organisation had become less oriented around processes of conscientisation. Meetings had become less regular, interactions between village-level sanghas fewer, and discussions of forms of class-, caste- and gender-based forms of oppression less frequent. Instead the organisation was focusing more on livelihood diversification programmes. Having secured funding from a donor for the production of bio-fertilisers and pesticides, there was an interest in securing further grants.

The JMS's priorities shifted again when one of the founders began to be heavily involved with the organisation once more. Instead of livelihood diversification, the focus switched back to organising to improve access to government poverty reduction programmes. Access to support networks and links to similar organisations in the area were re-strengthened. The organisation had moved back towards its roots as a small social movement of labouring class women trying to challenge existing power dynamics and improve economic conditions. Unlike livelihood diversification, this triggered dominant class resistance. Some months into the launch of a campaign aimed at increasing access to NREGS, core activists complained of interference and attempts to buy them off.

The remainder of the chapter analyses the uneven outcomes in the different villages. The sanghas of Chandapur, Bagaldini and Saraswati Camp (formed in 2000, 2003 and 2006, respectively) were selected as a representative core sample on the basis of a number of different variables – levels of irrigation and landlessness, degrees of economic dependence on the village/integration into non-agricultural labour markets, levels of remoteness, distributions of castes, political contexts, levels of social movement organising and outcomes.

Class relations in the villages

Labourers in the three villages of Chandapur, Bagaldini and Saraswati Camp were underemployed – somewhat more so in the largely unirrigated villages of Chandapur and Bagaldini than in the almost fully irrigated Saraswati Camp. With little non-agricultural wage-labour available locally, some labourers from all three villages migrated periodically to the construction sites of Bengaluru (as did the labourers from the villages of nearby Shiva Camp and Jagalwara discussed in Chapter 4).

Circular migration among sangha members from irrigated Saraswati Camp was somewhat less common than it was from Chandapur, which was a predominantly dryland village (where a minority of sangha members had marginal landholdings) around half an hour's walk from the main road; and largely unirrigated Bagaldini, where the majority of sangha members owned some (mostly dry) land. Their economic activities were slightly more village-oriented than sangha members in Chandapur, and slightly more independent of the dominant class than those in Saraswati Camp.

As well as being almost fully irrigated, Saraswati Camp had the most unequal distribution of land, and was more polarised in caste terms. It was also the furthest of the three villages from the main road, and its labourers were somewhat more dependent on the dominant class in their village for wage-labour and informal loans. These factors translated into higher levels of domination than in the other villages (as was the case in nearby Shiva Camp; see Chapter 4), and higher levels of poverty (Pattenden 2011b).

In Saraswati Camp a number of girls had been taken out of school to look after siblings (and in 2008 no one had attended school past the age of fifteen), there was a high number of health problems and relatively poor housing conditions. Pesticide-spraying prompted nausea and faintness in some, the number of skin complaints was high, and the prevalence of intense physical work late into pregnancy increased gynaecological problems. Almost one-third of sangha households included someone who was disabled. For example, Ratna's son was born with a growth adjacent to his spine. She and her husband borrowed money from their employer to pay for an operation that went wrong and left the child paralysed. Under pressure to start repaying the loan, they took their elder daughter out of school so that the mother could return to work.

Interviews with all households in the three sanghas in 2007 and 2008 showed that almost all of them were unable to consistently access three meals per day, clothing and basic healthcare, while in Saraswati Camp most were *usually unable* to do so. For the sangha members in Saraswati Camp, better delivery of public programmes was clearly urgent. If NREGS had been implemented, then their incomes during the summer months when agricultural employment is at its lowest would have more than trebled.[2] Instead NREGS had barely been implemented at all, and most households at that time did not have access to the PDS. In other words, the steeper socio-economic and socio-political hierarchies in Saraswati Camp translated into the lowest levels of access to poverty reduction programmes.

Uneven outcomes across three women's sanghas

The variations in the strength of the three village-level sanghas, which reflected uneven levels of organisation, and differences in class relations, led to marked differences in outcomes from social movement activity. The stories of the three sanghas is outlined in this section, beginning with the least successful sangha in Saraswati Camp, and finishing with a discussion of how the notable socio-political gains made in Chandapur were undermined to a degree by a donor-funded livelihood diversification programme.

Saraswati Sangha

Saraswati Sangha, only eighteen months old at the time of the main field-work, was relatively distant from the social movement headquarters, and its links to core activists were largely confined to one or two sangha members. Consequently, processes of conscientisation had been largely absent, and levels of organisation limited.

With a weaker level of organisation and greater socio-economic and socio-political inequality, the sangha members in Saraswati Camp saw little or no change in their situation. Its members had never approached the GP and knew nothing about gram sabhas (village assemblies where decisions about development programmes were supposed to be reached democratically). Their awareness of government programmes was more limited, and their access to them remained notably worse than in Chandapur in particular. They were aware that resources were being appropriated by GP members and officials, but did not entertain the idea that they might be able to challenge them. Their GP was well known for particularly high levels of appropriation of public resources by its dominant members, and for its hostility to interference (to the point, allegedly, of threatening physical violence). It was one of the most systematically privatised public institutions in the area (a visit to which in late 2011 had caused consternation – not least because the more remote GP offices in this area often seemed to be closed).[3] This helped to maintain dependence on the dominant class, and restricted labourers' ability to take political action.

Bagaldini Sangha

In Bagaldini, proximity to core activists and levels of conscientisation were higher than in Saraswati Camp, but lower than in Chandapur. Politically inactive with regard to its GP until 2007, it had become more assertive and begun to confront its GP, demanding that it allocate housing grants and implement PDS and NREGS correctly. Complaints were made to the ration shop licensee about the sporadic provision of foodgrains, to the anganwadi worker for failing to feed children and to the auxiliary nurse and midwife for failing to visit homes.

The upsurge in political action in the summer of 2007 coincided with land upgrade work organised by the JMS. Sangha members' land had been cleared, deep-ploughed, bunded and fertilised. This provided a short-term boost in income (as farmers were paid wages to upgrade their land) and the promise of higher yields. It had even reduced seasonal migration to some degree, and marginally reduced economic dependence on the villlage's dominant class. Moreover, support for the women's sangha among their husbands, which had hitherto been grudging and partial, became widespread in the wake of actual material benefits.

There were other factors at play in the increased assertiveness of Bagaldini Sangha. The mobilisation that took place against inter-caste rape in 2006 had occurred in a neighbouring village, which had heightened the women's sense of their own strength and had created a degree of fear among the GP's dominant men. Furthermore, the sangha's leaders had been galvanised by participation in a week-long rally in Delhi, and a national conference on health rights in Bhopal.[4]

In late 2007 a collective demand for NREGS work had led to fifteen days of work for each household – double the number of days that had been provided until that point. An earlier claim had been met with threats, whereas on this occasion it was said that the new GP President feared the sangha. The slight gains in their socio-political position were helped by less marked levels of inequality in Bagaldini GP. Land distribution was less unequal in this predominantly dryland village than it was in Saraswati Camp, and the number of Madigas in the GP was relatively high.

Although at times the GP ceded ground to the sangha, at others it back-tracked, or responded to claims made by certain individuals in order to foster divisions. Often it was the more assertive women who saw some improvement in access to public services. Collective claims for NREGS work, meanwhile, had been weakened through small payments to certain individuals. No work had been done on the flood-prone dirt lanes of their hamlet, no toilets had been built and no housing subsidies or grants had been received for over five years despite the trebling of housing expenditure in that period, and in spite of widespread low-quality housing among members.

The Bagaldini members' increased levels of political activism had not significantly altered the balance of power in the GP. It was harder to reach over the heads of the GP to higher levels of government than it was in Chandapur (see below) because Sindhanur sub-district's balance of political power has generally been less well disposed to labouring class Madiga assertiveness than is the case in neighbouring Manvi sub-district. In other words, increased levels of conscientisation and slight increases in agricultural productivity had galvanised increased levels of organisation and the claims being made of the GP, but with dominant class counter-strategies and the broader aggregation of class relations against it, there was no emergence of sustained collective action to significantly increase classes of labour's share of political power and public resources.

Chandapur Sangha

Chandapur Sangha had the closest links to core JMS activists. It had been one of the first sanghas to be formed and was situated just three kilometres from the movement's headquarters. With stronger links to core activists, meetings were more frequent, levels of conscientisation were greater and the sense of a wider support network more marked.

Having known little about them in the year 2000, sangha members had become much more aware of the provisions of government development and poverty reduction programmes. Whereas before they had not dared to approach GP members (besides the one member from their own caste), let alone members of the district and sub-district council, by 2007 the sangha was actively trying to increase labouring class access to public resources and routinely making demands of the GP. It had also made direct representations to the district and sub-district councils.

The sangha had demanded that the GP organise a (mandatory) village assembly. It had insisted on the payment of correct wages on public works by tying up a junior engineer and getting the MLA to intervene on their behalf. It had complained to the GP about the poor drainage facilities in their hamlet, which was contributing to a high incidence of illness in the wet season. Initially rebuffed by the GP, they took a sample of stagnant water to the sub-district council, and were subsequently awarded a contract to rectify the problem.

On another occasion, the sangha demanded work under NREGS and responded to GP members' threat to use a JCB instead of manual labour by threatening to set the JCB on fire. Partially as a result of this, their sangha received more employment under NREGS (thirty-one days in the early years of the programme) than any other. The socio-political gains of these labouring class women were not restricted to the sphere of LGIs alone. The women no longer lowered their heads and covered their faces when they saw members of the dominant caste approaching, and women reported a reduction in domestic violence as they were now more likely to resist it collectively.

Campaigns in Chandapur were assisted to some degree by the fact that the village's MLA at the time (Chandapur lay in a different assembly constituency and a different sub-district to Bagaldini and Saraswati Camp) was more somewhat concerned with securing labouring class Madiga votes than his counterpart in the neighbouring constituency,[5] and Madigas tended to have a stronger presence at all three levels of local government.

The socio-political gains were assisted by socio-economic ones that reduced their dependence on wage-labour in the village (and through that on the dominant class in their village). Access to non-agricultural labour markets had increased from the late 1990s through circulation to Bengaluru, and in 2003 the JMS had set up a donor-funded micro-enterprise that focused on the collection, processing and sale of neem fertiliser. In 2007, this was increasing annual household incomes by around 30 per cent – predominantly in the lean summer months.

The production of neem fertiliser increased incomes, improved economic conditions to some extent, augmented degrees of economic independence and may initially have further heightened willingness to challenge dominant class control of the GP. Over time, though, Chandapur Sangha became increasingly concerned with its micro-enterprise, which drew it away from broader forms of political mobilisation and generated contradictions that cut against wider labouring class struggles.

As a petty capitalist operation, it got caught up in dynamics of competition and began to hire wage-labour. The sangha women withdrew from seed collection and paid others a wage to collect instead, while initial expansion of production began to be pegged back in time by larger-scale competition. Rather than prioritising mobilisation to increase all labourers' share of government resources and generate pro-labour changes in class relations, they were increasingly weighed down by the need to keep their micro-enterprise competitive.

This has implications for the capacity of an organisation like the JMS to scale up its political activities. When the JMS focused on processes of conscientisation, organisation and mobilisation of labourers around issues of collective concern, it was able to make some socio-political and socio-economic gains – albeit unevenly. Even caste- and gender-based forms of oppression were challenged to some degree. Where the JMS began to replicate the practices of project-oriented NGOs, though, it provided economic gains for a few and possibly even increased political 'space' in the short term, but ultimately cut against broad-based mobilisation.

Conclusion

At the outset, this book underlined the significance of labouring class organisation. The JMS may be small-scale, and in over a decade of

organising its socio-political and material impacts may have been relatively minor, but gains have nevertheless been made in an area where
social hierarchies are relatively steep. The JMS's larger mobilisations
were shows of strength, which helped to expand the political 'space'
of particular sanghas – as the story of the Bagaldini Sangha shows.
The strategies of campaigning at different levels of government, building connections with similar organisations elsewhere and linking to
broader fronts increased the movement's sense of its own strength,
gave it greater political purchase and acted as a deterrent to concerted
dominant class resistance. By broadening its strength and political
reach, it became more likely to be able to deepen its organisation in
places like Saraswati Camp, where levels of inequality currently make
collective labouring class action difficult. If economic independence
from the dominant class can be increased without generating contradictions within such movements, if the government channels more
public resources in the direction of the labouring class and if the collective strength of organisations of the labouring class are able to with-
stand the inevitable counter-moves of the dominant, then scaling up
becomes feasible and the chances of modifying class relations in favour
of the labouring class greater.

The type of collective action engaged in by the JMS is distinct from
that of the neoliberal CSOs discussed in Chapter 7, which offer popular participation 'without the inconveniences of contestational politics'
(Harriss 2001:9). It is distinct because these are organisations of the
labouring class that seek an improvement in the political and economic
position of the poor *relative to other social classes*, and which do iden-
tify the roots of poverty and social deprivation in class relations (Harriss
2001:9).

Notes

1 With the exception of one where a faction of the Dalit Sangharsh Samiti (DSS)
  had a presence. This chapter draws on an article published in volume 42 of
  Development and Change.
2 Calculated from data on household employment for a period of 9.5 weeks
  starting on 7 April 2008.
3 A group of people rapidly gathered, including one or two GP members and the
  'peon'. Even though the questions during what was only a brief visit were kept
  very general, it seemed to cause a degree of discomfort. Two individuals were
  overheard discussing (almost trying to reassure one another) whether it would
  be possible to find out about the goings on in the GP.
4 At a point when the vast majority of sangha members were aware that they
  were entitled to 100 days of NREGS work, only 14 per cent of forty non-sangha
  members in three different villages knew this.

5 The party political context became less favourable as a result of local government elections in 2010 and January 2011 when the BJP significantly
increased its share of seats. It won twenty-eight out of sixty seats in Manvi
and Sindhanur taluk panchayats (securing a majority in the former), having previously held no seats on either (http://164.100.80.20/zptpresults
/TalukTP.aspx?district=6&taluk=3; http://164.100.80.20/zptpresults/TalukTP
.aspx?district=6&taluk=5 (accessed 28 January 2011)).

9

Conclusion: poverty and class

This book has argued for a class-relational approach to labour, state and society in rural India. In doing so it has sought to contribute to 'analysis of the social conditions of classes of labour in global capitalism, and the challenges their diverse forms of fragmentation present' (Bernstein 2006:457). In contrast to 'residual' and some 'semi-relational' approaches to poverty, it has argued that analysis of class relations is central to understanding the conditions of classes of labour and the possibilities for pro-labouring class change.

Class relations have been analysed primarily in terms of changing forms of domination and exploitation, and the ways in which they are mediated by forms of collective action and the state. As the bases of classes of labour's reproduction and patterns of capitalist accumulation are modified, so too are the ways in which labour is controlled and is able to seek concessions from capital and the state. Differences have been shown between villages where classes of labour are integrated into non-agricultural labour markets as commuters to nearby cities, or as circular migrants to more distant ones. These differences relate in turn to where forms of accumulation remain primarily focused on agriculture, and where they have diversified into agribusiness, formal employment or state-linked forms of expanded reproduction.

Rather than a singular identity, class has been understood as a multifaceted one that is inflected by a variety of forms of difference such as gender and caste. The interplay between class, caste and gender relations has been illustrated through fieldwork material focused on actually existing class relations in a number of South Indian villages. The use of detailed longitudinal primary research material gathered from a range of sites has underlined the uneven forms and trajectories of class relations at a variety of levels.

Labour relations were found to vary in their form between the countryside and the city, across different villages and over time as processes of structural change are interwoven with class-based agency. In the more remote irrigated villages where agrarian capital used interlocking mechanisms to control labour, forms of class-based domination were more pronounced, poverty levels were at their highest and government poverty reduction programmes were subverted to the greatest extent. In villages that were closer to urban labour markets, the dominant class made greater use of its control over the distribution of public resources through local government institutions to reproduce its position.

State mediations of class relations tended to maintain or strengthen the position of the dominant class. Decentralisation had increased the role played by local government institutions in the implementation of development and poverty reduction programmes, but usually in ways that allowed the dominant class to shape programmes to their own ends. Higher-level state institutions were found to be largely populated by capitalists. In the north-west of Karnataka, strong links were found between the state assembly and agrarian capital, while MLAs from other parts of the state reflected prominent forms of accumulation in those locations – mining in Bellary, for example, and real estate in Bengaluru.

The preponderance of informal labour relations meant that labour was afforded relatively little state protection – something that reflected its often threadbare capacity, but also its concern with maximising capitalist accumulation and the international competitiveness of Indian capital. This allowed construction capital to build offices for multinational companies and luxury apartments for IT workers with a labour force that lived in crowded camps under blue plastic sheets. Elsewhere large-scale industrial capital found ways to avoid the costs of the formal sector by hiring labour through intermediaries and terminating contracts before the payment of social security became mandatory.

It was found that the proliferation of civil society organisations in rural India, and of community-based organisations in particular, often reflected neoliberal policy agendas. Unsurprisingly in villages with marked social hierarchies, community-based organisations tended to be dominated by the better-off. The most common form of community-based organisation, the self-help group, fostered individualised approaches to development in ways that tended to exacerbate levels of inequality rather than reduce them. They also undermined forms of pro-labouring class collective action by drawing labourers into processes that underpinned rather than challenged the status quo, and crowded out possibilities for organisations of the labouring class.

The reworking of class relations through forms of labour relations, collective organisation and state practices tended to favour capital, but was not without counter-movements. Even though the state tends to serve the interests of capital, its need to maintain stability and governments' desire for re-election create openings for pro-labouring class change. Universal poverty reduction programmes not only have the capacity to weaken dominant class gatekeepers'control over the distribution of public resources, but critically they can also loosen labouring class dependence on capital for its material reproduction. By doing so they provide labour with greater room for political manoeuvre and a common agenda to unite them across their many forms of fragmentation. The extraction of pro-labouring class gains from the state is, of course, vulnerable in its turn to the counter-moves of capital, as has been shown to be the case with regard to the National Rural Employment Guarantee Scheme (NREGS).

A robust Unorganised Workers Social Security Act might have been derailed by (among other things) capital's need to compete in the global marketplace. Stronger legislation centred on a national minimum wage and a social floor based on universal security provisions could, though, be pushed through in the future. The election of the BJP government in 2014 has pushed the state more firmly in the direction of capital for the time being, but it will be voted out of office sooner or later, and at that point coalitions similar to those that pushed NREGS into being could exert even greater pressure than they did in 2004 when the erstwhile former UPA government was seeking broader support.

To do so they would need classes of labour to be much more organised than they are today. Despite some signs of rising labouring class strength, labour in rural India remains relatively weak, fragmented in a variety of ways and largely restricted to small-scale forms of collective action focused on the state. Although small in scale, it was argued in this book that these forms of organisation can be part of the push for broader change. Class-conscious forms of collective action by a small labouring class women's social movement were able to extract some concessions both from the state through poverty reduction programmes, and more directly from the dominant class in terms of gender- and caste-based forms of oppression. By scaling up such organisations and linking them into broader fronts, the possibility emerges for an agenda of pro-labouring class change that is not restricted to social floors and an increased share of public resources for the labouring class, but that moves India in the direction of more fundamental change. On the way there, degrees of material deprivation, which remain high across much of India, would be less severe than they are today.

References

Aakella, K.V. and Kidambi, S. (2007), 'Social audits in Andhra Pradesh: a process in evolution', *Economic and Political Weekly* 42:47, 18–19.

Agarwala, R. (2013), *Informal Labour, Formal Politics and Dignified Discontent* (Cambridge: Cambridge University Press).

Aiyar, A., Sharma, V., Narayanan, K., Jain, N., Bhat, P., Mahendiran, S. and Jha, J. (2013), *Rashtriya Swasthya Bima Yojana [A Study in Karnataka]* (New Delhi, Cairo and Washington, DC: Global Development Network (GDN)).

Alkire, S., Roche, J. and Sumner, A. (2013), 'Where do the world's multidimensionally poor people live?', *Oxford Poverty and Human Development Initiative Working Paper 61* (Oxford: OPHI, QEH, University of Oxford).

Ambasta, P., Shankar, P. and Shah, M. (2008), 'Two years of NREGA: The road ahead', *Economic and Political Weekly* 43:8, 41–50.

Amsden, A. (1989), *Asia's Next Giant: South Korea and Late Industrialisation* (Oxford: Oxford University Press).

Ananthpur, K. (2007), 'Dynamics of local governance in Karnataka', *Economic and Political Weekly* 42:8, 667–673.

Andrees, B. and Belser, P. (eds) (2009), *Forced Labor: Coercion and Exploitation in the Private Economy* (Boulder, CO: Lynne Rienner).

Anon. (2009), 'A different route to justice: the Lalith Mehta murder case', *Economic and Political Weekly* 44:12.

Arellano-Lopez, S. and Petras, J. (1994), 'Non-governmental organizations and poverty alleviation in Bolivia', *Development and Change* 25, 555–568.

Arun, T. and Hulme, D. (2009), 'Introduction', in D. Hulme and T. Arun (eds), *Microfinance: A Reader* (London and New York: Routledge), 1–6.

Assadi, M. (1997), *Peasant Movement in Karnataka 1980–1994* (Delhi: Shipra).

Association for Democratic Reforms [ADR]. (2013), 'Analysis of financial, criminal and other details of newly elected MLAs in the Karnataka Assembly Elections, 2013', Association for Democratic Reforms. Online: http://adrindia.org/download/file/fid/2840.

Association for Democratic Reforms Karnataka Election Watch Committee. (2008), *Karnataka Election Watch 2008: Criminal and Financial Background of MLAs and Candidates – 2008 Assembly Elections* (Bangalore: Association for Democratic Reforms).

Athrady, A. (2013), 'Karnataka may get more projects before LS poll', *Deccan Herald*, 19 May.

Athreya, V., Djurfeldt, G. and Lindberg, S. (1987), 'Identification of agrarian classes: a methodological essay with empirical material from south India', *Journal of Peasant Studies* 14:2, 147–190.

Azam, M. (2012), 'The impact of Indian job guarantee scheme on labour market outcomes: evidence from a natural experiment', *Institute for the Study of Labor Discussion Paper 6548* (Bonn: IZA).

Bailey, F. (1963), *Politics and Social Change: Orissa in 1959* (Berkeley: University of California Press).

Banaji, J. (1994), 'The farmers' movement: a critique of conservative rural coalitions', *Journal of Peasant Studies* 21:3/4, 228–245.

Banaji, J. (2003), 'The fictions of free labour: contract, coercion and so-called unfree labour', *Historical Materialism* 11:3, 69–95.

Banaji, J. (2010), *Theory as History: Essays on Modes of Production and Exploitation* (Chicago, IL: Haymarket Books).

Bandyopadhyay, D. (2002), 'Panchayats in Karnataka: two steps back', *Economic and Political Weekly* 37:35, 3572–3577.

Bardhan, P. (1998), *The Political Economy of Development in India* (Oxford: Blackwell).

Bardhan, P. (2011), 'Our self-righteous civil society', *Economic and Political Weekly* 46:29, 16–18.

Barrientos, A. (2010), 'Should poverty researchers worry about inequality', Brooks World Poverty Institute Working Paper 118 (Manchester: BWPI, University of Manchester).

Basole, A. and Basu, D. (2011), 'Relations of production and modes of surplus extraction in India: Part I – agriculture', *Economic and Political Weekly* 46:14, 41–58.

Baviskar, B.S. (2009), 'Including the excluded: empowering the powerless through Panchayati Raj in Maharashtra', in B.S. Baviskar and G. Mathew (eds), *Inclusion and Exclusion in Local Governance: Field Studies from Rural India* (New Delhi: Sage).

Baviskar, B.S. and Mathew, G. (eds) (2009), *Inclusion and Exlcusion in Local Governance: Field Studies from Rural India* (New Delhi: Sage).

Benbabaali, D. (2013), 'Caste dominante et territoire en Inde du Sud: Migration et ascension sociale des Kamma d'Andhra côtier', Unpublished PhD thesis (Universite Paris Ouest Nanterre La Defense).

Berenschot, W. (2011), *Riot Politics: Hindu–Muslim Violence and the Indian State* (London: Hurst).

Berg, E., Bhattacharyya, S., Durgam, R. and Ramachandra, M. (2012), 'Can rural public wages affect agricultural wages? Evidence from India', *Centre for the Study of African Economies Working Paper WPS/2012-05* (Oxford: CSAE University of Oxford).

Bernstein, H. (1988), 'Capitalism and petty-bourgeois production: class relations and divisions of labour', *Journal of Peasant Studies* 15:2, 258–271.

Bernstein, H. (1992), 'Poverty and the poor', in H. Bernstein, B. Crow, H. Johnson and K.Y. Lee (eds), *Rural Livelihoods: Crises and Responses* (Oxford: Oxford University Press), 13–27.

Bernstein, H. (2006), 'Is there an agrarian question in the twenty-first century?', *Canadian Journal of Development Studies* 27:4, 449–460.

Bernstein, H. (2007), 'Capital and labour from centre to margins', paper presented at the *Living on the Margins* conference, Stellenbosch, 26–28 March.

Bernstein, H. (2008), 'Agrarian change in a globalising world: (final) farewells to the peasantry?', paper presented at the Journal of Agrarian Change *Workshop on Agrarian Change: Lineages and Prospects*, SOAS, University of London, 1–2 May.

Bernstein, H. (2010), *Class Dynamics of Agrarian Change* (Halifax: Fernwood and Sterling, VA: Kumarian).

Besley, T., Pandey, R. and Rao, V. (2007), 'Political economy of panchayats in south India', *Economic and Political Weekly* 42:8, 661–666.

Bhalla, S. (1999), 'Liberalisation, rural labour markets and the mobilisation of farm workers: the Haryana story in an all-India context', *Journal of Peasant Studies* 26:2/3, 25–70.

Bharadwaj, K. (1985), 'A view on commercialisation in Indian agriculture and the development of capitalism', *Journal of Peasant Studies* 12:4, 7–25.

Bhatia, B. and Drèze, J. (2006), 'Employment Guarantee in Jharkhand: ground realities', *Economic and Political Weekly* 41:29, 3198–3202.

Bhowmik, S. (2008), 'Labour organisations in the twenty-first century', *Indian Journal of Labour Economics* 51:4, 959–968.

Bourdieu, P. (1986), 'The forms of capital', in J.G. Richardson (ed.), *Handbook of Theory and Research for the Sociology of Education* (New York: Greenwood), 83–95.

Bourdieu, P. (1990), *The Logic of Practice* (Cambridge: Polity).

Bracking, S. (2003), 'The political economy of chronic poverty', *Institute for Development Policy and Management, University of Manchester Working Paper 23* (Manchester: IDPM, University of Manchester).

Brass, P. (1997), *Theft of an Idol: Text and Context in the Representation of Collective Violence* (Princeton, NJ: Princeton University Press).

Brass, T. (1990), 'Class struggle and the deproletarianisation of agricultural labour in Haryana (India)', *Journal of Peasant Studies* 18:1, 36–65.

Breen, R. (2005), 'Foundations of a neo-Weberian class analysis', in E.O. Wright (ed.), *Approaches to Class Analysis* (Cambridge: Cambridge University Press).

Breman, J. (1974), *Patronage and Exploitation: Changing Agrarian Relations in South Gujarat, India* (Berkeley: University of California Press).

Breman, J. (1985), *Of Peasants, Migrants and Paupers: Rural Labour Circulation and Capitalist Production in West India* (Oxford: Clarendon Press and Delhi: Oxford University Press.

Breman, J. (1990), '"Even dogs are better off": the ongoing battle between capital and labour in the cane-fields of Gujarat', *Journal of Peasant Studies* 17:4, 546–608.

Breman, J. (1996), *Footloose Labour: Working in India's Informal Economy* (Cambridge: Cambridge University Press).

Breman, J. (1999), 'The study of industrial labour in post-colonial India: the informal sector – a concluding review', in J. Parry, J. Breman and K. Kapadia (eds), *The Worlds of Indian Industrial Labour* (New Delhi, Thousand Oaks and London: Sage).

Breman, J. (2007a), *The Poverty Regime in Village India: Half a Century of Work and Life at the Bottom of the Rural Economy in South Gujarat* (New Delhi: Oxford University Press).

Breman, J. (2007b), *Labour Bondage in West India: From Past to Present* (New Delhi: Oxford University Press).

Breman, J. and Guérin, I. (2009), 'Introduction: of bondage old and new', in J. Breman, I. Guérin and A. Prakash (eds), *India's Workforce: Of Bondage Old and New* (Oxford: Oxford University Press).

Breman, J., Guérin, I. and Prakash, A. (2009), *India's Workforce: Of Bondage Old and New* (Oxford: Oxford University Press).

Breman, J. and Kannan, K.P. (2013), 'Introduction: unto the last?', in K.P. Kannan and J. Breman (eds), *The Long Road to Social Security* (New Delhi: Oxford University Press).

Business Standard. (2014), 'Rajasthan Assembly passes labour law changes', *Business Standard*, 1 August. Online: www.business-standard.com/article/economy-policy /rajasthan-assembly-passes-four-labour-reform-bills-114073101662_1.html.

Byres, T. (1981), 'The new technology, class formation and class action in the Indian countryside', *Journal of Peasant Studies* 8:4, 405–454.

Camfield, L. (2012), 'Resilience and well-being among urban Ethiopian children: what role do social resources and competencies play?', *Social Indicators Research* 107, 393–410.

Cammack, P. (2002), 'Attacking the poor', *New Left Review* 13, 125–134.

Cammack, P. (2003), 'What the World Bank means by poverty reduction', paper presented at Chronic Poverty Research Centre Conference *Staying Poor: Chronic Poverty and Development Policy*. Online: www.chronicpoverty .org/publications/details/what-the-world-bank-means-by-poverty-reduction (accessed 4 July 2013).

Campling, L. (2014), 'Debating modes of production and forms of exploitation: introduction to the symposium on Jairus Banaji's Theory as History', *Historical Materialism* 21:4, 3–10.

CIDA [Canada International Development Agency]. (1997), 'The role of microcredit in poverty reduction and promoting gender equity: a discussion paper' (Quebec: CIDA).

Carswell, G. and De Neve, G. (2013), 'From field to factory: tracing transformations in bonded labour in the Tiruppur region, Tamil Nadu', *Economy and Society* 42:3, 430–454.

Carswell, G. and De Neve, G. (2014), 'MGNREGA in Tamil Nadu: a tale of success and transformation', *Journal of Agrarian Change* 14:4, 564–585.

Chambers, R. (1983), *Rural Development: Putting the Last First* (London: Longman).

Chandhoke, N. (1995), *State and Civil Society: Explorations in Political Theory* (New Delhi: Sage).

Chandhoke, N. (2003), 'The "civil" and the "political" in civil society', in C. Elliot (ed.), *Civil Society and Democracy: A Reader* (New Delhi: Oxford University Press).

Chandhoke, N. (2012), 'Whatever has happened to civil society?', *Economic and Political Weekly* 47:23, 39–45.

Chandrasekhar, C.P. (2007), 'The progress of "reform" and the retrogression of agriculture', *Macroscan*. Online: www.macroscan.org/anl/apr07/pdf/Agriculture.pdf (accessed 25 April 2007).

Chandrasekhar, C.P. and Ghosh, J. (2006), 'Employment trends: the latest trends', *Macroscan*. Online: www.macroscan.org/fet/nov06/fet171106Employment_Growth.htm (accessed 17 November 2006).

Chandrasekhar, C.P. and Ghosh, J. (2007), 'Self-employment as opportunity or challenge?', *Macroscan*. Online: www.macroscan.org/fet/nov06/fet171106Employment_Growth.htm (accessed 30 March 2007).

Chandrashekhar, L. (2009), 'Caste, party and democratic decentralisation in Karnataka', in B.S. Aviskar and G. Mathew (eds), *Inclusion and Exclusion in Local Governance: Field Studies from Rural India* (New Delhi: Sage).

Chatterjee, P. (2004), *The Politics of the Governed: Reflections on Popular Politics in Most of the World* (New Delhi: Permanent Black).

Chavan, P. and Bedamatta, R. (2006), 'Trends in agricultural wages in India', *Economic and Political Weekly* 41:38, 4041–4051.

Chibber, V. (2003), *Locked in Place: State-building and Late Industrialization in India* (Princeton, NJ: Princeton University Press and New Dehi: Tulika).

Chibber, V. (2013), *Postcolonial Theory and the Specter of Capital* (London and New York: Verso).

Chhotray, V. (2011), *The Anti-Politics Machine in India: State, Decentralization and Participatory Watershed Development* (London: Anthem).

Chopra, D. (2011), 'Interactions of "power" in the making and shaping of social policy', *Contemporary South Asia* 19:2, 153–171.

Chopra, D. (2014), 'The Indian case: towards a rights-based welfare state?', in G. Koehler and D. Chopra (eds), *Development and Welfare Policy in South Asia* (London and New York: Routledge).

Chopra, D. and te Lintelo, D. (2011), 'Democratic governance for social justice: the politics of social protection', *IDS Bulletin* 42:6, 10–12.

Coelho, K. and Venkat, T. (2009), 'The politics of civil society: neighbourhood associationism in Chennai', *Economic and Political Weekly* 44:26/27, 358–367.

Corbridge, S. and Harriss, J. (2000), *Reinventing India: Liberalisation, Hindu Nationalism and Popular Democracy* (Cambridge: Polity).

Corbridge, S., Harriss, J. and Jeffrey, C. (2013), *India Today: Economy, Politics and Society* (Cambridge and Malden, MA: Polity).

Corbridge, S., Williams, G., Srivastava, M. and Veron, R. (2005), *Seeing the State: Governance and Governmentality in India* (Cambridge: Cambridge University Press).

Crook, R. and Manor, J. (1998), *Democracy and Decentralization in South Asia and West Africa: Participation, Accountability and Performance* (Cambridge: Cambridge University Press).

Crook, R. and Sverisson, A. (1999), 'To what extent can decentralised forms of government enhance the development of pro-poor policies and improve poverty-alleviation outcomes?', Background Paper for the *World Development Report* 2000. Online: http://siteresources.worldbank.org/INTPOVERTY/Resources/WDR/DfiD-Project-Papers/crook.pdf.

Da Corta, L. and Venkateshwarlu, D. (1999), 'Unfree relations and the feminisation of agricultural Labour in Andhra Pradesh 1970–1995', *Journal of Peasant Studies* 26:2/3, 71–139.

Damle, C. (1993), *Land Reforms and Changing Agrarian Relations* (Jaipur and New Delhi: Rawat Publications).

Damodaran, H. (2008), *India's New Capitalists: Caste, Business, and Industry in a Modern Nation* (Basingstoke: Palgrave Macmillan).

Das, R. (2011), 'Reconceptualizing capitalism: forms of subsumption of labor, class struggle, and uneven development', *Review of Radical Political Economics* 20:10, 1–23.

Davis, M. (2001), *Late Victorian Holocausts: El Nino Famines and the Making of the Third World* (London and New York: Verso).

Deccan Herald. (2013a), 'Cabinet rejigs rice for Re 1 per kilo scheme', *Deccan Herald*, 13 June.

Deccan Herald. (2013b), 'Siddu cracks whip for graft-free governance', *Deccan Herald*, 18 June.

de Haan, A. (1989), '"Social exclusion": an alternative concept for the study of deprivation?', *IDS Bulletin* 29:1, 10–19.

De Neve, G. (2005), *The Everyday Politics of Labour: Working Lives in India's Informal Economy* (Delhi: Social Science Press).

De Neve, G. (forthcoming), 'Predatory property: urban land acquisition, housing and class formation in a south Indian city', *Journal of South Asian Development*.

Deshingkar, P. and Akter, S. (2009), 'Migration and human development in India', Working Paper (New York: UNDP).

Deshingkar, P. and Farrington, J. (2009), *Circular Migration and Multilocal Livelihood Strategies in Rural India* (Delhi: Oxford University Press).

Devereux, S., McGregor, A. and Sabates-Wheeler, R. (2011), 'Introduction: social protection for social justice', *IDS Bulletin* 42:6, 1–9.

Devereux, S. and Sabates-Wheeler, R. (2004), 'Transformative social protection', *IDS Working Paper 232* (Brighton: Institute of Development Studies).

Devereux, S. and Sabates-Wheeler, R. (2007), 'Debating social protection', *IDS Bulletin* 38:3, 1–7.

Djurfeldt, G., Athreya, V., Jayakumar, N., Lindberg, S., Rajagopal, A. and Vidyasagar, R. (2008), 'Agrarian change and social mobility in Tamil Nadu', *Economic and Political Weekly* 43:45, 50–61.

Drèze, J. (2011), 'Employment guarantee and the right to work', in R. Khera (ed.), *The Battle for Employment Guarantee* (New Delhi: Oxford University Press).

Drèze, J. and Khera, R. (2009), 'The battle for employment guarantee', *Frontline*, 3 January.

Drèze, J. and Sen, A. (2013), *An Uncertain Glory: India and Its Contradictions* (London: Allen Lane).

Edward, P. and Olsen, W. (2006), 'Paradigms and reality in micro-finance: the Indian case' *Perspectives on Global Development and Technology* 5:1/2, 31–54.

Economic Times. (2013), 'Agriculture's share in GDP declines to 13.7 per cent in 2012–13', *Economic Times*, 30 August. Online: http://articles.economictimes .indiatimes.com/2013-08-30/news/41618996_1_gdp-foodgrains-allied -sectors (accessed 16 August 2014).

The Economist. (2013a), 'Memento Modi', *The Economist*, 24 January.

The Economist. (2013b), 'Memento Modi', *The Economist*, 13 April.

The Economist. (2013c), 'Steamroller', *The Economist*, 13 April.

Elliot, C. (2011), 'Moving from clientelist politics toward a welfare regime: evidence from the 2009 assembly election in Andhra Pradesh', *Commonwealth and Comparative Politics* 49:1, 48–79.

Engberg-Pedersen, L. and Rovnborg, H. (2010), 'Conceptualisations of poverty', *Danish Institute for International Studies Report 2010:01* (Copenhagen: DIIS).

Epstein, T.S. (1973), *South India – Yesterday, Today and Tomorrow: Mysore Villages Revisited* (London: Macmillan).

Epstein, T.S., Suryanarayana, A.P. and Thimmegowda, T. (1998), *Village Voices: Forty Years of Rural Transformation in South India* (New Delhi: Sage).

Escobar, A. (1995), *Encountering Development: The Making and Unmaking of the Third World* (Princeton, NJ: Princeton University Press).

Esping-Andersen, G. (1990), *The Three Worlds of Welfare Capitalism* (Princeton, NJ: Princeton University Press).

Evans, P. (1995), *Embedded Autonomy: States and Industrial Transformation* (Princeton, NJ: Princeton University Press).

Evans, P., Rueschemeyer, D. and Skocpol, T. (1985), 'On the road toward a more adequate understanding of the state', in P. Evans, D. Rueschemeyer and T. Skocpol (eds), *Bringing the State Back in* (Cambridge: Cambridge University Press).

Frankel, F. (2004), *India's Political Economy 1947–1977: The Gradual Revolution* (New Delhi: Oxford University Press).

Fuller, C. and Harriss, J. (2001), 'For an anthropology of the Indian state', in C. Fuller and V. Benei (eds), *The Everyday State and Society in Modern India* (London: Hurst).

Garikipati, S. (2008), 'Agricultural wage work, seasonal migration and the widening gender gap: evidence from a semi-arid region of Andhra Pradesh', *European Journal of Development Research* 20:4, 629–648.

Garikipati, S. (2009), 'Landless but not assetless: female agricultural labour on the road to better status, evidence from India', *Journal of Peasant Studies* 36:3, 517–545.

Gerry, C. (1978), 'Petty production and capitalist production in Dakar: the crisis of the self—employed', *World Development* 6:9/10, 1147–1160.

Ghosh, J. (2010), 'The unnatural coupling: food and global finance', *Journal of Agrarian Change* 10:1, 72–86.

Ghosh, J. (2011a), 'Dealing with "the poor"', *Development and Change* 42:3, 849–858.

Ghosh, J. (2011b), 'Is the MNREGS affecting rural wages?', *Macroscan*, 4 February. Online: www.macroscan.com/cur/feb11/cur040211MNREGS.htm.

Gibbon, P. and Neocosmos, M. (1985), 'Some problems in the political economy of "African Socialism"', in H. Bernstein and B.K. Campbell (eds), *Contradictions of Accumulation in Africa: Studies in Economy and State* (Beverly Hills, CA: Sage).

Gill, S.S., Singh, S. and Brar, J.S. (2013), 'Functioning of NREGS in a prosperous state: a study in Punjab', in K.P. Kannan and J. Breman (eds), *The Long Road to Social Security: Assessing the Implementation of National Social Security Initiatives for the Working Poor in India* (New Delhi: Oxford University Press).

Gledhill, J. (2001), 'Disappearing the poor? A critique of the new wisdoms of social democracy in an age of globalisation', *Urban Anthropology and Studies of Cultural Systems and World Economic Development* 30:2/3, 123–156.

Goetz, A.-M. and Jenkins, R. (1999), 'Accounts and accountability: theoretical implications of the right-to-information movement in India', *Third World Quarterly* 20:3, 603–622.

Goetz, A.M. and Sen Gupta, R. (1996), 'Who takes the credit? Gender, power and control over loan use in rural credit programs in Bangladesh', *World Development* 24:1, 45–63.

Gooptu, N. and Harriss-White, B. (2001), 'Mapping India's world of unorganised labour', *Socialist Register* 37. Online: http://socialistregister.com/index.php/srv/article/view/5757#.VcKFsWctDIU.

Gough, I., Mcallister, G. and Camfield, L. (2006), 'Wellbeing in developing countries: conceptual foundations of the WeD programme', *WeD Programme Working Paper 19* (ESRC Working Group on Wellbeing in Developing Countries). Online: www.welldev.org.uk/research/workingpaperpdf/wed19.pdf (accessed 29 May 2014).

Gough, K. (1981), *Rural Society in South-East India* (Cambridge: Cambridge University Press).

Government of India Census. (2011), 'Districts of Karnataka'. Online: www.census2011.co.in/census/state/districtlist/karnataka.html   (accessed   1 November 2014).

Government of India, Central Statistics Office (Industrial Statistics Wing), MOSPI [GoI CSO]. (2014), *Annual Survey of Industry 2011–12* (Kolkata: CSO).

GoI LB [Government of India, Labour Bureau]. (2010), 'Wage rates in rural India 2008–09', (Shimla and Chandigarh: Labour Bureau). Online: http://labourbureau.nic.in/Wage_Rates_Rural_India_2008_09.pdf   (accessed   21 July 2014).

GoI LB [Government of India, Labour Bureau]. (2012), 'Wage rates in rural India 2010–11', (Shimla and Chandigarh: Labour Bureau). Online: http://labourbureau.nic.in/Wage_Rates_2010_11_New.pdf (accessed 21 July 2014).

GoI LB [Government of India, Labour Bureau]. (2013), 'Wage rates in rural India December 2013' (Shimla and Chandigarh: Labour Bureau). Online: http://labourbureau.nic.in/WRRI_DEC_2013.pdf (accessed 21 July 2014).

GoI LB [Government of India, Labour Bureau]. (2014), 'Wage rates in rural India 2012–13' (Shimla and Chandigarh: Labour Bureau).

GoI LB [Government of India, Labour Bureau]. (n.d.(a)), 'Wage rates in rural India 2006–7' (Shimla and Chandigarh: Labour Bureau). Online: http://labourbureau.nic.in/WR%202k6-7%20Table%208%20(a).htm (accessed 21 July 2014).

GoI LB [Government of India, Labour Bureau]. (n.d.(b)), 'Consumer price index for agricultural labourers' (Shimla and Chandigarh: Labour Bureau). Online: http://labourbureau.nic.in/indtab.html (accessed 11 July 2014).

GoI MoF [Government of India, Ministry of Finance]. (2014), *Economic Survey 2013–2014* (New Delhi: Ministry of Finance). Online: http://indiabudget.nic.in/es2013-14/echap-13.pdf (accessed 6 August 2014).

Government of India, Ministry of Finance (Department of Economic Affairs, Economic Division). (n.d.), 'Mid-year economic analysis 2014–2015' (New Delhi: Ministry of Finance).

GoI MOSPI [Government of India, Ministry of Statistics and Programme Implementation]. (2012), Annual Report (New Delhi: MOSPI).

GoI MOSPI [Government of India, Ministry of Statistics and Programme Implementation]. (n.d.), 'Consumer price indices warehouse: general index, Karnataka' (New Delhi: MOSPI), http://164.100.34.62:8080/CPIIndex/TimeSeries.aspx, accessed 21 July 2014.

GoI MWCD [Government of India, Ministry of Women and Child Development]. (2006), *Report of the Working Group on Empowerment of Women for the 11th Plan* (New Delhi: Ministry of Women and Child Development).

GoI NSSO [Government of India, National Sample Survey Organisation, Ministry of Statistics and Programme Implementation] (2008), 'Employment and unemployment situation in India, NSS 62nd Round, July 2005–June 2006' (New Delhi: NSSO).

GoI NSSO [Government of India, National Sample Survey Office, Ministry of Statistics and Programme Indicators]. (2013), 'Key indicators of employment and unemployment in India 2011–12' (New Delhi: NSSO).

GoI NSSO [Government of India, National Sample Survey Organisation, Ministry of Statistics and Programme Implementation]. (2014), 'Employment and unemployment situation in India, NSS 68th round, July 2011–June 2012' (New Delhi: NSSO).

GoI NSO [Government of India, National Statistical Office]. (2001) (Ministry of Statistics and Programme Indicators), 'Employment and Unemployment Conditions among Social Groups, Report 469', NSS 55th Round July 1999–June 2000 (New Delhi: MOSPI).

GoI NSO [Government of India, National Statistical Office, Ministry of Statistics and Programme Indicators]. (2007), 'Key indicators of employment and unemployment in India 2005–06' (New Delhi: National Sample Survey Organisation [NSSO]).

GoI NSO [Government of India, National Statistical Office, Ministry of Statistics and Programme Indicators]. (2009), 'Key indicators of employment and unemployment in India 2007 08' (New Delhi: NSSO).

GoI NSO [Government of India, National Statistical Office, Ministry of Statistics and Programme Indicators]. (2011), 'Key indicators of employment and unemployment in India 2009–10' (New Delhi: NSSO).

GoI NSO [Government of India, National Statistical Office, Ministry of Statistics and Programme Indicators]. (2012), 'Employment and unemployment situation among social groups in India', NSS 66th round July 2009–June 2010, Report 543 (New Delhi: NSSO).

GoI PC [Government of India, Planning Commission]. (2006), 'Report of the Eleventh Plan Working Group on Poverty Elimination Programmes' (New Delhi: Planning Commission).

GoI PC [Government of India, Planning Commission]. (2007), 'Report of the Steering Committee on Micro-Finance and Poverty Alleviation for the Eleventh Five-Year Plan' (New Delhi: Planning Commission).

GoI PC [Government of India, Planning Commission]. (2009), 'Report of the Expert Group to Review the Methodology for Estimation of Poverty' (New Delhi: Planning Commission).

GoI PC [Government of India, Planning Commission]. (2011), 'Report of the Working Group on the National Rural Health Mission (NRHM) for the Twelfth Five Year Plan (2012–2017)' (New Delhi: Planning Commission).

GoI PC [Government of India, Planning Commission]. (2012), 'Press note on poverty estimates, 2009–2010' (New Delhi: Planning Commission).

GoI PC [Government of India, Planning Commission]. (2013), 'Press note on poverty estimates, 2011–2012' (New Delhi: Planning Commission).

GoI PC [Government of India, Planning Commission]. (2014a), 'Report of the Expert Group to Review the Methodology for Measurement of Poverty' (New Delhi: Planning Commission).

GoI PC [Government of India, Planning Commission]. (2014b), 'Sectoral breakup of employment and value added per worker (93–94, 99–00, 04–05)' (New Delhi: Planning Commission). Online: http://planningcommission.nic .in/data/datatable/0306/table%20118.pdf (accessed 17 August 2014).

Government of India, Press Information Bureau, Ministry of Rural Development. (2010), 'Recommendations of the N.C. Saxena Committee', 6 December 2010 (New Delhi: Ministry of Rural Development).

Government of Karnataka. (1989), *Karnataka State Gazetteer* (Bangalore: Government of Karnataka).

Government of Karnataka. (n.d.), *Buildings and Other Construction Workers Act* (Kaushila Bhavan, Bangalore: Government of Karnataka).

Government of Karnataka, Buildings and Other Construction Workers Welfare Board. (2010), Document showing the lists of benefits available to beneficiaries, handed to author by Welfare Board officials on 14 June 2010 (Koushalya Bhavan, Banerghatta Road, Bangalore).

Government of Karnataka, Buildings and Other Construction Workers Welfare Board. (n.d.), Kannada document showing implementation of the BOCWA, handed to author by Welfare Board officials on 14 June 2010 (Koushalya Bhavan, Banergatta Road, Bangalore).

Government of Karnataka Lokayukta. (2011), *Report on the Reference Made by the Government under Section 7(2-A) of the Karnataka Lokayukta Act, 1984 (Part-II)* (27 July 2011) (Bangalore: Government of Karnataka Lokayukta).

Gramsci, A. (1971), *Selections from the Prison Notebooks* (London: Lawrence and Wishart).

Guérin, I. (2013), 'Bonded labour, agrarian changes and capitalism: emerging patterns in South India', *Journal of Agrarian Change* 13:3, 405–423.

Guérin, I., Bhukhut, A., Marius-Gnanou, K. and Venkatasubramanian, G. (2009b), 'Neo-bondage, seasonal migration, and job brokers: cane cutters in Tamil Nadu', in J. Breman, I. Guérin and A. Prakash (eds), *India's Unfree Workforce: Of Bondage Old and New* (Delhi: Oxford University Press), 233–258.

Guérin, I. and Palier, J. (eds) (2005), *Microfinance Challenges: Empowerment or Disempowerment of the Poor?* (Pondichery: French Institute of Pondichery).

Guérin, I., Roesch, M., Venkatasubramanian, G. and Kumar, S. (2011), 'The social meaning of over-indebtedness and creditworthiness in the context of poor rural South Indian households (Tamil Nadu)' (Nogent-sur-Marne: Rural Microfinance and Employment Project).

Guérin, I., Subramanian, P., Venkatasubramanian, G. and Michiels, S. (2012), 'Ambiguities and paradoxes of the decent work deficit: bonded migrants in Tamil Nadu', *Global Labour Journal* 3:1, 118–142.

Guérin, I. with Venkatasubramanian, G. (2009a), 'Corridors of migration and dependence: brick kiln moulders in Tamil Nadu', in J. Breman, I. Guérin and A. Prakash (eds), *India's Unfree Workforce: Of Bondage Old and New* (Delhi: Oxford University Press), 170–197.

Gupta, A. (1998), *Postcolonial Developments: Agriculture in the Making of Modern India* (Durham, NC and London: Duke University Press).

Hanlon, J., Barrientos, A. and Hulme, D. (2010), *Just Give Money to the Poor: The Development Revolution from the Global South* (Sterling, VA: Kumarian Press).

Hard News (n.d.) 'Who killed Lalith Mehta and Kameshwar Yadav?' Online: www.hardnewsmedia.com/2008/07/2264 (accessed 21 July 2014).

Harriss, J. (1982), *Capitalism and Peasant Farming: Agrarian Structure and Ideology in Northern Tamil Nadu* (Bombay: Oxford University Press).

Harriss, J. (1992), 'Does the depressor still work? Agrarian structure and development in India: a review of evidence and argument', *Journal of Peasant Studies* 19:2, 189–227.

Harriss, J. (1999), 'Comparing political regimes across Indian states: a preliminary essay', *Economic and Political Weekly* 34:48, 3367–3377.

Harriss, J. (2001), *Depoliticizing Development: The World Bank and Social Capital* (New Delhi: Leftword).

Harriss, J. (2005), 'Political participation, representation and the urban poor findings from research in Delhi', *Economic and Political Weekly* 40:11, 1041–1054.

Harriss, J. (2006), 'Middle-class activism and the politics of the informal working class', *Critical Asian Studies* 38:4, 445–465.

Harriss, J. (2007a), 'Bringing politics back into poverty analysis: why understanding social relations matters more for policy on chronic poverty than measurement', *CPRC Working Paper 77* (Manchester: Chronic Poverty Research Centre).

Harriss, J. (2007b), 'Antinomies of empowerment: observations of civil society, politics and urban governance in India', *Economic and Political Weekly* 42:26, 2716–2724.

Harriss, J. (2012), 'Reflections on caste and class, hierarchy and dominance', *Seminar*. Online: www.india-seminar.com/2012/633.htm (accessed 14 November 2014).

Harriss, J. (2013), 'Does landlordism still matter? Reflections on agrarian change in India', *Journal of Agrarian Change* 13:3, 351–364.

Harriss, J., Jeyaranjan, J. and Nagaraj, K. (2010), 'Land, labour and caste politics in rural Tamil Nadu in the twentieth century: Iruvelpatu (1916–2008)', *Economic and Political Weekly* 45:31, 47–61.

Harriss, J., Stokke, K. and Tornquist, O. (eds) (2004), *Politicising Democracy: The New Local Politics of Democratisation* (Basingstoke: Palgrave Macmillan).

Harriss-White, B. (1990), 'The intrafamily distribution of hunger in South Asia', in J. Drèze, A. Sen and A. Hussain (eds), *The Political Economy of Hunger: Selected Essays* (Oxford: Clarendon Press).

Harriss-White, B. (1996), *A Political Economy of Agricultural Markets in South India: Masters of the Countryside* (New Delhi, Thousand Oaks and London: Sage).

Harriss-White, B. (2003), *India Working: Essays on Society and Economy* (Cambridge: Cambridge University Press).

Harriss-White, B. (2005), 'Poverty and capitalism', *Queen Elizabeth Hall Working Paper No.134* (Oxford: QEH, University of Oxford).

Harriss-White, B. (2008), *Rural Commercial Capital: Agricultural Markets in West Bengal* (New Delhi: Oxford University Press).

Harriss-White, B. (2010), 'Work and wellbeing in informal economies: the regulative roles of institutions of identity and the state', *World Development* 38:2, 170–183.

Harriss-White, B. (2014), 'Labour and petty production', *Development and Change* 45:5, 981–1000.

Hart, G. (1986), *Power, Labour and Livelihood: Processes of Change in Rural Java* (Berkeley, Los Angeles and London: University of California Press).

Harvey, D. (2004), 'The "new" imperialism', *Socialist Register* 40, 63–87.

Hearn, J. (2007), 'African NGOs: the new compradors?', *Development and Change* 38:6, 1095–1110.

Heller, P. (1995), 'From class struggle to class compromise: redistribution and growth in a South Indian state', *Journal of Development Studies* 31:5, 645–672.

Heller, P. (1999), *The Labor of Development: Workers and the Transformation of Capitalism in Kerala, India* (Ithaca, NY: Cornell University Press).

Heller, P., Harilal, K. and Chaudhuri, S. (2007), 'Building local democracy: evaluating the impact of decentralization in Kerala, India', *World Development* 35:4, 626–648.

Herring, R. and Agarwala, R. (2006), 'Restoring agency to class: puzzles from the subcontinent', *Critical Asian Studies* 38:4, 323–356.

Herring, R. and Edwards, R. (1983), 'Guaranteeing employment to the rural poor: social functions and class interests in the employment guarantee scheme in Western India', *World Development* 11:7, 575–592.

Heyer, J. (2012), 'Labour standards and social policy: a South Indian case study', *Global Labour Journal* 3:1, 91–117.

Hickey, S. (2010), 'The government of chronic poverty: from exclusion to citizenship?', *Journal of Development Studies* 46:7, 1139–1155.

Hickey, S. and Bracking, S. (2005), 'Exploring the politics of chronic poverty: from representation to a politics of justice?', *World Development* 33:6, 851–865.

Hickey, S. and Du Toit, A. (2007), 'Adverse incorporation, social exclusion and chronic poverty', *CPRC Working Paper 81* (Manchester: Chronic Poverty Research Centre).

Himanshu. (2007), 'Recent trends in poverty and inequality: some preliminary results', *Economic and Political Weekly* 42:6, 497–508.

Himanshu. (2008a), 'Social sector: continuation of past priorities', *Economic and Political Weekly* 43:15, 29–32.

Himanshu. (2008b), 'What are these new poverty estimates and what do they imply?', *Economic and Political Weekly* 43:43, 38–43.

Himanshu. (2008c), 'Towards new poverty lines', *Economic and Political Weekly* 45:1, 38–48.

Himanshu. (2011), 'Employment trends in India: a re-examination', *Economic and Political Weekly* 46:37, 43–59.

Himanshu and Sen, A. (2011), 'Why not a universal food security legislation?', *Economic and Political Weekly* 46:12, 38–47.

The Hindu. (2013), 'For 97 "bonded labourers" in Athani taluk, freedom continues to be a distant dream', *The Hindu*, 24 March.

The Hindu. (2014a), 'Congress fails to impress in Karnataka', *The Hindu*, 24 May.

The Hindu. (2014b), 'UPA flagship scheme to be rejigged', *The Hindu*, 1 June.

The Hindu. (2014c), 'Village plans focus of revamped MGNREGS', *The Hindu*, 1 June.

The Hindu. (2014d), 'CITU slams Centre's labour law amendments', *The Hindu*, 16 September.

Houtzager, P., Gurza Lavalle, A. and Acharya, A. (2007), 'Associations and the exercise of citizenship in new democracies: evidence from Sao Paulo and Mexico City', *IDS Working Paper 285* (Brighton: Institute of Development Studies).

Hulme, D. and Arun, T. (2009), *Microfinance: A Reader* (London and New York: Routledge).

Hulme, D. and Shepherd, A. (2003), 'Conceptualising chronic poverty', *World Development* 31:3, 403–423.

Inbanathan, A. and Gopalappa, D. (2002), 'Fixers, patronage, "fixing" and local governance in Karnataka', *Working Paper 112* (Bangalore: Institute for Social and Economic Change).

Indian Express. (2014a), 'Rajasthan shows way in labour reforms', *Indian Express*, 8 June. Online: http://indianexpress.com/article/india/india-others/rajasthan-shows-way-in-labour-reforms (accessed 11 September 2014).

Indian Express. (2014b), 'Key labour reforms get central push', *Indian Express*, 31 July. Online: http://indianexpress.com/article/india/india-others/key-labour-reforms-get-central-push (accessed 11 September 2014).

International Institute for Population Sciences and Macro International. (2000), *National Family Health Survey (NFHS-2) 1998–99: India* (Mumbai: International Institute for Population Studies).

International Institute for Population Sciences and Macro International. (2007), *National Family Health Survey (NFHS-3), 2005–06: India, Volume I* (Mumbai: International Institute for Population Studies).

International Labour Organisation. (n.d.), 'Data on strikes of 10+ workers 1980–2008', Table 9a. Online: http://laboursta.ilo.org (accessed 8 August 2014).

Iyer, A. (2005), 'Gender, caste, class, and health care access: experiences of rural households in Koppal District, Karnataka', *Research Report* (Trivandrum: Achutha Menon Centre for Health Science Studies, Sree Chitra Tirunal Institute for Medical Sciences and Technology Medical College).

Iyer, G. (2004), *Distressed Migrant Labour in India: Key Human Rights Issues* (New Delhi: Kanishka).

Jankimow, T. (2014), '"Breaking the backbone of farmers": contestations in a rural employment guarantee programme', *Journal of Peasant Studies* 41:2, 263–281.

Jeffrey, C. (2000), 'Democratisation without representation? The power and political strategies of a rural elite in North India'. *Political Geography* 19, 1013–1036.

Jeffrey, C. and Lerche, J. (2000), 'Stating the difference: state, discourse and class reproduction in Uttar Pradesh, India', *Development and Change* 31:4, 857–878.

Jenkins, R. (1999), *Democratic Politics and Economic Reform in India* (Cambridge: Cambridge University Press).

Jenkins, R. (2004), *Regional Reflections: Comparing Politics Across India's States* (Oxford: Oxford University Press).

Jha, P. (2004), 'Continuity and change: some observations on the landscape of agricultural labourers in North Bihar, India', *Journal of Agrarian Change* 4:4, 509–531.

Jodhka, S. (1994), 'Agrarian changes and attached labour: emerging patterns in Haryana agriculture', *Economic and Political Weekly* 29:39, A102–116.

Johnson, C., Deshingkar, P. and Start, D. (2005), 'Grounding the state: devolution and development in India's Panchayats', *Journal of Development Studies* 41:6, 937–970.

Judge, P. (2011), 'An ambiguous actor: "people" in the movement', *Economic and Political Weekly* 46:46, 19–22.

Kadekodi, G., Kanbur, R. and Rao, V. (2007), 'Governance and the "Karnataka Model of Development"', *Economic and Political Weekly* 42:8, 649–652.

Kalpana, K. (2005), 'Shifting trajectories in microfinance discourse', *Economic and Political Weekly* 40:51, 5400–5409.

Kamat, S. (2002), *Development Hegemony: NGOs and the State in India* (New Delhi: Oxford University Press).

Kamat, S. (2004), 'The privatization of public interest: theorizing NGO discourse in a neoliberal era', *Review of International Political Economy* 11:1, 155–176.

Kamath, L. and Vijayabaskar, M. (2009), 'Limits and possibilities of middle class associations as urban collective actors', *Economic and Political Weekly* 44:26/27, 368–375.

Kannan, K.P. (2012), 'How inclusive is inclusive growth in India', *Indian Journal of Labour Economics* 55:1, 31–35.

Kannan, K.P. and Breman, J. (eds) (2013), *The Long Road to Social Security: Assessing the Implementation of National Social Security Initiatives for the Working Poor in India* (New Delhi: Oxford University Press).

Kannan, K.P. and Jagajeevan, N. (2013), 'Beneficiary as agency: role of women's agency and the Panchayat in implementing NREGA – a study in Kerala', in K.P. Kannan and J. Breman (eds), *The Long Road to Social Security: Assessing the Implementation of National Social Security Initiatives for the Working Poor in India* (New Delhi: Oxford University Press).

Kannan, K.P. and Jain, V. (2013a), 'National health insurance for the poor: a review of the implementation of RSBY', in K.P. Kannan and J. Breman (eds), *The Long Road to Social Security: Assessing the Implementation of National Social Security Initiatives for the Working Poor in India* (New Delhi: Oxford University Press).

Kannan, K.P. and Jain, V. (2013b), 'Historic initiative, limited by design and implementation: a national overview of the implementation of NREGA', in K.P. Kannan and J. Breman (eds), *The Long Road to Social Security: Assessing the Implementation of National Social Security Initiatives for the Working Poor in India* (New Delhi: Oxford University Press).

Kapadia, K. (1993), 'Mutuality and competition: female landless labour and wage rates in Tamil Nadu', *Journal of Peasant Studies* 20:20, 296–316.

Kapadia, K. (1995), *Siva and Her Sisters: Gender, Caste and Class in Rural South India* (Boulder, CO: Westview Press).

Khan, M. (2005), 'Markets, states and democracy: patron–client networks and the case for democracy in developing countries', *Democratization* 12:5, 705–725.

Khera, R. (ed.) (2011), *The Battle for Employment Guarantee* (New Delhi: Oxford University Press).

Khera, R. and Nayak, N. (2008), 'Women workers and perceptions of the National Rural Employment Guarantee Act', *Economic and Political Weekly* 44:43, 49–57.

Khera, R. and Nayak, N. (2011), 'Women workers and perceptions of the NREGA', in R. Khera (ed.), *The Battle for Employment Guarantee* (New Delhi: Oxford University Press).

Koehler, H. (2011), 'Transformative social protection: reflections on South Asian policy experiences', *IDS Bulletin* 42:6, 96–103.

Kohli, A. (1987), *The State and Poverty in India* (Cambridge: Cambridge University Press).

Kohli, A. (2011), *Poverty amid Plenty in the New India* (Cambridge: Cambridge University Press).

Krishna, A. (2003), *Active Social Capital: Tracing the Roots of Development and Democracy* (New Delhi: Oxford University Press).

Krishna, A., Kapila, M., Porwal, M. and Singh, V. (2005), 'Why growth is not enough: household poverty dynamics in Northeast Gujarat, India', *Journal of Development Studies* 41:7, 1163–1192.

Krishna, A., Lumonya, D., Markiewicz, M., Mugumya, F., Kafuko, A. and Wegoye, J. (2006), 'Escaping poverty and becoming poor in 36 villages of Central and Western Uganda', *Journal of Development Studies* 42:2, 346–370.

Kumbhar, R.K. (2013), 'Structural legacy, inefficacy and weakening social securities: a study of NREGS in a Panchayat in Odisha', in K.P. Kannan and J. Breman (eds), *The Long Road to Social Security: Assessing the Implementation of National Social Security Initiatives for the Working Poor in India* (New Delhi: Oxford University Press).

Kunnath, G. (2009), 'Smouldering Dalit fires in Bihar, India', *Dialectical Anthropology* 33, 309–325.

Laclau, E. and Mouffe, C. (1985), *Hegemony and Socialist Strategy: Towards a Radical Democratic Politics* (London and New York: Verso).

Lange, S. (2008), 'The depoliticisation of development and the democratisation of politics in Tanzania', *Journal of Development Studies* 44:8, 1122–1144.

Lerche, J. (1995), 'Is bonded labour a bound category? Reconceptualising agrarian conflict in India', *Journal of Peasant Studies* 22:3, 484–515.

Lerche, J. (1999), 'Politics of the poor: agricultural labourers and political transformations in Uttar Pradesh', *Journal of Peasant Studies* 26:2/3, 182–241.

Lerche, J. (2003), 'Hamlet, village and region: caste and class differences between low-caste mobilization between East and West Uttar Pradesh', in R. Jeffery and J. Lerche (eds), *Social and Political Change in Uttar Pradesh: European Perspectives* (New Delhi: Manohar), 181–198.

Lerche, J. (2007), 'A global alliance against forced labour? Unfree labour, neo-liberal globalisation and the International Labour Organisation', *Journal of Agrarian Change* 7:4, 424–452.

Lerche, J. (2010), 'From "rural labour" to "classes of labour": class fragmentation, caste and class struggle at the bottom of the Indian labour hierarchy', in

B. Harriss-White and J. Heyer (eds), *The Comparative Political Economy of Development: Africa and South Asia* (London: Routledge).

Lerche, J. (2011), 'Review essay: agarian crisis and agrarian questions in India', *Journal of Agrarian Change* 11:1, 104–118.

Lerche, J. (2012), 'Labour regulations and labour standards in India: Decent work?', *Global Labour Journal* 3:1, 16–39.

Lerche, J. (2013), 'The agrarian question in neoliberal India: Agrarian transition bypassed?', *Journal of Agrarian Change* 13:3, 382–404.

Lerche, J. (2014), 'Regional patterns of agrarian accumulation in India', draft paper for the *Tenth Anniversary Conference of the Foundation for Agrarian Studies*, Kochi, 9–12 January 2014.

Lerche, J., Shah, A. and Harriss-White, B. (2013), 'Introduction: agrarian politics and left politics in India', *Journal of Agrarian Change* 13:3, 337–350.

Levien, M. (2011), 'The land question: special economic zones and the political economy of dispossession in India', *Journal of Peasant Studies* 39:3/4, 933–969.

Lewis, D. and Mosse, D. (eds) (2006), *Development Brokers and Translators: The Ethnography of Aid and Agencies* (Bloomfield, CT: Kumarian Press).

Lieten, G. and Srivastava, R. (1999), *Unequal Partners: Power Relations, Devolution and Development in Uttar Pradesh* (New Delhi: Sage).

Lieten, K. and Breman, J. (2002), 'A pro-poor development project in rural Pakistan: An academic analysis and a non-intervention', *Journal of Agrarian Change* 2:3, 331–355.

Locke, C. and Lloyd-Sherlock, P. (2011), 'Qualitative life course methodologies: critical reflections from development studies', *Development and Change* 42:5, 1131–1152.

Ludden, D. (2005), *Early Capitalism and Local History in South India* (Delhi: Oxford University Press).

Manor, J. (1989), 'Karnataka: caste, class, dominance and politics in a cohesive society', in F. Frankel and M. Rao (eds), *Dominance and State Power in Modern India: Decline of a Social Order, Volume 1* (New Delhi: Oxford University Press).

Manor, J. (1998), *The Political Economy of Democratic Decentralization* (Washington, DC: World Bank).

Manor, J. (2004a), 'Towel over armpit: small-time political "fixers" in India's states', in A. Varshney (ed.), *India and the Politics of Developing Countries: Essays in Memory of Myron Wiener* (New Delhi: Sage).

Manor, J. (2004b), 'Explaining political trajectories in Andhra Pradesh and Karnataka', in R. Jenkins (ed.), *Regional Reflections: Comparing Politics across India's States* (Oxford: Oxford University Press).

Manor, J. (2007), 'Change in Karnataka over the last generation: villages and the wider context', *Economic and Political Weekly* 42:8, 653–660.

Manor, J. (2010), 'What do they know of India who only India know? The uses of comparative politics', *Commonwealth and Comparative Politics* 48:4, 505–516.

Manor, J. (2012), 'Accommodation and conflict', *Seminar*, May. Online: www.india-seminar.com/2012/633.htm (accessed 12 December 2014).

Martin, N. (2014), 'The dark side of political society: patronage and the reproduction of social inequality', *Journal of Agrarian Change* 13:4, 419–434.

Marx, K. (1973), *Grundrisse: Foundations of the Critique of Political Economy* (London: Penguin).

Marx, K. (1976), *Capital: A Critique of Political Economy, Volume I* (London: Penguin).

Marx, K. (1978), *Capital: A Critique of Political Economy, Volume II* (London: Penguin).

Marx, K. (1990), *The Eighteenth Brumaire of Louis Bonaparte* (London: Lawrence and Wishart).

Matin, I. and Hulme, D. (2009), 'Programs for the poorest: learning from the IGVGD Program in Bangladesh', in D. Hulme and T. Arun (eds), *Microfinance: A Reader* (London and New York: Routledge), 78–107.

Menon, S. (2013), 'Indian trade unions are getting bigger, coinciding with slow-down', *Business Standard*, 6 April.

Mezzadri, A. (2014), 'Indian garment clusters and CSR Norms: incompatible agendas at the bottom of the garment commodity chain', *Oxford Development Studies* 42:2.

Migdal, J. (2001), *State in Society: Studying How States and Societies Transform and Constitute One Another* (Cambridge: Cambridge University Press).

Miliband, R. (1973a), *The State in Capitalist Society* (London: Quartet Books).

Milband, R. (1973b), 'Poulantzas the capitalist state', *New Left Review* I/82, 83–92.

Miyamura, S. (2011), 'Diversity of labour market institutions in Indian industry: a comparison of Mumbai and Kolkata', *The Indian Journal of Labour Economics* 54:1, 113–130.

Miyamura, S. (forthcoming), 'Industrial restructuring, organisations of labour and patterns of accumulation in India', *Third World Quarterly*.

Mobile Crèches. (2008), *Distress Migration: Identity and Entitlements – A Study on Migrant Construction Workers and the Health Status of Their Children in the National Capital Region 2007–2008* (New Delhi: Mobile Crèches).

Mohanty, B.B. (2009), 'Power to the excluded groups and Panchayati Raj in Coastal Orissa', in B.S. Baviskar and G. Mathew (eds), *Inclusion and Exlcusion in Local Governance: Field Studies from Rural India* (New Delhi: Sage).

Mollinga, P. (2003), *On the Waterfront: Water Distribution, Technology and Agrarian Change in a South Indian Canal Irrigation System* (Hyderabad: Orient Longman).

Monaco, L. (2015), 'Bringing Operaismo Gurgaon: a study of labour composition and resistance practices in the Indian Auto Industry', unpublished PhD thesis (SOAS, University of London).

Montgomery, H. and Weiss, J. (2005), 'Great expectations: microfinance and poverty reduction in Asia and Latin America', *ADB Institute Research Paper Series* 63 (Tokyo: Asian Development Bank Institute).

Mooij, J. (1999), *Food Policy and the Indian State: The Public Distribution System in South India* (New Delhi: Oxford University Press).

Mooij, J. (2001), 'Food and power in Bihar and Jharkhand: power and its functioning', *Economic and Political Weekly* 36:34, 3289–3299.

Moore, B. (1966), *Social Origins of Dictatorship and Democracy: Lord and Peasant in the Making of the Modern World* (Harmondsworth: Penguin).

Moore, M. and Putzel, J. (1999), *Thinking Strategically about Politics and Poverty* (London: CIIR).

Mosley, P. and Hulme, D. (1998), 'Microenterprise finance: is there a conflict between growth and poverty alleviation?', *World Development* 26:5, 783–790.

Mosley, P. and Hulme, D. (2009), 'Microenterprise finance: is there a conflict between growth and poverty alleviation?', in D. Hulme and T. Arun (eds), *Microfinance: A Reader* (London and New York: Routledge), 65–77.

Mosse, D. (2004), *The Rule of Water: Statecraft, Ecology, and Collective Action in South India* (New Delhi: Oxford University Press).

Mosse, D. (2005), *Cultivating Development: An Ethnography of Aid Policy and Practice* (New Delhi: Vistaar Publications).

Mosse, D. (2010), 'A relational approach to durable poverty, inequality and power', *Journal of Development Studies* 46:7, 1156–1178.

Mosse, D., Gupta, S., Mehta, M., Shah, V. and Rees, J. (2002), 'Brokered livelihoods: debt, labour migration and development in tribal Western India', *Journal of Development Studies* 38:5, 59–88.

Mosse, D., Gupta, S. and Shah, V. (2005), 'On the margins in the city: Adivasi seasonal labour migration in Western India', *Economic and Political Weekly* 40:28, 3025–3038.

Nadkarni, M. (1987), *Farmers' Movements in India* (Ahmedabad: Allied).

Nair, R.P. (2004), 'The Kerala Construction Labour Welfare Fund', Sectoral Activities Programme in Cooperation with the Employment-Intensive Investment Programme, *Working Paper 219* (Geneva: International Labour Organisation).

Narasimha Reddy, D. (2013), 'Functioning of NREGS in Andhra Pradesh', in K.P. Kannan and J. Breman (eds), *The Long Road to Social Security: Assessing the Implementation of National Social Security Initiatives for the Working Poor in India* (New Delhi: Oxford University Press).

NABARD [National Bank for Agriculture and Rural Development]. (2006), *SHG-Bank Linkage Programme Karnataka 2005–2006: The Success Story of Micro-Finance through SHGs in Karnataka* (Bangalore: NABARD).

NCEUS [National Commission for Enterprises in the Unorganised Sector]. (2007), *Report on Conditions of Work and Promotion of Livelihoods in the Unorganized Sector* (New Delhi: NCEUS).

NCEUS [National Commission for Enterprises in the Unorganised Sector]. (2009), *The Challenge of Employment in India: An Informal Economy Perspective – Volume 1, Main Report* (New Delhi: NCEUS).

NIC [National Informatics Centre]. (n.d.), 'Statewise notified wages for MGNREGA (Rs/day)'. Online: http://nrega.nic.in/nerega_statewise.pdf (accessed 15 July 2014).

Neocosmos, M. (1986), 'Marx's third class: capitalist landed property and capitalist development', *Journal of Peasant Studies* 13:3, 5–44.

New Indian Express. (2013), 'Tendulkar Panel to be examined by PM', *New Indian Express*, 30 July. Online: http://newindianexpress.com/states/tamil_nadu/Tendulkar-panel-report-to-be-examined-by-PM/2013/07/30/article1708223.ece (accessed 12 August 2013).

Nilsen, A. (2010), *Disposession and Resistance in India: The River and the Rage* (London: Routledge).

Nirantar. (2007), 'Executive summary: examining power and literacy within self-help groups: a quantitative study' (New Delhi: Nirantar, A Centre of Gender and Education).

Nordholt, H. (2004), 'Decentralisation in Indonesia: less state, more democracy?', in J. Harriss, K Stokke and O. Tornquist (eds), *Politicising Democracy: The New Local Politics of Democratisation* (Basingstoke: Palgrave Macmillan).

Offe, C. (1984), *Contradictions of the Welfare State* (London: Hutchinson).

Omvedt, G. (1993), *Reinventing Revolution: New Social Movements and the Socialist Tradition in India* (Armonk: M.E. Sharpe).

Pankaj, A. and Tankha, R. (2010), 'Empowerment effects of the NREGS on women workers: a study in four states', *Economic and Political Weekly* 45:30, 45–55.

Parry, J. (2008), 'The sacrifices of modernity in a Soviet-built steel town in Central India', in F. Pine and D. De Cabral (eds), *On the Margins of Religion* (Oxford and New York: Berghann).

Patnaik, P. and Chandra Sekhar, C.P. (2004), 'A perspective on migration', in K. Gopal Iyer (ed.), *Distressed Migrant Labour in India: Key Human Rights Issues* (New Delhi: Kanishka), 11–21.

Patnaik, U. (1976), 'Class differentiation within the peasantry: an approach to analysis of Indian agriculture', *Economic and Political Weekly* 11:39, A82–101.

Patnaik, U. (1986), 'The agrarian question and development of capitalism in India', *Economic and Political Weekly* 21:18, 781–793.

Patnaik, U. (2007), 'Neoliberalism and rural poverty in India', *Economic & Political Weekly* 42:30, 3132–3150.

Pattenden, J. (2005), 'Trickle-down solidarity, globalisation and dynamics of social transformation in a South India village', *Economic and Political Weekly* 40:19, 1975–1985.

Pattenden, J. (2010), 'A neoliberalisation of civil society? Self-help groups and the labouring class poor', *Journal of Peasant Studies* 37:3, 485–512.

Pattenden, J. (2011a), 'Gatekeeping as accumulation and domination: evidence from South India', *Journal of Agrarian Change* 11:2, 164–194.

Pattenden, J. (2011b), 'Social protection and class relations: evidence from scheduled caste women's associations in rural South India', *Development and Change* 42:2, 469–498.

Pattenden, J. (2012), 'Migrating between rural Raichur and boomtown Bangalore: class relations and the circulation of labour in South India', *Global Labour Journal* 3:1, 163–190.

Pellissery, S. and Kumar Jalan, S. (2011), 'Towards transformative social protection: a gendered analysis of the Employment GuaranteeAct of India (MGNREGA)', *Gender and Development* 19:2, 283–294.

Picherit, D. (2009), 'Workers trust us! Labour middlemen and the rise of the lower castes in Andhra Pradesh', in J. Breman, I. Guérin and A. Prakash (eds), *India's Unfree Workforce: Of Bondage Old and New* (New Delhi: Oxford University Press), 259–283.

Picherit, D. (2012), 'Migrant labourers' struggles between village and urban migration sites: labour standards, rural development and politics in South India', *Global Labour Journal* 3:1, 143–162.

Picherit, D. (2014), 'Neither a dog nor a beggar: seasonal labour migration, development and poverty in Andhra Pradesh', paper presented at the London School of Economics Inequality and Poverty Research Programme Workshop, 24–25 April 2014.

Poulantzas, N. (1976), 'The capitalist state: a reply to Miliband and Laclau', *New Left Review* 95.

Prosperi, V. (2009), 'Labour relations in the construction industry: a case study from Delhi', paper presented at the *IIPPE Workshop*, Ankara, September.

Putnam, R. with Leonardi, R. and Nannetti, R. (1993), *Making Democracy Work: Civic Traditions in Modern Italy* (Princeton, NJ: Princeton University Press).

Raghavan, E. and Manor, J. (2009), *Broadening and Deepening Democracy: Political Innovation in Karnataka* (New Delhi: Routledge).

Ramachandran, V.K. (1990), *Wage Labour and Unfreedom in Agriculture: An Indian Case Study* (Oxford: Clarendon).

Ramachandran, V.K. and Rawal, V. (2010), 'The impact of liberalisation and globalisation on India's agrarian economy', *Global Labour Journal* 1:1, 56–91.

Ramachandran, V.K., Rawal, V. and Swaminathan, M. (2010), *Socio-Economic Surveys of Three Villages in Andhra Pradesh: A Study of Agrarian Relations* (New Delhi: Tulika).

Ram Reddy, G. and Haragopal, G. (1985), 'The pyraveekar: "the fixer" in rural India', *Asian Survey* 25:11, 1148–1162.

Rawal, V. (2006), 'The labour process in rural Haryana (India): a field-report from two villages', *Journal of Agrarian Change* 6:4, 538–583.

Rawal, V. and Swaminathan, M. (2011), 'Returns from crop cultivation and scale of production', *Indira Gandhi Institute for Development Research Proceedings/Projects Series*, Workshop on Policy Options and Investment Priorities for Accelerating Agricultural Productivity and Development in India, November 2011 (Mumbai: IGIDR).

Reddy, N. and Acharya, D. (2007), 'Striking at the roots of democracy', *Economic and Political Weekly* 42:18, 1601–1603.

Reserve Bank of India. (n.d.), *Economic Review 2012–2013*. Online: http://rbi-docs.rbi.org.in/rdocs/AnnualReport/PDFs/P1_02ECRV220813.pdf (accessed 16 August 2014).

Reserve Bank of India Bulletin. (various), 'Consumer price index for agricultural labourers'. Online: http://rbidocs.rbi.org.in/rdocs/Bulletin/PDFs/82605.pdf; http://rbidocs.rbi.org.in/rdocs/Bulletin/PDFs/37T_EBU70110.pdf; http://rbi-docs.rbi.org.in/rdocs/Bulletin/PDFs/37T_CS100112B.pdf, 9–10; www.rbi.org.in/scripts/BS_ViewBulletin.aspx?Id=13802 (all accessed 21 July 2014).

Robinson, M. (1988), *Local Politics: The Law of the Fishes – Development through Political Change in Medak District, Andhra Pradesh (South India)* (Delhi: Oxford University Press).

Rodgers, G. and Rodgers, J. (2011), 'Inclusive development? Migration, governance and social change in rural Bihar', *Economic and Political Weekly* 46:23, 43–50.

Roesch, M., Venkatasubramanian, G. and Guérin, I. (2009), 'Bonded labour in rice mills: fate or opportunity?', in J. Breman, I. Guérin and A. Prakash (eds), *India's Unfree Workforce: Of Bondage Old and New* (New Delhi: Oxford University Press), 284–311.

Rogaly, B., Biswas, J., Coppard, D., Rafique, A., Rana, K. and Sengupta, A. (2001), 'Seasonal migration, social change and migrants' rights', *Economic and Political Weekly* 36:49, 4547–4559.

Roy, R. (1996), 'State failure in India: political-fiscal implications of the black economy', in B. Harriss-White and G. White (eds), *Liberalization and the New Corruption IDS Bulletin* 27:2, 31–39.

RoyChowdury, S. (2003), 'Old classes and new spaces: urban poverty, unorganised labour and new unions', *Economic and Political Weekly* 38:50, 5277–5284.

RoyChowdhury, S. (2005), 'Labour activism and women in the unorganised sector: garment export industry in Bangalore', *Economic and Political Weekly* 40:22/23, 2250–2255.

Ruckert, A. (2006), 'Towards an inclusive-neoliberal regime of development: from the Washington to the Post-Washington Consensus', *Labour, Capital and Society* 39:1, 36–67.

Rudolph, L. and Rudolph, S. (1987), *In Pursuit of Lakshmi: The Political Economy of the Indian State* (Chicago: University of Chicago Press).

Rutten, M. (2003), *Rural Capitalists in Asia: A Comparative Analysis of India, Indonesia and Malaysia* (London: Routledge).

Sabates-Wheeler, R. and Devereux, S. (2008), 'Transformative social protection: the currency of social justice', in A. Barrientos and D. Hulme (eds), *Social Protection for the Poor and Poorest: Risk, Needs and Rights* (Basingstoke: Palgrave Macmillan), 64–84.

Sanyal, K. and Bhattacharyya, R. (2009), 'Beyond the factory: globalisation, informalisation of production and the new locations of labour', *Economic and Political Weekly* 44:22, 35–44.

Satish, S. (2005), 'Mainstreaming of Indian microfinance', *Economic and Political Weekly* 40:17, 1731–1739.

Scott, J. (1985), *Weapons of the Weak: Everyday Forms of Peasant Resistance* (New Haven, CT and London: Yale University Press).

Selwyn, B. (2011), 'Liberty limited? A sympathetic re-engagement with Amartya Sen's *Development as Freedom*', *Economic and Political Weekly* 46:37, 68–76.

Selwyn, S. (2014), *The Global Development Crisis* (Cambridge: Polity).

Sen, A. (1981), *Poverty and Famines: An Essay on Entitlement and Deprivation* (Oxford: Clarendon).

Sen, A. (1999), *Development as Freedom* (Oxford: Oxford University Press).

Sen, A. and Himanshu. (2004), 'Poverty and inequality in India: II – widening disparities during the 1990s', *Economic and Political Weekly* 39, 4361–4375.

Shah, A. (2010), *In the Shadows of the State: Indigenous Politics, Environmentalism and Insurgency in Jharkhand, India* (Durham, NC: Duke University Press).

Shah, A. (2013), 'The agrarian question in a Maoist guerilla zone: land, labour and capital in the forests and hills of Jharkhand, India', *Journal of Agrarian Change* 13:3, 424–450.

Shah, A. and Kapur Mehta, A. (2008), 'Experience of the Maharashtra Employment Guarantee Scheme: are there lessons for NREGS?'. *Chronic Poverty Research Centre Working Paper 118* (Manchester: Chronic Poverty Research Centre).

Shahi, D. (2014), 'India in the emerging world order: a status quo power or a revisionist force', *Shifting Power/Critical Perspectives on Emerging Economies TNI Working Papers* (Amsterdam: Transnational Institute).

Shivakumar, M.S., Sheng, Y.K. and Weber, K. (1991), 'Recruitment and employment practices in the construction industry: a case study of Bangalore', *Economic and Political Weekly* 26:8, M27–M40.

Shyam Sundar, K.R. (2008), 'Measuring an international core labour convention: a study of freedom of association', *Indian Journal of Labour Economics* 51:2.

Sidel, J. (1996), 'Siam and its twin? Democratization and bossism in contemporary Thailand and the Philippines', in B. Harriss-White and G. White (eds), *Liberalization and the New Corruption IDS Bulletin* 27:2, 31–39.

Sidel, J. (2004), 'Bossism and democracy in the Philippines, Thailand and Indonesia: towards an alternative framework for the study of local strongmen', in J. Harriss, K. Stokke and O. Tornquist (eds), *Politicising Democracy: The New Local Politics of Democratisation* (Basingstoke: Palgrave Macmillan).

Sidhu, H.S. (2005), 'Production conditions in contemporary Punjab agriculture', *Journal of Punjab Studies* 12:2, 197–218.

Sidhu, M.S., Rangi, P.S. and Singh, K. (2004), 'Migrant agricultural labour in the Punjab', in K. Gopal Iyer (ed.), *Distressed Migrant Labour in India: Key Human Rights Issues* (New Delhi: Kanishka), 141–154.

Silver, H. (1994), 'Social exclusion and social solidarity: three paradigms', *International Labour Review* 133, 531–578.

Silver, B. (2003), *Forces of Labor: Workers' Movements and Globalization since 1870* (Cambridge: Cambridge University Press).

Sivakumar, S. (2010), 'A political agenda to minimise wages', *Economic and Political Weekly* 45:50, 10–12.

Skocpol, T. (1985), 'Bringing the state back in: strategies of analysis in current research', in P. Evans, D. Rueschemeyer and T. Skocpol (eds), *Bringing the State Back in* (Cambridge: Cambridge University Press).

Smith, A. (1970 [1776]), *The Wealth of Nations, Books I–III* (London: Penguin).

So, A. (2007), 'Peasant conflict and the local predatory state in the Chinese countryside', *Journal of Peasant Studies* 34:3/4, 560–581.

Srinivas, M.N. (1963), *The Dominant Caste and Other Essays* (New Delhi: Oxford University Press).

Srivastava, R. (1989), 'Tenancy contracts during transition: a study based on fieldwork in Uttar Pradesh', *Journal of Peasant Studies* 16:3, 339–395.

Srivastava, R. (1999), 'Rural labour in Uttar Pradesh: emerging features of subsistence, contradiction and resistance', *Journal of Peasant Studies* 26:2/3, 263–315.

Srivastava, R. (2009), 'Conceptualizing continuity and change in emerging forms of labour bondage', in J. Breman, I. Guérin and A. Prakash (eds), *India's Unfree Workforce: Of Bondage Old and New* (New Delhi: Oxford University Press), 129–146.

Srivastava, R. (2011), 'Internal migration in India: an overview of its features, trends and policy challenges', in *Workshop Compendium*, Vol. 2, National Workshop on Internal Migration and Human Development in India, Indian Council of Social Science Research, New Delhi, 6–7 December 2011. UNESCO.

Srivastava, R. (2012), 'Changing employment conditions of the Indian workforce and implications for decent work', *Global Labour Journal* 3:1, 63–90.

Srivastava, R. and Singh, R. (2005), 'Economic reforms and agricultural wages in India', *The Indian Journal of Labour Economics* 48:2, 407–424.

Srivastava, R. and Singh, R. (2006), 'Rural wages during the 1990s: a re-estimation', *Economic and Political Weekly* 41:38, 4053–4062.

Standing, G. (2012), 'Cash transfers: a review of the issues in India' (New Delhi: UNICEF).

Stewart, F., Saith, R. and Harriss-White, B. (2007), *Defining Poverty in the Developing World* (Basingstoke: Palgrave Macmillan).

Still, C. (2009), 'From militant rejection to pragmatic consensus: caste among Madigas in Andhra Pradesh', *Journal of South Asian Development* 4:1, 7–23.

Sud, N. (2003), 'Experiences of SGSY in Gujarat: from process-oriented theory to deterministic practice', *Economic and Political Weekly*, 38:39, 4085–4087.

Suresh, T.G. (2009), 'Understanding grassroots power and excluded communities in Kerala', in B.S. Baviskar and G. Mathew (eds), *Inclusion and Exclusion in Local Governance: Field Studies from Rural India* (New Delhi: Sage).

Suryanarayana, M., Agrawal, A. and Seeta Prabhu, K. (2011), *Inequality-Adjusted Human Development Index for India's States* (New Delhi: UNDP).

Tarrow, S. (1998), *Power in Movement: Social Movements, Collective Action and Politics* (Cambridge: Cambridge University Press).

Taylor, M. (2011), ' "Freedom from poverty is not for free": rural development and the microfinance crisis in Andhra Pradesh, India', *Journal of Agrarian Change* 11:4, 484–504.

Thara Bhai, L. (2009), 'Gender, caste and politics in rural Tamil Nadu', in B.S. Baviskar and G. Mathew (eds), *Inclusion and Exlcusion in Local Governance: Field Studies from Rural India* (New Delhi: Sage).

Thomas, J.J. (2012), 'India's labour market during the 2000s: surveying the changes', *Economic and Political Weekly* 47:51, 39–51.

Thompson, E.P. (1991), *The Making of the English Working Class* (London: Penguin).

Thorner, A. (1982), 'Semi-feudalism or capitalism? Contemporary debate on classes and modes of production in India', *Economic and Political Weekly* 17, 49–51.

Thorner, D. and Thorner, A. (1962), *Land and Labour in India* (Bombay: Asia Publishing House).

UNDP. (2005), *Karnataka Human Development Report 2005* (Bangalore: Government of Karnataka Planning and Statistics Department).

Usami, Y. (2011), 'A note on recent trends in wage rates in rural India', *Review of Agrarian Studies* 1:1.

Usami, Y. and Rawal, V. (2012), 'Some aspects of the implementation of India's employment guarantee', *Review of Agrarian Studies* 2:2.

Van der Loop, T. (1996), *Industrial Dynamics and Fragmented Labour Markets: Construction Firms and Labourers in India* (Thousand Oaks, CA: Sage).

Varshney, A. (1995), *Democracy, Development and the Countryside: Urban–Rural Struggles in India* (Cambridge: Cambridge University Press).

Veron, R., Williams, G., Corbridge, S. and Srivastava, M. (2006), 'Decentralised corruption or corrupt decentralisation? Community monitoring of poverty-alleviation schemes in Eastern India', *World Development* 34:11, 1922–1941.

Vijayabaskar, M. (2010), 'Saving agricultural labour from agriculture: SEZs and politics of silence in Tamil Nadu', *Economic and Political Weekly* 45:6, 36–43.

Virk, R. (2004), 'Women construction workers in Amritsar City', in K. Gopal Iyer (ed.), *Distressed Migrant Labour in India: Key Human Rights Issues* (New Delhi: Kanishka), 162–177.

Wade, R. (1982), 'The system of administrative and political corruption: canal irrigation in South India', *Journal of Development Studies* 18:3, 287–328.

Wade, R. (1988), *Village Republics: Economic Conditions for Collective Action in South India* (Cambridge: Cambridge University Press).

Walker, K. Le Mons. (2008), 'Neoliberalism on the ground in rural India: predatory growth, agrarian crisis, internal colonization, and the intensification of class struggle', *Journal of Peasant Studies* 35:4, 557–620.

Weber, M. (1978), *Economy and Society: An Outline of Interpretive Sociology*, ed. by G. Roth and C. Wittich (Berkeley, Los Angeles and London: University of California Press).

White, B. and Wiradi, G. (1989), 'Agrarian and non-agrarian bases of inequality in nine Javanese villages', in G. Hart, A. Turton and B. White (eds), *Agrarian Transformations: Local Processes and the State in Southeast Asia* (Berkeley, CA: Berkeley University Press).

Wilson, K. (1999), 'Patterns of accumulation and struggles of rural labour: some aspects of agrarian change in Central Bihar', in T. Byres, K. Kapadia and J. Lerche (eds), *Rural Labour Relations in India* (Frank Cass: London), 316–354.

Wolf, E. (1982), *Europe and the People without History* (Berkeley, Los Angeles and London: University of California Press).

Wood, E.M. (1981), 'The separation of the economic and the political in capitalism', *New Left Review* 127, 66–95.

Wood, E.M. (1986), *The Retreat from Class: A New 'True' Socialism* (London and New York: Verso).

Wood, E.M. (1995), *Democracy against Capitalism: Renewing Historical Materialism* (Cambridge: Cambridge University Press).

Wood, G. (2003), 'Staying secure, staying poor: the "Faustian bargain"', *World Development* 31:3, 455–471.

World Bank. (2001), *World Development Report, 2000/2001: Attacking Poverty* (Oxford: Oxford University Press).

World Bank. (2004), *World Development Report 2004:Making Services Work for Poor People* (Washington, DC: World Bank).

World Bank. (2006), 'India: inclusive growth and service delivery – building on India's success', Development Policy Review (Washington, DC: World Bank).

World Bank. (2007), *Strengthening World Bank Group Engagement on Governance and Anti-Corruption* (Washington, DC: World Bank).

World Bank. (2011), 'Social protection for a changing India: volume II' (Washington, DC: World Bank).

Wright, E.O. (2000), 'Working-class power, capitalist-class interests and class compromise', *American Journal of Sociology* 105:4, 957–1002.

Wright, E.O. (2005), 'Foundations of a neo-Marxist class analysis', in E.O. Wright (ed.), *Approaches to Class Analysis* (Cambridge: Cambridge University Press).

Wright, E.O. (2009), 'Understanding class: towards an integrated analytical approach', *New Left Review* 60, 101–116.

Index

Italic page numbers indicate tables, **bold** indicate figures.

EU authorised representative for GPSR:
Easy Access System Europe, Mustamäe tee 50,
10621 Tallinn, Estonia
gpsr.requests@easproject.com

www.ingramcontent.com/pod-product-compliance
Lightning Source LLC
Chambersburg PA
CBHW071413290326
41932CB00047B/2827